Kind Soul, Closet Maniac

Kind Soul, Closet Maniac

A Memoir

Edward Cleaves

Copyright

Kind Soul, Closet Maniac: A Memoir
Written by Edward Cleaves

Copyright @ 2022 by Edward Cleaves

Cover design, formatting and layout by Evening Sky Publishing Services

Published in United States of America
ISBN (Hardback): 978–
ISBN (Paperback): 978-
ISBN (eBook): 978–

Dedication

For Brian

Contents

Foreword

Alan R. Warren

For anybody who has ever tried to write a book, no matter what type of book it is, you know how much work it is, the time it takes, and what an emotional journey it can be. You have to be able to pour your heart out as you would in a diary. Only the pages where you write your innermost thoughts and feelings are available for everyone to read.

Kind Soul Closet Maniac is one of those books that will stay with you for life. This memoir is the personal journey of the author Ed Cleaves. Cleaves might not have chosen the same road you have traveled through your life, as there are so many roads to choose from, but you will find that Cleaves's journey was for the same reasons that many of us have for our own.

His raw, honest words will resonate with anybody who has found love in their life. When we find love, we find a freedom that can never be forgotten. And this freedom is what powers our strength throughout our lives. This power creates something required to become a new person. Love is our common bond, a bond that we all can understand.

The book reminds us that even though our time seems to be

moving so slowly when we're counting the minutes throughout our days at work or school, those minutes we can never get back.

The changes in our life are subtle. We give away our time freely for no reason believing that there is an endless supply of it and it'll never run out. How often have you found yourself waiting for something in a lineup at a store or waiting for a bus? I have often looked back and thought about how great it would be if we could gather up all of that lost time and use it again, more usefully.

By the end of *Kind Soul Closet Maniac*, you'll be faced with knowing what lies ahead for all of us in our life. And that everything we have in our life, in this world, is just on loan to us. We have to remember that every person who passes through our lives will leave, whether they want to.

Hopefully, all we are left with is a meaning in our life for the losses we have, to try and learn from it and carry it forward to the next step that we're about to take.

One thing is for sure, everything and everyone we experience throughout our life changes us, whether we want it to or not. So, the most important thing that we can do is to learn from it to be ready for what's next.

Alan R. Warren

NBC Radio KCAA 106.5 F.M. Los Angeles, Palm Springs, San Bernardino

Best Selling True Crime Author

Chapter One

Brian

February 9th, 2016, 6:11 p.m.

As I turned away from the hospital bed we kept in our living room, out of the corner of my eye, I saw his chest rise as he inhaled and his chest fall for the last time. He was gone. After a long and painful battle with cancer, I lost the love of my life and the best thing that ever happened to me.

We fought together as best we could for two years against stage four lung cancer. I have never witnessed someone handle so much pain with such dignity and grace. He never complained.

I'll never forget the look on his face when we found out that there was no coming back from it. It was heartbreaking. I begged God to take me instead. He did not.

Brian was an innocent. He was kind to a fault and about as gentle a human being one could ask for. How lucky I was to have him for the short time that I did. I wish I could have found him sooner in life. Innocent souls are rare in this world, so if you're lucky enough to find one, be sure to hold on tight and take damn good care of it.

We met in November 2007 at a place called Madison Pub in Seattle. It was my local watering hole. It was the only Gay sports pub in town at the time—peanut shells on the floor and good whiskey. I still go there from time to time. It was a good place to watch football and watch men at the same time.

I was finishing my pint and was about to leave when Brian walked in, and everything I thought I knew had changed. Oh, how beautiful he was. I fell for him almost right away. He still has the most beautiful face I have ever seen. I couldn't keep my eyes off of him. He seemed so humble. So kind. I couldn't let him go without telling him how handsome I thought he was.

I was about to make my move when he walked right up to me and introduced himself. Not so shy after all, I thought. By this time, I had several beers in me and a few shots of whiskey, so my inhibitions were low. I asked him for his phone number and if he would like to meet for coffee sometime. I had no idea this was the beginning of something that would change my life forever. We made a date for coffee, and I dashed out the door. I had a little too much in me and didn't want to make a bad impression. I went outside and lit up a cigarette as I made my way home in the rain.

I was excited for his call, but he decided to keep me waiting for two days. I started to realize this was more than just a crush I had on this man. So strange. We had only just met. I was pissed off that he kept me waiting. He would later tell me that he was playing it cool.

I, myself, had the same plan, however. Two days wasted, I thought. I was about to ring him when he called me, and we set a date for coffee at a Starbucks on Broadway. I got there early. He arrived right on time wearing a navy blue button-down with the collar open at the top with a tuft of hair poking out. How handsome he looked. I wanted to kiss him right then and there. No little peck on the cheek. It was a sunny, crisp Fall day in Seattle. Brian had the bluest of eyes, and they reflected off the blue on his shirt. I couldn't take my eyes off him. The innocent, humble nature I witnessed at Mad Pub was sitting across from me in the daylight, and I was all in. Smitten by his kind nature. Was this guy for real? I don't remember all that we talked about apart from where we were from, our jobs, and the city. It turned into a three-hour coffee date, and at the end, he agreed to let me walk him home. I remember noticing every little bit of flora on the way up to 15th Avenue on Capitol Hill – a mostly gay neighborhood at the time. Small coffee shops and boutique restaurants. We got to the front door, and I was so eager to kiss him on the mouth, but I didn't want to push my luck or seem too forward.

As I do with most things in my life, I just closed my eyes and jumped. He kissed me back. The first kiss. Tender, beautiful, and real. We made plans to have dinner together, and I left him at his doorway. I headed back to my place to finish a bottle of wine I had and the rest of some book I was into.

My place was classic Seattle at the time. An old apartment building surrounded by trees so close to the windows I could barely see outside. Dark, old, hardwood floors. A one-bedroom with a beautiful claw-foot bathtub. Other than that, it was kind of a dump. I loved it, though—the perfect place to read or hide or just get drunk and write nonsense into a journal. I like to drink. In fact, I love it. More about that later. Strangely enough, though, an apartment became available just two blocks from Brian's apartment. A more modern place with plenty of sunshine. When it's available. It is Seattle, after all. I didn't realize how close it was to his place, but I took it anyway. Much better on the soul to have as much sunshine in when it did decide to show. I moved in no time and took over a new position as a waiter at a local restaurant down on 12th Avenue and East Pine Street. I called Brian and asked him to come down for a drink. He did. A different button-down showed this time in the same beautiful face staring at me while I worked. The last thing I wanted to do was to wait on people, but I got to see him hanging out at the bar. I finished the shift and promptly joined him for a drink.

We sat a lot closer this time. I didn't waste any time putting my arm around him or touching his arm or his leg. His shy and innocent nature was driving me crazy. It wasn't an act. For the first time in a long time, I felt good again. Being with Brian felt natural right away, and it certainly didn't hurt that he was so very handsome. We drank together there for a while and then confirmed our date for dinner. I barely noticed the November rain as I walked home on cloud nine, wondering what I had found.

That's the thing about Seattle weather for me. I love the Fall, especially here in the Pacific Northwest.

It's dark. It gets colder. It's really the only way for me to know that time is passing. The Fall season begins with fantastic windstorms that blast through Seattle and strip the trees of their leaves. Everything stays wet for a long time, and then the cloud level drops, and the "Mighty Grey" rolls in. It's fantastic, and it stays that way for a long time.

It doesn't downpour as much as people outside of the Pacific Northwest think, but after a while, every day looks and feels the same. Time flies by in Seattle. I have learned to adapt to almost anything as a result of a really fucked up childhood. I had no problem switching from introvert to extrovert. In the offseason, I would sit and read all day in my apartment with a few bottles of 2 Buck Chuck. Or go out on Puget Sound riding the ferry to Bainbridge Island or Bremerton Island.

Seattle is a great place to get lost if one chooses to. I never really suffered the depression I had heard so much about from so many. I enjoyed looking at the misty mountains across the Sound or walking around Gasworks Park in the rain on a handful of mushrooms. Mostly, I would hang out at a dive bar somewhere, pounding Rainier beer and chatting up the locals. I rarely left Capitol Hill. Everything I needed was in a five-block radius, and now so was Brian. I had a rare weekend off, and Brian offered to cook for us on a Friday night.

Our first official date. I was so excited. On that Friday, I was home drinking a couple of beers when Brian called and said that he needed a little more time to get ready. That worked for me as I forgot to hit the wine shop for a bottle of red and some flowers from the local florist on my way. I arrived at Brian's for the first time with a slight buzz and an armful of fresh sunflowers.

I crossed his threshold and found myself at home. I knew this was who I wanted to be with from now on. He was so sweet and so humble. His apartment, however, was another story altogether. God bless my dear boy, but his housekeeping skills were nonexistent. Holy cow! I thought he got robbed or something. There was crap everywhere. He went into the kitchen to crack a bottle of vino, so I walked around for a bit. He wasn't the type to leave empty food containers around or anything like that, but laundry, delivery boxes, and paperwork were everywhere. It was kind of overwhelming for a neat freak like me. It didn't matter, though. All I wanted was to be there with him.

We shared a bottle of Bordeaux and smoked a couple of cigarettes before dinner. We both smoked. It was a bit of a relief to know that he smoked also. I used to worry about stinking of tobacco in a social situation. After a great dinner, we were sitting on his couch next to each other, and I leaned in for a kiss from him. A real kiss. Deep and passionate. You know how when you kiss someone, it can be awkward. Or it doesn't match up properly, or there's too much pressure or too little? This was not the case with my Brian. We locked in right away— a perfect match. An hour later, we came up for air. I, standing at full mast, was losing my mind. I lit up a cigarette, and we relaxed for a bit, finishing the rest of the Bordeaux. As it turned out, his second favorite thing to do was watch movies, as was mine. We watched *Love Actually* – a Christmas favorite of mine – and snuggled up on his couch. A great first date.

Brian once told me that he was lucky to have met me. When all the while, it was I who was the lucky one.

———————————

If I haven't told you already, I like to drink. A bit of an understatement, really. The fact is that my appetite for destruction is absolutely fucking insatiable. *My name is Edward, and I'm an alcoholic.* As it stands, I am writing from a regeneration/rehab facility called Justin's Place, also known as St. Matthew's house in Naples, Florida. I've traded Mt. Rainier and the Misty Mountains of the Pacific Northwest for the enormous skies of southern Florida. The endless shades of grey, snowcapped peaks, and constant dampness for massive billowing clouds that blanket the horizon and seem to stretch all the way to the Heavens.

With beautiful hues of pink, indigo, and blue-green. So pretty. I had forgotten how big the skies are down here. It made me want to sail away. The last time I was here was in 2004. Seasonal work as a waiter at a restaurant called Touch on Lincoln Road on Miami beach. I rented a two-bedroom condo on Pennsylvania and 13th Avenue. A few blocks from the beach in October of that year. A lot of things seem to happen or begin in October or November for some reason. The apartment belonged to some friends of mine up in Boston. I had mentioned that I was moving to Miami and looking to rent. They mailed the keys; I mailed a check, and that was it. The place was fantastic—a perfect bachelor pad for a single guy on South Beach with a split floor plan, a big living room, and a wall of windows facing the beach. I couldn't see the ocean, but I had a nice view of Washington Street and the post office. I had the time of my life. I still love South Beach to this day. It's one of my favorite places in the country. I hit the ground running.

The mornings brought me to the beach with such gorgeous tropical blue waters. Then off to work in the evenings, and after that, I would hunt the middle-aged clean-cut, married dad types who came to South Beach to prey upon the bevy of Cuban, Central, and South American men that dominated the Gay scene. The bars on South Beach were fantastic. They stayed open until 5:00 a.m. I would get home from work around midnight, take a shower, pour a glass of Scotch, and slap on some music. Then off to the bars I went. I only lived a couple of blocks away from a club called Twist. Five different bars under one roof. The cocaine was unbelievably good and extremely cheap. I had a lot of fun. I scored an eight ball from a girl at work and took it home to try it out with a glass of Scotch before I went out clubbing. I chopped up a fat line and snorted it, waited, waited... nothing. I called the girl I scored from and said, "Hey, what the hell?" She said, "Give it 15 minutes and call me back." Then, I couldn't feel my face.

That shit was extremely potent. Welcome to Miami. I would go out at least three nights a week minimum seeing as I didn't have to be at work until 5:00 p.m. the next day. It left a lot of time for me to party, recover, and hit the beach in the morning before work. I loved it. I loved prowling the beach at 3:00 a.m. like Lestat the fucking Vampire.

That first season on South Beach was ridiculous. To say I was a bit of a man whore would be an understatement. It's rare that I see my type of man in a bar, but my type was everywhere that first season. Stocky, hairy men, doughboys were everywhere, and I'd scoop them up and take them home to console them after they would strike out with one Latin Adonis or another. The winter of 2004 was a lot of fun. I'd never been laid so much in my life by men who were so close to my type!

Chapter Two
Revere, Massachusetts

My drinking life started when I was around thirteen or so in Revere, Massachusetts. Bon Jovi and big hair was everywhere. I had just come from San Jose, California, by way of Greyhound. Cross country on a bus was a fucking nightmare. I was put on a bus with my older brother Jimmy and sent on my way. I had my older sister Debbie's address, but I wasn't sure if she knew I was coming, and I didn't know if I would make it there. I was scared.

Revere, Massachusetts, in the early 80s, was all Italian-American. Hair metal bands dominated the radio, including Journey, Def Leppard, and a never-ending array of glam rock. Guns and Roses finally came along and changed everything. I was a hypersensitive kid. I liked 70s classic rock and the singers and songwriters of that era. Loggins and Messina, Bread, and Joni Mitchell. My love of music takes me from the Bee Gees to Slipknot and everywhere in between. So long as it matches the fire inside. I like for my music to rip me in half, and I still do.

I can't listen to the song "River" by Joni Mitchell too often. It reminds me of Brian. It hurts too much. The places I get to go by way of music are unlike anything I've ever felt before. Music is my other constant companion. I take it with me everywhere I go. If I don't have to talk to anyone, my music is on. Always there to comfort me, console me, and motivate me at every turn. It's my second-best friend in life. Sometimes my moods can change like the wind. The highs are very high the lows are very low. And there's always a soundtrack or a song to match it: all-day, every day. Music takes me into the depths of my sorrow and to ethereal heights that no psychedelic drug could ever give me. It never hurts to tune in and drop out occasionally, however.

Around April or May of 1984, I remember walking up the stairs to my sister Debbie's apartment on a warm Spring night with a suitcase, not knowing for sure if she lived there. I knocked on the door. I heard, "Who is it?" "It's Eddie." "Eddie who?" "Your little brother." Thank God she let me in. I had nowhere to go. She was surprised to see me, to say the least. She let me live with her in a tiny two-bedroom apartment on the 2nd floor on Garfield Ave. Two blocks from Revere beach. My first night there, I threw my suitcase in the corner of the bedroom, opened all the windows, and just lay there crying. I remember falling asleep to smell the salty air blowing in from the window, relieved to be off that fucking bus once and for all. I didn't know what was coming next, and I didn't care. I just wanted to sleep. I didn't even shower to try and wash the bus off me. I was exhausted. Mentally, physically and spiritually exhausted.

Not knowing what was coming next in my life was no big deal to me. So, I compartmentalized that shit and faded off to sleep. Summer was coming to Revere, and I was so close to the beach. My plan was to get up, visit with Debbie, let her know what was going on and what happened, and then go to the beach to sort of wash all of the stress off of me by jumping into the ocean.

Revere was a culture shock for me. My sister worked nights and slept late during the day, so I never saw her much that first Summer. I spent all my time at the beach. Bianchi's pizza and the boardwalk at

Revere Beach Train Station were the places to be that Summer. So, there I went. I didn't know anybody at first, so I kind of kept to myself eating pizza while sitting on the seawall, staring out at the ocean, or watching all the "guidos" walk by with their big hair, playing Bon Jovi music. Gotta love "guidos." It was fun to watch.

There were a few kids I met on "The Ave," as it was called. Shirley Ave., to be precise. All Italians. They were all related to someone who knew someone who knew someone who was in the mob. It was funny. The truth of it was that some of these kids were connected. We ranged in age from 13 to 17 years, and most of us were to attend Revere High School in the Fall. I loved that first summer drinking with everyone. Again, it was all Bon Jovi and Def Leppard. Songs of bravado and unrequited love, and for some reason, everyone was named Gina. Go figure.

I didn't notice it right away, but after a while, it dawned on me that I drank way faster than everyone else in our crew. I would slam my beer so quickly that I would get attention—the wrong attention. I also had a basketball with me everywhere I went, so I got the nickname "The White Shadow" after an early 80s television show. Then, after that, it was just "Shadow"—a nickname I still have to this day. Basketball was my first love. I was hoping to play in the NBA until I stopped growing at 6' 2" and started getting wider. There was a place called Breakheart Reservation in Saugus, Ma. We would all go to drink beers and light campfires. Again, 80s hair metal was everywhere. I still listen to all that shit today.

We would all pile into whoever had a car at the time, fill the trunk with Budweiser, and head out for the day to swim and drink and listen to music. It was always a lot of fun. Debbie slept in late, so I would normally just leave her a note letting her know in which general area I would be for that day, so she didn't worry too much. It was always the beach or Breakheart anyway. Or up at my buddy Jim's house at the top of Garfield Avenue. That was sort of the central meeting place for all the neighborhood kids to drink. His mother worked nights as a bartender on the beach, so we would just take over his house and drink and smoke cigarettes. At least 20 strong. Fucking kids everywhere slamming beers and talking shit. I still talk to a couple of those kids to this day. A few still live in the same neighborhood. Jim still lives in the same house. Some people never leave their neighborhood. Townie mentality, I guess.

That first summer on Revere Beach was a lot of fun. Sunburns, sand, Budweisers, and Bon Jovi. I remember it fondly. We would save all the empty Budweiser cans as sort of mini trophies of our nightly adventures drinking and talking crap to each other. There had to be hundreds and hundreds of cans in the backyard of Jimmy's house. I don't know how his mother never found out. Maybe she knew, and she just didn't care.

Fall arrived, and with it, the first day of high school. Revere High. Giant hair, Aqua net, dungaree jackets, and cologne and perfume that stunk up the hallways.

I stood out like a sore thumb. The high school was predominantly Italian. Everybody smoked, and in between classes, it seemed like everyone, I mean everyone, was making plans to do one thing or another after school or in between periods, at recess, and at lunch. It's like these little Italian kids all needed a fucking secretary. It was hilarious. And it was all very hush-hush for some reason. Guidos are a trip. I love 'em. My high school was like being in the movie *Grease*, except one hundred percent Italian. One of the funniest things I heard in the lunch line was a student saying, "I can't eat this. My mother would kill me. Mingya!" I laughed my ass off. The little mobsters that they were. The first day of high school didn't exactly go as planned for me, however. I was told to go home before I ever got to homeroom. I wore a Pussycat Lounge T-shirt from a strip club in the infamous combat zone in Boston. The combat zone was a den of iniquity, Sodom and Gomorrah, a seething cauldron of shitty bars and strip clubs and sex shops in between Chinatown and Back Bay. It was fabulous. All manner of sin was represented within three square blocks. Seedy, nasty, and perfect.

My sister was a bartender and a dancer at the Pussycat Lounge, and after work, she would bring her fellow dancers home or friends, and I would wake up and watch them party. Coke, weed, and booze were made readily available, and I remember feeling so cool watching these people get high and telling war stories about their night at work. I learned a hell of a lot about what not to do when it came to drugs. I only got high occasionally. It was only weed. I was still a weekend warrior at that point. Being there watching them party felt so bohemian to me. No one seemed to care about time or responsibilities the next day. It was a big party, and consequences be damned. They played Black Sabbath, Jefferson Airplane, and Janis Joplin on LP. I would sit in the corner of the room and learn, jam out with them, and occasionally smoke weed. They called it diesel. It smelled like pickles. Two of Debbie's friends, Gina (another Gina) and Brittany, dancers at the Pussycat and lovers, turned me onto it.

I got extremely high. I loved it when they all came over. Occasionally the sweet smell of the salty air would sweep across the room, and I felt like I had found a home. My sister felt more like a roommate than a guardian. I would wake up to go to school, and there would be a note, always with a song reference thrown in, like from the band Wham, and there would be $5 or $10 on top of the note. She made me feel like an adult. I loved that about her. School lunch was free, so I would pocket the money and buy smokes or pizza on the beach. Don't get me wrong; if I screwed up, she was all over me. But it was more like a look she would give me. Sort of saying, "Really, dude?"

If I did get punished, it was never severe and never lasted that long. Most of the time, it was extra babysitting duty for her daughter, my niece Desiree. I was left to my own devices for most of that Summer and pretty much all the Fall. I never got into any real trouble. Not yet anyway. The freedom that Debbie offered me in a strange way taught me a lot of responsibility. I could come and go as I pleased if I wasn't out all night and if I didn't come home fucked up. Which never really happened. My disease hadn't progressed at all. In fact, it had only just begun. At that age, I had no idea I was an alcoholic. Nor did I give a shit, really. To me, it was only beer, and it wasn't every night. So I didn't see a problem at all.

Everyone in the neighborhood drank the same way. I miss that time in Revere with Debbie. I miss that early age of discovery and feeling free. She taught me a valuable lesson. Not to take life too seriously. It's gonna happen anyway. Debbie passed away from stomach cancer not long after my Brian died. At this time, she was living in Clemson, South Carolina, with her daughter Desiree. She didn't let on as to how serious it was until the very end, and by then, she was gone—another loss.

High school didn't last very long. I left school in my freshman year. I went to work doing anything and everything I could to make money legally. I ended up on a framing crew in Revere with a high school buddy and his brother-in-law, building houses. They started their own business, and business was good. I was learning a new trade, working outside, and having a great time making good money. We were a four-man crew, and it would usually take us about seven days to frame a house from form to finish, which is rather good for four guys.

By this time, I had found an apartment on McClure Street right behind the high school. A furnished one bedroom with a landline. An old rotary phone. The drapes in the bedroom were so thick that not a ray of sunlight could get in. A dark, dark maroon. Vampiric. It had a queen-size bed and a kitchenette. Everything a kid needed. $400 a month. And with my framing job, I was making $400 a week in cash. So, I had a little bit of savings going. The weekend warrior in me was still alive and kicking. I was very disciplined during the week, but come Friday night, it was on. Usually the same thing, a shitload of beers, and riding around with friends, listening to music, and smoking weed.

I loved that little apartment. It was my first time living all alone. I was very disciplined. Food shopping, bills, work. I never missed a day of work. The weekends brought the beers and riding around, and all-day Saturday meant basketball. Pickup games with friends. Serious competition, though. I loved it. This was when I began lifting weights. I had grown to 6' 2" in height, but I was skinny. I witnessed a pretty bad bar fight, and it triggered something in me. I joined a gym the next day and got after it. Seeing that fight brought me back to the helplessness I felt as a kid being physically unable to stop the violence I witnessed and was subject to. No more! I was determined to become as strong as I possibly could so that no one could ever hurt me or a loved one again.

So that's what I did and still do to this day. I never need motivation to tear it up at the gym. Everything I do is done with full force and all my strength. To make it impossible for you to hurt me. I have done well. Thanks to my rage and my insatiable appetite, I am still the same height but much larger and much stronger.

My home, work, and gym routine went on for quite some time. Dare I say I might have been happy for a little bit? I enjoyed it all. I became an expert thrift shopper—a bargain hunter for food, clothing, and anything I could get on the cheap.

Revere is not that big of a town, so on those Friday nights, we would drive around to different pockets of the city to drink and smoke with different clicks. Fistfights never lasted long, and the beefs were usually squashed right away, or lifelong grudges were born. No in-between, really.

Chapter Three
Coming Up

At around seventeen, I started to explore my homosexuality. I always knew I was gay. By the way, people, and I can't believe everybody doesn't know this, being gay is not a choice. I've been asked many times when I "decided" to be gay. I usually ask straight people the same question. When did you decide to be heterosexual? They usually shut up after that.

After a night of drinking and riding around listening to rock and roll (David Coverdale and the mighty Whitesnake took over the country that summer with their self-titled album, that shit was everywhere), I would split off from the crew and walk to a stretch of the beach known for late-night cruising for gay men. I couldn't wait to get there on a Friday or Saturday night. Usually both. What seemed like an endless menu of strangers making themselves available for sins of the flesh were readily abundant. And I, with a good buzz going from a night of beers and Bon Jovi, was like a kid in a candy store. It was fantastic.

It was about a 100 yard stretch of seawall directly across the street from the M.D.C Police Department. The Metropolitan District

Commission. It always made me laugh. Directly across the stretch of beach that was infamous for late-night hookups. I loved the smell of the sea on the air at night, and I loved cruising men.

Anonymous sex is a hell of a lot of fun for a 17-year-old horny kid. Men would line up with their backs to the seawall, opposite the police station, and cruise each other all night long. It was all so very exciting. And addicting. I started cruising the beach on a nightly basis.

Just across the street from the M.D.C was an area where cars would park, and people would hop in and out of each other's rides. It always made me laugh. If I was parked behind a car with a couple of strangers looking for love, I would suddenly see one head disappear into the lap of another. It was hot.

There's a place in the Fenway neighborhood in Boston called "The Fens" that is infamous for late-night cruising. It has been there for a long time. If you know The Fens, then you know what I mean—so much fun. There was something so exciting about outdoor public sex. I think it was the fear of being caught. That, combined with hunting the chubby, straight married types, I think, is what kept me coming back— and getting off, of course. I think more than anything, I was lonely, though. I couldn't come out of the closet yet to any of my friends, but I started to realize just how lonely I was. And cruising the beach at night would fill that void, even if only temporarily. By this time, I was 18 years old, and I was horny all the damn time. So, it only makes sense I'd go down there as often as I possibly could. I usually hooked up with married men who got to do things and have things done to them that their wives would never do. They were always so eager. The beer is what made it possible, though. It gave me the courage to go down there and to do what I did.

I started venturing out to nightclubs in Boston. Looking for love, lust, or whatever would come my way. It was all so exciting. I was looking for Mr. Right or even Mr. Right Now. Napoleon Club in Bay Village was a favorite spot of mine—a gentleman's bar, really. It was beautiful. It was dimly lit. It had brass and glass everywhere, sparkly things, and shiny objects reflecting here and there. It was one of the oldest clubs in the city, and back in the day, a jacket and tie were required for entry. That tradition still seemed to hold true when I became a regular patron. The bartenders wore jackets and bow ties. They look very professional. Upstairs was a dance floor and another bar. Downstairs, upon entry, was a coat check and a host to greet you. It was lovely. There was a room off to the left with a baby grand piano and the legendary Mary Faith at the helm. She had been playing show tunes and the like for the gentlemen of Napoleon Club for as long as anyone could remember—an absolute legend. In fact, it was at her piano that I met my dear friend Peter. It was a late-night, early morning on a Saturday, almost closing time when I glanced across the room, and I saw him. He was just standing there with a mischievous grin on his face, holding a martini, staring at me. How handsome, I thought, he was. I said to myself I had better investigate! I sauntered over to his smile and introduced myself.

"Hey, I'm Ed," I said. "Hey, I'm Peter. Nice to meet you." We went to the main bar to grab another round and returned to the piano room. Mary Faith was just finishing her night and was about to leave, leaving Peter and me alone. We seemed to hit it off right away. It felt natural. Organic. I felt like I had known him for a long time, even though we had only just met. With his easygoing demeanor and tempting smile, I felt comfortable right away. We drank and chatted and flirted until the lights came on for last call! That was fast, I thought. Peter invited me back to his place for a nightcap. Yes, please! I was more than happy to. He lived on the 3rd or 4th floor of a brownstone on Commonwealth Ave in the Back Bay in a lovely little apartment. We had a couple of cocktails and listened to Elton John on L.P, I think. It felt good being there with him. It was the first time I had been inside one of the brownstones. I had always wondered what they were like. We chatted on the couch for a while, and again, as I do with most things in life, I dove right in. I planted a kiss on that beautiful mouth of his. It was so alluring. I couldn't wait. Peter was a wonderful lover—sweet, playful, and kind. We were hot and heavy for a while. I'm proud to now be able to call him family after almost 30 years. He and his partner Roy sort of became mentors for me. I love them. Sadly, Peter would lose Roy shortly after I lost my Brian. He knows the pain. I love Peter B. I am grateful and lucky that he is in my life.

For most of my early life, trial and error have been my stepping stone. So many mistakes were made because I wasn't shown or didn't have the basic knowledge or stable foundation early on that so many take for granted. I would trip and fall repeatedly. I'm going to jump ahead to this date.

Chapter Four

Drinking Life

September 28th, 2019

And so, I begin yet another treatment center here at St. Matthew's house—Justin's place Regeneration Program in Naples FL. The third inpatient treatment center in as many years. When my Brian died, I climbed into a bottle with absolutely no intention of climbing out. The pain was too much to bear. I would wander the streets of Seattle at all hours, drunk, and in the grips of a sorrow the likes of which I never felt before. I cared for nothing and no one, least of all myself. All that mattered was that there was a half-gallon of vodka in my gym bag slung over my shoulder. I hated the world. Brian's parents lived in Colorado, and it was his wish to be cremated. His ashes went to Colorado with them. I didn't fight it. They were old and in pain. We didn't have a burial plot for him, so I had no specific place to mourn him. I felt so very lost. I felt the pain of his loss as if it were a palpable, tangible entity. I'm accustomed to pain, but this was something on a level I had never experienced before. It was all-consuming. It was all over me. And it would not go away. I was in agony over it and I could not get it off me.

The first inpatient program I went to was a 28-day stay in Seattle called Sea Mar. Useless! I was surrounded by infants coming off methamphetamine and heroin, and they were bouncing off the fucking walls. All day. Every day I had to fight to hear the message. My first night there was just before the one-year anniversary of Brian's death. I was basically homeless, almost without hope, and buried in despair. I felt like a worthless piece of shit.

However, I was born with this thing inside me that doesn't give up. To me, there's always something good that can come out of a bad situation if you know how to look for it. There's always something good that can come out of my pain and sorrow, I thought. After a futile 28 days, I was kicked to the curb. Set free as I saw it. I lit up a smoke and walked into the city with some hope, but not feeling any different from when I walked in. It wasn't long before I filled my gym bag with vodka and picked up right where I left off. It's easy to get lost in pain.

A good friend once quoted Frederick Nietzsche, something along the lines of "Don't let the darkness take you." Suicide was never an option for me. It's just not who I am. I continued to wander the neighborhoods near where Brian and I lived, listening to an old Ozzy Osbourne song called "Tonight," wallowing in an agonizing cocktail of pain, anger, and indignation. I would sit on the pews at Saint Joseph's Catholic Church in between masses, crying and searching for some sign of Brian. A clue, a word, anything to let me know he was okay. Nothing. It went this way for a long time until my second stint in a Native American rehab called Thunderbird.

Thunderbird had twice as many kids as the first rehab. Romper room rehab as I like to call it. Again, heroin and meth were the drugs of choice for most of the inpatients. There were only three alcoholics other than me. Another rehab and another anniversary of Brian's passing.

I was lucky enough to get a moment to myself at 6:11 p.m. on February 9th and said a little prayer for him. I didn't care about much anymore. Thunderbird was comprised mostly of Native Americans from tribes in Seattle and around the Pacific Northwest. They were a federally-funded program, however white people were allowed in. I was most definitely a minority there and was made to feel so just about every day. No big deal. I grew up in Roxbury, Massachusetts. An all-black and Puerto Rican neighborhood. Being the minority was nothing new to me. Fuck 'em. Most of the residents had little or no teeth in their heads. Don't smoke meth kids. I don't judge anyone based on appearance. But what I'm not is a morally bankrupt piece of shit. Being an addict doesn't give anyone the right to take way more than they need or at the expense of others. There are people in rehab truly looking for a change, but they are few. Most are court-ordered and looking to lay up and do nothing instead of going to jail. Which brings me back to St. Matthew's house.

I was in Seattle working for a French Bistro called Maximilien, located in the historic Pike Place Market, near the waterfront in Seattle. A great little restaurant with a killer view of Puget Sound and the mountains. Spectacular sunsets. Some friends on Bainbridge Island introduced me to St. Matthew's house while I was still drinking.

They told me it was a one year inpatient program and that it was faith-based. Fuck that. I'd much rather be out there, running and gunning. I sobered up after about a month, briefly. I did a little more research. It sounded pretty good on paper. I thought of it as a mashup of a 12-step and a faith-based program. I said screw it, what have I got to lose? I was required to go to a detox at N.C.H, North Collier County Hospital in Naples, FL. They basically kept me on Librium, and would monitor vitals every six hours. If I didn't detox medically, I ran the risk of a seizure or suffering delirium tremens. No fun. Normally I would try to wean myself off the booze.

It takes about a week for me to come down from a gallon of vodka a day. Two half-gallons in about 18 hours to be precise. Usually some rot-gut Russian vodka. That was the norm for a long time. It took that much booze to bury the pain of my childhood, the loss of Brian, and the loss of Debbie.

After detox, I was admitted. The campus, called Justin's place in LaBelle, Florida, is an hour or so Northeast of Naples, in the middle of nowhere. It serves as a functioning three-story, old, Miami-style stucco hotel. Fifty-eight other men and I walked the halls, trying to stay out of each other's way. A Jesus camp is what it was.

Again, there was some 12-step and N.A (Narcotics Anonymous) here, but it leaned way more toward Christianity. A Jesus boot camp. Hence, the term faith-based. I genuinely believe the staff means well, but the problems I have here are twofold: one is that, in my experience, a lot of fledgling Christians tend to live by a "Do as I say not as I do" philosophy. The hypocrisy is always just on the other side of their mouths. The second is that I hear homophobic comments from people and from staff members occasionally, and it pisses me off to no end. For this reason alone, I don't think I will stay. St. Matthew's is geared more toward creating Christians out of heathens than it is anything else. If you're looking for a militant-style Jesus bootcamp, then this is the place for you. There are kind, caring people here, but if you stray from the Christian way, then all that love that comes your way is gone. Fuck that shit.

This will most likely be my last attempt at sobriety at a rehab facility or anything of this kind. The fact is I don't think I ever want to stop drinking. I don't think I ever really did. I did it for other people. Or to try and save money, keep my place, to live, or get myself back in shape. Or to not lose the people in my life that I loved. I may be too long in the tooth to change. More likely, after Brian died, a part of me just stopped caring. I may just wander, and expatriate in my own country, traveling, and drinking. It will take miracle to keep me from doing what it seems to be in my nature to do (and I don't just mean drinking). I keep my skeptical ears open for now.

At least the campus here is beautiful. The hotel is a bit rundown, but the landscaping is lovely. A creek surrounds the western side of the hotel. The Oxbow it is called. Funky ass swamp water with two gators and a shit load of water moccasins. Oh joy. But the problem with this program was that you couldn't go anywhere by yourself. They had this thing where they wanted residents to hold each other accountable 24-hours a day. What they meant was, rat on your fellow inmate the first opportunity you get. In the eyes of these Christians, being a rat bastard was ok in the eyes of Jesus. Hard for me being around residents that I knew didn't give a shit about recovery. They were there because they were given an option other than prison. I don't blame them. I would have done the same thing. Their "I don't give a fuck" attitude was so blatantly obvious to me. And again, the ever-present noise. Always loud bangs. Sudden changes in volume, and some of the dumbest motherfuckers I've ever seen in my life. Some of the things they would say and do, I wondered how the hell they got through life. They stood on the legs of other people, that's how. Their parents most likely. If they had any.

I always wondered how some of them could ever hold down a job. Truth is that a lot of these young kids had no skill set to use. Addiction hit them at an early age. Before they got to develop some of these things. They're kind of screwed in that sense. It still doesn't give you a reason to be a thieving piece of shit though. These guys would steal pretty much anything simply for the thrill of it, I think.

Activities and little extras that were thrown our way once in a great while, like television privileges, were always being taken away because someone stole a roll of toilet paper from the communal bathroom. Or something as equally stupid. It didn't really matter. Residents ranged in age from 18-years old up to almost 70-years old. Men who had been through programs time and time and time again. St.

Matthew's House boasted a success rate of 95%. This was not true, but was one of the main attractions for me. I thought to myself, well, maybe these guys know something other places don't. I've got to at least give it a shot. That number turned out to be a crock of shit!

The bottom line is this, at St. Matthew's House, the whole idea was to turn you into a God-fearing Christian. Then, God would cure you of your addiction. But not before. It just doesn't work that way. I can't tell you how many times I begged God on my knees ripping the hair out of my head to please help me. I gave up on that notion. I have come to realize that perhaps this is just what I am.

I looked forward to every evening in the LaBelle dining room, however. The sunsets from the westerly view were fantastic. I could see spectacular sunsets on a nightly basis. What a beautiful gift. With Winter almost here in LaBelle Florida, my body's clock told me it's time for the dark and the cold the rainy nights of Seattle. How I so enjoyed my walks in the mist and rain. The leaves stuck to the sidewalks created a never-ending puzzle pattern to stroll by. I rarely looked up. I could feel the cocoon of the dark and the damp, and it felt comfortable to me.

I never thought I would get used to it let alone miss it. It was always nice to cross the threshold of some random cafe or neighborhood pub that I've never been to after walking for hours aimlessly. People in Seattle rarely talk to one another unless they know each other. It's the one thing I like the most about it. I can be left the hell alone. It's a gift really. The "Seattle Freeze" they call it. The bare minimum in conversation needed to order a beer or a cup of coffee is perfect. After losing Brian, I had no desire to speak to anyone. For a relatively small city, it's easy to disappear into Seattle. So that's what I did, riding buses, the light rail, and walking around endlessly. Stopping only to load up on vodka and cigarettes and charge my phone. I would sit in a coffee house up on 15th Ave. Starbucks or Victrola and order something warm, dump half of it out, and fill the rest with vodka. All while charging my phone and watching people as if I were The Vampire Lestat. And always, always there was my music. I had to have it. The driving force in my life. It was and still is my constant companion, breaking my heart at every turn, consoling me, wrapping me in a warm blanket and putting me to bed.

After reloading walking supplies and having a fully charged battery, I would move on. Anywhere. A left turn, or right turn. It didn't matter. As long as I had the cloud cover, the rain, and my vodka.

I remember getting caught in a snowstorm one night down by the Convention Center. It had started snowing heavily, which happens very rarely in Seattle. But when it does, it comes down hard. It was coming down hard on this night. I was on my way back up to the Hill, when I passed a woman in a wheelchair who was stuck. The buses had stopped running, and she needed to get up to the Safeway on 15th, which was where I was going anyway. I couldn't believe no one would help her. They just kept walking by. I said, "OK, I gotcha. Let's go!" I got in behind her ,and pushed her up the hill through the snow, up Pike Street, all the way down Broadway to East John, and then up the Hill to Safeway. We were both buried in snow. It was kind of fun. I was fucking exhausted. We made it up there finally, and I dropped her off to a waiting friend. She thanked me repeatedly, and I went on my way, good deed for the day accomplished. The snow kept falling, and I had nowhere to go. So, I walked down 15th to Volunteer Park. I had vodka in my bag and cigarettes. But the snow would not stop. What the fuck was I going to do?

I went into the park and found a huge pine tree with boughs that hung all the way to the ground. I climbed underneath. It was dry and a little warm, and I hunkered down for the night. I drank my vodka, curled up, and fell asleep. It had continued to snow throughout the night. I awoke to the sound of a dog barking, and a little kid laughing. I was still kind of out of it from the vodka. I'll never forget this; I laughed my ass off.

I poked my head out through the snow-covered bottom boughs of this tree, and I scared the shit out of a little kid that was about three feet away from me. All I could hear was his dog and his laughter, and I didn't know what it was. I poked my head out as if to say, "What the hell is going on?" His little eyes got so wide, he screamed, and bolted off to find his mother. I rolled over on my back, good morning. I had to laugh to myself. I scared the shit out of that kid. "Mommy, I saw a snowman, and he smelled like Kettle One!" After walking around forever, eventually, I would tire of it, and find a shitty motel somewhere to crash if I had the money. Usually, by then, the booze had done its job, and I didn't care for anything but sleep. A lot of times I would check into one of the local bath houses on Capitol Hill. $40 for 12 hours.

Anonymous sex with "whom the fuck ever." Or just a crash pad for the night. It didn't matter. I would check in, go to my room, set up my bar, and smoke a cigarette before heading to the showers to wash up and see what kind of men were on the prowl that night. Time didn't matter anymore. I would make a strong drink in my room, put on my headphones, and tune the world out in a darkened room no bigger than an average jail cell. It was warm, and I was away from people for the next 12 hours. Unless I wandered the halls of the bath house looking for love.

In pretty much any bath house, or at least the ones in Seattle, all the windows are blacked out. No light. No sense of time. I've walked out thinking it was 7 a.m., and it would be black as pitch and raining. That always took some getting used to. My only concern was not timing it properly, and running out of booze, missing a liquor store before it closed.

There are a few 24-hour places in Seattle I would go to in the early hours of the morning if I wanted to get warm, or just be around other people without having to talk to them. Lost Lake Cafe being one of them. My favorite. There are two sides to this place separated by a fire wall. On one side is the 24-hour diner with a dozen or so half swivel stools posted up to the waist high cafe counter. The breakfast looked good even though I rarely ate. I'd order something just for the familiarity of it. I only ate every three or four days, and that was just to stay alive so I could continue to drink. No food, no drink. It's that simple. I looked at food as an annoyance that had to be tolerated. On the other side was the bar, my favorite of the two. Not for obvious reasons, but because it was always dark, and the clientele was straight out of the Cantina bar from Star Wars. There were freaks from every corner of society, and it was fabulous. Gay, straight, trans, black, white, steampunk, goth and people like me. Whatever the hell I am? At any time of the day or night, it's a good place to hide in plain sight. I spent almost an entire day there last Halloween, drinking and watching movies with other misfits and lost souls, vicariously enjoying the parade of costumes and the endless menu of strangers. It was a lot of fun. I tip waitstaff very well being in the industry myself so I could stay as long as I wanted. Usually never more than an hour or two or the time it took to charge my phone. Lost Lake is a haven for me. I was there on Halloween for at least one shift change, having tipped in excess of $100 the bar staff who were well aware of my presence and took good care of me. Heavy handed pours and free shots came my way every once in a while. It was a mutual respect thing.

If I did engage someone, it was out of loneliness, or a need for affection. Having moved around so much and being thrust into so many situations and scenarios, it's rather easy for me to adjust to most people or environments. Winning the confidence of someone is not difficult. My philosophy about life is simple, don't be a dick! Easier said than done sometimes. If I were in the drink to just the right amount, I would find someone suitable to make out with. This was simple physical contact. No one would ever get my true affection or heart again. Nothing or no one could ever compare to kissing my Brian. Especially the first kiss we ever shared together and the intimacy we enjoyed in one another. Everything else is second. Making out with a stranger in a bar was a mere distraction. It very rarely happened. Sometimes I just didn't care.

Unlike at the bath houses, I prefer to see men fully clothed before we engage. Something about leaving more to the imagination I should think. Undressing a man was half the fun. I've been in LaBelle for a little while now and I can't believe that I'm starting to miss Seattle. The short-term goal if I don't stay the whole year is to get to Key West in time for the season to begin. Restaurant work. It's about five weeks from now. I can't see myself staying a whole year in club Jesus.

My particular brand of destruction always ends up in overdrive so Key West is not exactly the best place for an alcoholic to be, but I'm broke and it's the perfect place to stack money quickly. From December to May I can make a lot of money. I just have to stay sober for the season. This I can do. Usually not for more than six to eight months though. By that time, my head is a hornets nest of anger from the overall stress of the restaurant business and the pain from the past. If you really want to see just how stupid some people are, become a waiter or bartender. Anything in the service industry, really. The idiocy is fucking rampant. As is the entitlement. There is a page on Facebook called "Server Life." It's all about nightmare guests, told from the point of view of waitstaff and bar staff. If you need a good laugh, I highly recommend it. Everything from two well-dressed senior citizens fist-fighting in the dining room at Ruth's Chris steakhouse—I saw that one personally—to a woman absolutely losing her mind because we didn't have an extra seat on a busy Saturday evening for her son's imaginary friend. Unbelievable! That poor kid.

The Florida Keys may present a challenge initially because I'm technically homeless. When I look back in detail over my life, I realize I've been homeless off and on for most of it. It hurts too much to think about, so I don't go there very often. Not without booze handy. Having

25-plus years as a professional waiter and bartender, I usually find work within a day or two, so I'm not worried about that part of it.

The Jimmy Buffett lifestyle in the Florida Keys is incredibly attractive and a recipe for disaster at the same time. Bring it on. I'll keep you posted. For some reason I'm reminded of Bob Seger's song "Turn the Page." Always a good one. Maybe I'll find a lover down in the Keys. I'm lonely. It would be nice to feel someone lying next to me in bed. Someone to have fun with, go sailing with, get naked with. Or just hightail it to the Bahamas.

There's something about the Caribbean that I can't get enough of. Perhaps I'll disappear and spend the rest of my days with rose-colored glasses on somewhere in Bimini or Treasure cay. Time stands still for me when I'm in the Caribbean. I lose all track of it in a good way. I feel free. I can swim all day, wait tables, or tend bar at night. And just get lost. Island time hits me right away and I just don't rush around anymore with barely a thought to the mainland. I could live in the Bahamas easily. The white sand and turquoise waters are awfully hard to get away from. So lovely. Soon enough.

Chapter Five

Roxbury, MA and the Adventures of a Scared White Boy

"The Berry," as it is called is where I'm from. On December 14th, 1969, I was born at Boston City Hospital, to Juanita and Thomas Cleaves III. From what I was told, we lived on Haverford Street in Jamaica Plain, the next town over. But I have no memory of that place. All my memories begin at 44 West Walnut Park.

Good Lord, where do I begin? Roxbury in the early to mid-70s was a predominantly black and Puerto Rican neighborhood. We had Orchard Park and Bromley Heath Housing Projects up the road, Egleston square was at the top of my street, and there was crime everywhere. The white neighborhood was my house. I lived in constant fear most of the time. I honestly thought my name was "White Boy" for so long because the only people that called me Eddie were my siblings and my mother. My brothers, sister, and I were constantly harassed. I got beat up a lot. I got punked, slapped, and made to feel that I was gonna get my ask kicked at any moment. All the time being chased home from school got to the point where I would think, really? Again?

The fastest kid in an all-black neighborhood was me. Actually, it was my sister Michelle. Being caught meant getting a beating. It always made me furious after. However, I was being chased home to a place much scarier than the streets of Roxbury.

By the way, most of this is written from memory. I'm still here at club Jesus and have no access to my phone or Internet or any research material. Not having vodka on the brain affords me some clarity, however. So here we go.

We lived in a single-family three-bedroom house that was so rundown it was condemned by the city. There was no heat most of the time, so during winter, we all slept in one room with the beds pushed together. Every blanket we owned was on this makeshift fort. I am the second-youngest of seven children. My three oldest siblings Patty, Debbie, and Butchie had all made their escape in their mid-teens. And that's exactly what the fuck it was—an escape. My biological parents were not together. I don't know if they ever married or divorced. My mother had a live-in boyfriend named Amos. He was about as white trash as they come. They were both blackout drunk, violent alcoholics. So was my biological father. Imagine Hannibal Lecter from the movie *Silence of the Lambs*, only blacked out and murderous most of the time. I watched Amos grit his teeth and snarl at something across the room that wasn't there, and it scared the life out of me. It scares me still. I think I was six years old when I first met him, and it was a terrible experience. He was pissed drunk but seemed to still have his balance and his faculties for the most part. He had a knife in his hand, and he kept throwing it at the floor, and it would stick. Over and over, he did this with the crazed look in his eye. I was terrified. He drank Jack Daniels like water, and he smelled like Aqua Velva aftershave. To this day, I hate the smell of both. So, left in the house in Roxbury were myself, my older sister Michelle, and my little brother Johnny. Johnny was Amos' son. Half-brother to me, but my brother, nonetheless. My older brother Jimmy was with us for a little bit but at 15 or 16 years old, he escaped.

As bad as the crime and the violence was in Roxbury, I still managed to have one friend, a kid named Terry Dixon White. Terry White. I used to ask him if his middle name was "Ain't." He never got the joke. West Walnut Park, from my house to the top of the street, was a bit of a haven from the rest of the area. There were a few families with kids, and we would all play football when I was allowed to join. Until the streetlights came on. I hated those fucking streetlights. It meant I had to go back inside, back to "them."

Our house was constantly filthy. Roaches and rodents were always there. Trash everywhere, clutter, and chaos. It looked like a bomb went off. Almost literally. In a poor neighborhood, we stood out as being really, really poor. There was always booze though. Not always food, but always booze. Smirnoff vodka for my mother. She would put it in her coffee first thing in the morning.

One of us kids would have to go and knock on the neighbor's door to ask for $5 so we could buy cereal for breakfast. I hated doing this. I felt so ashamed. I was six years old and one of my earliest feelings in life was shame. If not constantly being sent out to borrow money to eat, then being sent up to Egleston Square to a small supermarket with a grocery list and a note for the clerk with a promise to pay later. Sometimes they gave us food, sometimes not. Always there was shame.

I ate lunch in school most of the time anyway. That was one meal that was guaranteed at least.

My mother's boyfriend Amos was a piece of shit. White trash. I never saw him drink in the morning. He was usually passed out. He was a gangly man with a pigeon chest, an overbearing and abrasively loud laugh, and bad teeth. I hated him. I saw him as the reason why we lived the way we did. Anything he fixed around the house never worked again, heating, the television, etc. We had the classic TV on top of the div.

I remember watching *The Brady Bunch* and seeing how clean their home was and that there was always food. I would look around me and think, *what the hell*? This isn't normal. This isn't right. If food was spilled on the floor, it stayed there. Clothing was everywhere. There was one room on the first floor that I just didn't go into. There was something ominous and frightening about that room. The kitchen table was littered with ashtrays, cigarette butts, and cans of beer. It smelled like stale booze, and always, the ever-present roaches.

If there was cereal to eat, we would have to shake the box before pouring any out just in case there were bugs in it. The weekends brought the struggle for breakfast from time to time, and off I went with note in hand. During the week, we ate in school: breakfast and lunch, guaranteed food. Every time I walked into my friend Terry's house, I looked around thinking, *wow, you guys must be rich!* This was still the ghetto, by the way. Their place was clean, and nothing was sticky. I didn't see any bugs. I wanted to stay there, except I was afraid of his parents. They always referred to me as "White Boy."

When I was invited to come along with some of the neighborhood kids, my brother Jimmy, when he was still with us and I would wander the outskirts of the neighborhood, avoiding the projects at the end of the street at all costs. The black kids would walk through the projects. We always went around. Going in there meant getting beaten up. I did not go in there. They were different people inside those projects. Mean people. They didn't like white people.

Behind those projects was a fire station and next to it was a massive field with a six-foot rod iron fence surrounding it. There was an abandoned factory on the opposite side of the field and someone long before us built a tree house and one of the many apple trees on the property. This became our base of operation for the Ghetto Scooby-doo gang. The floor of the treehouse was at least seven feet off the ground, so the challenge was to see who could jump and land on their feet without falling over.

It took me most of the summer to work up the balls to do it. Nailed it! I felt bionic. The Six Million Dollar Kid. For some reason, the kids in the neighborhood were all into Bruce Lee that summer. In the front of the tree house, we laid out some carpet torn from the floor, and this became our dojo. I was considered a white belt because I didn't know anything about karate, and because I was white. The older black kids were black belts because they were black. Ghetto logic. We would re-enact fight scenes from Bruce Lee movies. I never saw any Bruce Lee movies. I usually just got beat up a lot. Fun though.

The field before the factory was a great place to hunt snakes and hunt them, we did. Garter snakes mostly. I loved flipping over a door or piece of plywood in hopes of catching one. No fear at that age. Oddly enough, I'm scared shitless of snakes now.

I remember wandering off a little bit from my usual hunting grounds and coming across an abandoned door lying in the middle of a rhubarb patch. Good eating, by the way, rhubarb, that is. I flipped over the door and there was a giant milk snake coiled up and staring at me. I screamed for the guys to come check it out. We were all scared of this thing so none of us dared to try and pick it up. I was a legend in the Ghetto Scooby-doo gang for about five minutes that summer, and then back to just regular old white boy again.

The abandoned factory was the perfect place to play "hide and seek" or "army men." We would scatter in all different directions, hide, and then hunt each other like we were in combat. I was good at "army men" because I could run like the wind, and I knew how to hide well. It reminds me of a song entitled "Leave the Light On" by Beth Hart. One of my favorite songs. I played outside every chance I got. All day, every day if I wasn't in school. We had a backyard with one pear tree directly behind the bulkhead leading to the dreaded basement.

I didn't go in that way either. The pear tree was my favorite thing about the backyard other than being outside. It had a plastic milk crate nailed to it with the bottom cut out. Ghetto basketball. Almost impossible to make a basket in that thing. The pears were sweet and delicious. They provided a quick easy snack if I was hungry. I had a lot of fun playing back there.

The houses on either side had connecting backyards so there was even more room to roam. I was a spider monkey by the age of seven. If there was something to climb on or up, I was there. Climbing became another way to escape. And boy could I ever get after it. Getting down, I'd come to find, was another story altogether. Many times, I got stuck way too high in a pear tree chasing a snack or on top of someone's garage, too scared to climb down. The climb up was half the fun.

Then came the day I worked up the courage to go into the dreaded basement. Holy hell! My little brother Johnny and I were home alone. That happened a lot, and one day we dared each other to go and open the basement door. Just walking by the damn thing scared the life out of me. I would scurry past it on my way to the kitchen at night. I don't know what possessed me to do it, but I reached for the door, turned the knob, and I remember thinking, *we're gonna die*. We were so scared. The door was stuck, so I pulled on it and it broke free with a loud, crisp bang. It scared the crap out of us. Our courage was hanging by a thread, and either of us at any second could have slammed the door shut and bolted out the front. I found the light switch and clicked it on. Nothing. I tried it again, and a dim light came on, illuminating only the staircase heading into the basement. A dim, yellow haze.

We're never gonna get out of here alive, I thought to myself. "You go first," I said to Johnny." "No way. You go," he shot back. Down the staircase we went. I remember thinking that as soon as we got to the bottom something was going to pounce on us and swallow us whole. Johnny was clung to my back. There was no space between us. We got down to the last step and under the dirty yellow haze was a second light switch just off to the left. It was as if there was a dingy spotlight on it saying, "Go ahead, I fucking dare you!" I reached out for it, terrified, and switched it on. It crackled, and the whole basement was suddenly illuminated. There were no monsters.

What there was, however, was a complete and total disaster. There was crap everywhere. The parts of the floor that you could see, that weren't covered in old clothes garbage and debris, was covered in about 1/2 an inch of water. It was awful. It had no rhyme or reason to it. Not even a path to walk on. It was damp and dirty, and smelled like oil. We had oil heat, but since there was never any oil, there was never any heat.

We were on welfare from the state, and from time to time I would see my mother using food stamps to pay for groceries. I always felt like people were looking at us differently because of this. Just under the staircase to the basement, we found a little food pantry. It was lined with boxes of potato spuds, instant potatoes. And there was a massive block of orange government cheese. We only knew that because it said "Government Cheese" all down the side of the packaging. One bite of that, and you would never take a crap again. Even the roaches were afraid of it. It wasn't even safe to scavenge and look for things we might want to play with.

It was just wet, smelly, and depressing. We heard something scurry across the other side of the room, so we bolted back upstairs and outside. Crisis averted. The basement wasn't so scary after that. All that time we spent afraid of nothing. I never really went back down there again. There was no reason to.

Looking back on the living conditions of that house, I'm amazed none of us got sick. There were a lot of break-ins in the neighborhood, but no one really messed with us. From time to time, we would hear someone trying to get in through the front or back door. I can only assume after looking around, they realized we had absolutely nothing worth stealing.

My mother's boyfriend kept a closet full of rifles in the bedroom, and would fire a round down the staircase in the dark at any would-be intruder. He never went down there himself. One of the many ways we were woken up in the middle of the night by them. The front door didn't have a lock on it, so we would push an old floor-model freezer up against it at night for security. Again, we had nothing to steal. I never went downstairs after dark anyway. It was way too scary. If we were lucky enough to watch a movie on a working TV, we would gather every blanket in the house, light a Coleman camping stove for heat, and hunker down to stay warm. I would hold my pee for as long as I could, so I didn't have to freeze my ass off going to the bathroom. I can only assume that the bank owned the house, and wanted us out. In addition to not having heat, the lights would go out from time to time. My mother would say it was a fuse, but after a few days, we would always ask why they were still out. A question we didn't ask more than twice.

Because there was no heat, that also meant no hot water. Once, there was no running water for some time. No running water! This was the 70s. What the fuck? One of the most depressing memories I have for my childhood was having to carry buckets of water from the next-door neighbor's spigot. We would use it to flush the upstairs toilet. I would sit to poop, and feces, someone else's feces, would touch my butt from the inside of the toilet because we were unable to flush it without water. I told my mother this, and she laughed. She thought it was cute. It wasn't. We, or I, would have to pour half of the bucket directly into the toilet to make it flush. No running water, but there was always booze.

When the water was running, my mother would boil pots of it, and put it in the tub so we could all bathe. We didn't bathe every day, and had to share the same bathwater. I was reminded of how dirty I was by the kids at school, and by a teacher named Mrs. Harris, I think. She would ridicule me in front of the class, and make me wash my face and hands every morning. I hated her for it. When there were periods without running water, we would all pile into the piece-of-shit station wagon and head to Brockton, Mass to Amos' parent's house to bathe. Usually once a week. We would pile into the tub while they drank, and played cribbage. His parents looked Native American. They had dark skin, and jet-black hair. Everyone stunk of booze. At least their place was clean, and there was food. I can only assume the city shut off the water to force us out.

There are still so many unanswered questions. Summertime in the neighborhood was a blast, however. And in true ghetto fashion, one of the older kids would produce a massive wrench, and pop the fire hydrant directly in front of my house. Such anticipation, I remember. The water would come out ever so slowly, the color of rust, and then, at long last, crystal clear and gushing out in a torrent. Such a relief from the heat and humidity of the unforgiving Boston Summer.

Oh how I loved playing in the fire hydrant, as we called it. I got to cool down, and get clean at the same time. The Fire Department was only a block away or so, and would come turn it off, eventually. As soon as they left, the other kids would turn it right back on. I loved it. I didn't have to look like Pigpen from the Peanuts Gang that day.Going to bed clean was a rare and wonderful experience. To this day, I still shower before bed. Everything is washed away.

The worst part about living in that house, apart from the filth and roaches, was the drinking and fighting. They were daily drinkers, and by the end of the evening, they were both wasted. Blacked out. The fights always started with yelling and screaming about God knows what. We would all lie in bed together, huddled up against the cold, praying it would stop. Then something would smash, furniture would be knocked over, and then the real fighting would begin. We would panic. I was terrified.

Sometimes, they would fight in silence, which was even scarier because we knew they were trying to kill each other. I was never so afraid. We would scream and cry from the top of the stairs to no avail. When they took a break, usually between rounds. One of us, usually me, or Michelle, because she was the fastest, would run to the neighbors, and ask them to call the police. The cops were always at our house. My mother and Amos would be panting, sweating, and one or both would be bleeding. This happened all the time.

Amos had a closet full of rifles, as I'd mentioned, but the cops never took them away from him. It was only a matter of time I thought to myself. Their fights got worse and worse towards the end. As I write this, I'm 49 years old, and still, every time I hear raised voices and drunken arguing, I bristle. I can't take it. Being shocked awake in the middle of the night was common. Something smashing, something breaking, glass shattering. If an argument didn't precede it, then we knew it was serious. More serious than them just beating each other up.

During one particularly violent fight, we ran into their bedroom. Why, I don't know. We usually hid under the bed. They were fighting over a loaded rifle. The barrel was pointed toward the ceiling and my mother was on my right, Amos on the left. My sister Michelle bolted down the stairs to ask a neighbor to call the police again, because, of course, we had no phone. My older brother Jimmy was fearless. He was at the house for some reason. He hated them. He basically ripped the rifle out of their grips, and ran down the stairs with it. They started fighting on the bed. It was awful. We went downstairs into the kitchen, huddled up, and waited for the police. A typical day at 44 West Walnut Park.

My sister Michelle was very fast. My heart still breaks for her. I could always see the look of pain, fear, and downright terror on her face at any given moment in that house. She had such an angelic and apostolic face, so innocent with her long brown hair and hopeful smile. They ruined it. They fucking ruined it. I think she was damaged more than the rest of us by all the violence and intimidation. The uncertainty of our day-to-day, and the unpredictability of their behavior had affected all of us, I fear. At the very least, it has made us all adaptable to almost any situation. Roll with it, and roll with it quickly, became a motto. It has made me able to assess a situation in the blink of an eye. Poor Michelle wasn't that way, I think. She would stand there and cry, with her eyes closed as if she was trying to wish it all away. She was my favorite sibling, and the only girl in the house since Patty and Debbie made their escape long ago.

She seemed to feel things more deeply than everyone else. And when the bad things would come, I could see a change in her, physically. After a while, it became almost second nature for us to dodge that shit because we could see it coming. Still, the crashing and breaking of things that preceded the fight had taken its toll on us all. Breaking glass, or a loud bang, and I became hyper-aware of everything around me. I am still this way today.

I miss Michelle. She's the one sibling I've always worried for more than everyone else. She always seemed so lost.

I remember a day sitting on the front stairs of the house, and I looked down to the end of the street to see my sister Michelle hauling ass, with three girls chasing after her.

She was flying! I had never seen her run so fast. There were three sisters at our school, the John F. Kennedy Grade School, in Roxbury. Triplets in fact, with long thick braids. They look like The Pointer Sisters, and they were bullies. They would beat the crap out of me if I got caught off guard before or after school. It was easy to tell when I had been crying because my face was always dirty. Not to worry though. There was always the lovely Mrs. Harris there to shame me, and make me wash up in front of the class. The bitch.

Watching my sister run like that in some way made me proud. She smoked The Pointer Sisters, and we ran inside and pushed the freezer against the door to block them from getting it. We suffered the usual chants of "You're fucking dead you white bitch," or "We're gonna beat your ass tomorrow at school Honky." People still used the word "Honky" in the mid-70s. I still use it when I watch old white men on T.V. Honkys! I still can't listen to The Pointer Sisters to this day.

Then came the fateful day that I stole fifty cents from my mother's purse to buy candy. Big mistake. I showed it to my friend Terry "Ain't"

White on the way to school, and he took it from me, and ran back home to tell my mother. The little snitch. Terrified, I bolted off to school with the hopes that I could at least delay the beating until the end of the day. I showed up to school sweating, dirty, of course, and panicked. She didn't wait until school was over. She pulled me out of school, and beat me with one of those white aluminum curtain rods. Cheap, but sturdy. The kind that was manufactured by machine so that the backside of them was folded over and still had a sharp edge to it. She hit me over and over, on my back, butt, and legs in the backseat of that shitty fucking station wagon. I screamed and wailed for her to stop. She was drunk, and the look on her face told me I was in for a good one. She then drove me around to show people what she had done. All I wanted was some fucking candy.

She drove me over to my biological father's house, but he was either not home, or passed out drunk. To tell you the truth, I have no idea why she paraded me around to the neighbors, my father's, or to anyone else. I also have no idea as to why no one tried to stop her.

Chapter Six
The Neighborhood

My mother was 42 years old when she died from fire. She always wore a kerchief on her head, and she looked so much older than her 42 years. She had long grey hair. She was underweight, and very frail. She seemed to move, at times, slowly, methodically. Looking back, it makes sense. She was a "round the clock" drinker, and would need to drink first thing in the morning to be able to function. Something I would come to know all too well. She hailed from Valdosta, Georgia, but I never really heard an accent.

The older siblings drove the rest of us from Boston to Georgia for her funeral service. In the short time I spent with my mother, she always seemed to be suffering from something. It broke my heart to see her in pain all the time. She always seemed to be locked in her head. She would put her head down, place her hands on her temples, and sort of moan in pain. I don't know if it was from drinking, being hungover, or some sort of mental health issue. Maybe all the above.

She would pour vodka into her morning coffee, and slowly stand up to get us on our way to school. We were experts by this point. I would dash off to school, usually cutting through the backyards on the way, to avoid getting my ass kicked. It was a good morning when I made it there untouched. Breakfast!

There were moments of sobriety in my mother's life, and in our household. They were very few and far between, but when they happened, there was some sense of normalcy. There would be food. The house would be cleaned. It usually took us all about two days to get it looking like a habitable environment, but when we did, oh boy! I felt like we were worth something. It felt so much better being able to see the floors again. They were usually covered in trash and clothing. But we did have some moments of happiness, or what I considered happiness when they were sober, and usually for brief periods in time. My mother came home one afternoon, we didn't know where she was, with bag after bag of groceries. I had never seen so much food in one place before. The cupboards were full. This was living! The house was clean and there was food.

I brought Terry "Ain't" White over so I could proudly show off all the food we had. He just looked at me like I was crazy. I felt like a king. One of the reasons that Michelle was my favorite was that she would take me to the supermarket. She was a couple years older than me. We would fill the cart with everything we ever wanted to eat from meats to candy soda pop. It would be overflowing with food. Then, we would just push it into the corner, and leave. The first time we did it, it was kind of fun and mischievous. After that, it just seemed sad. I stopped doing it.

Michelle always seemed like she had something going on just under the surface. It was as if she had something painful and pressing on her mind all the time. When the mischievous and playful side of her did come out, we had so much fun. She wasn't a tomboy, but woe to me or any of my other siblings if we pissed her off. She hit awfully hard. I remember pulling the head, arms, and legs off her Barbie doll, throwing them at her, saying, "Oh my God, what happened to Barbie? She doesn't look so good." She just lowered head about 6 inches, staring at me the whole time, and I thought "Oh shit, I'm a dead man." I didn't even make it out of the bedroom before she was on me. She slapped me silly. I never did that again.

Roxbury, or at least my neighborhood, being as poor as it was, had a welfare program or an after-school program rather that kept kids occupied while their parent(s) worked. It was just at the end of West Walnut Park and up about two blocks East. They kept us busy with arts, crafts, and coloring. We never went outside for some reason, which was weird. They also had snacks! Usually peanut butter and jelly sandwiches, and milk. Fine by me. They were mostly kids from my neighborhood, so it was just the usual taunting instead of getting beat up.

I enjoyed it. Monday through Friday. On the weekends, Terry and I would explore some of the abandoned buildings that were at the top of my street near Egleston square. Three and four level apartment buildings that were either burned out or completely empty and abandoned. We fixed one of them up to make a clubhouse. No one ever went in there. They were falling apart and dangerous to be in. Extremely dangerous, especially on the top floors. Holes in the floors and exposed beams were everywhere. Stairs were missing. It was very rickety. We could have fallen at any time, and gotten seriously hurt. I don't think we cared. I know I didn't. Another escape.

There was a walkway behind the tenement building that we played in. An alleyway, really, but it faced my street. The front of the tenement building faced Columbus Avenue which went from Egleston Square directly into downtown Boston. Some of the tenants would throw the garbage over their back-porch railings, and it would pile up in the walkway. Nobody ever cleaned it up. Then, in the heat of the Boston Summer, all you could smell was hot garbage. It was awful. There was another tenement building that had a lot of Puerto Rican families in it. It always smelled so good walking by there. At pretty much any time of the day, someone was cooking. The music was loud and tremendous. Lots of horns and drums. There was a small bodega at the bottom of the building. It smelled like stale everything. I very rarely went in there. No money, and God forbid, I was tempted to steal something to eat. My mother would have beaten the shit out of me.

I was afraid of the clerk anyway. He had a look on his face like he literally wanted to eat me. If I was lucky, I would stumble across some loose change. Or, if I was really lucky, a quarter found somewhere in the household, buried in all the garbage and clothing, I would use it to buy a Honey Bun Glazed cake snack and a pack of Now or Later candies, and devour them both on the way to school. Terry always made me get grape-flavored Now or Later. What is it with the brothers and the color purple? Keeping it real, I guess.

The drinking and the fighting got worse at home. It became a nightly thing. Something smashing, screaming, and the terrifying silence before the real fighting began. The cops were there all the time, and that's the first time I saw a social worker come to the door. I didn't know that that's what she was at the time. Just a stranger. She was tall, and had long grey hair, pulled back into a ponytail, and thick rimmed glasses. Picture a 1960s secretary from any TV show. She was nice enough, but whenever she came over, my mother would begin to cry. She would cry the whole time that the woman was there.

I never understood why until the day came when a bag was packed for me. My mother and the social worker were standing next to it at the front door when I was summoned. I was confused, scared mostly, because my mother was hysterical. I couldn't tell if it was because she was drunk again, or something was really, really wrong this time.

Every time this woman came over, my mother was different. Panicky. I didn't like the social worker for this reason. Go away! We had enough problems. It was early Summer when I was removed from the house, and brought to what seemed like a campground somewhere. We pulled up in front of a silver stream camper, with a picnic table in front of it, and bikes lying around over the fallen pine needles. A barbecue grill, and the smell of food cooking made me hungry. Leaving my house that morning was confusing and extremely chaotic. My mother was losing her mind. I was freaked out because she was. I had no idea what was going on. I was told it was only temporary, and to try to enjoy myself.

In front of the silver stream stood a young couple, and a boy about my age. He came up to me right away and asked me if I wanted to go bike riding around the camp. I told him I didn't have a bike, and he pointed to a beat up old huffy lying on the ground, and said, "It's yours!" Even if it was just a loaner, I was very excited. Terry "Ain't" White taught me how to ride his bike, so I knew how to ride, and off we went.

This place was vastly different from 44 West Walnut Park. No cars, no noise, no fighting, and no one was drunk. No one was passed out or bleeding. It was peaceful. I remember gliding on the huffy, with the sun on my face and feeling the warm breeze wash over me as I rode around the campground. I was on that thing for hours. The insects buzzing here and there over a sunflower patch next to the silver stream made me happy. I got to smell and taste fresh mint for the first time.

I didn't feel stress or anxiety. I didn't feel an impending sense of doom heading off to school. Or running off to school, I should say. I wasn't afraid of the end of the day or fearing another night of fighting. I had no idea this kind of world existed. At all. I missed Michelle and Johnny though. I wished that they could have shared in all of this with me. That was the first time I'd ever really relaxed at night. Sitting around a campfire and thinking, this is the life for me!

Even now at 50 years old, whenever I get the chance to get out into nature or go camping, I feel so much more at ease. City life and the problems and hassles that come with it are gone. Also gone is the obsession and compulsion to drink. I'm not in pain when I'm in the woods. No pain means no booze. Maybe that deserves a little more investigation.

I still never knew why I was brought there that summer. I can only assume I was removed from the house because of the living conditions. We were on welfare, and I think the social worker had seen enough. I don't know why I was the only one chosen. I wish we all could have gotten to go, but it really was the summer of a lifetime. It exposed me to a brand-new world. The smell of pine, swimming in a lake, campfires, food, starry nights, and best of all, peace. It was priceless.

I still never knew where they brought me that summer. I should like to find out. I would like to go back.

At the end of that summer season of magic, I felt like a new person. I was calm. I ate every day and more than once. I took to that life very quickly, and wasn't too keen on letting it go, but when you live at 44 West Walnut Park, you learn young that nothing lasts, and you'd better learn to roll with it and roll with it quickly.

After another day of bike riding and chewing on mint leaves, I returned to the silver stream to see the foster family standing out front with the social worker. My heart sunk. I knew it was over. I cried, and for the first time, I realized I was crying tears of anger. Back to Roxbury. Back to that other life. I felt a shift in my attitude and demeanor. I became more aware of everything again. I was afraid again for the unknown. Would I be in trouble for leaving even though I didn't have a say in the matter?

This time, heading back to Roxbury I had a new and constant companion, anger. Fuck everyone, I thought. Nothing good lasts. I was heading to a new season with a sense of foreboding. Like driving toward a thunderstorm. Everything had a shadow over it again, or some sort of veil or charcoal filter. I was excited to see Johnny and Michelle again, but fuck everything else.

The social worker bombarded me with questions on the way back. I gave her nothing. I tuned her out completely. I had more important things on my mind. Pulling up in front of the house, I felt as if I were betrayed by something or someone. Something was different about me.

Chapter Seven

Early Life

Looking around me and at the condition of the house, I became officially aware that we sucked. That we were white trash. That we were "less than." I felt as if coming back to that house was a giant step backward. I bristled, and for the first time ever, I became aware of a sense of power.

I didn't care anymore. One of the neighborhood kids yelled, "Welcome back, white boy," and I glared at him, unafraid. I pushed the door open, no lock, of course, with the social worker in tow, and I looked around, and, to my surprise, it was spotless. The whole house had been scrubbed clean. It still sucked, however. Everything was old and shitty and broken, but it was clean.

My mother was sitting on the couch with what looked like hopeful anticipation. I'd never seen the house so clean before. Ever. She always wore rayon mom slacks that went up slightly past her stomach, and a blouse with her ever-present kerchief on her head. She seemed so worn down by something in life. I always sensed a mental fatigue emanating from her. The joys of being an empath I suppose. God bless her struggle, but fuck her cruelty.

I didn't know where Michelle and Johnny were. I couldn't wait to see them again. I sat down on the couch to be talked over by those two, looking out the window. I think I was seven years old at this time.

I still got chased home from school from time to time, but only when I was outnumbered, which was pretty much all the time. It became more of a nuisance than anything else. Instead of leaving them in the dust, I would stop when I was far enough away, and taunt them. I was tired of their bullshit. I would unleash profanity laced tirades towards them. Fuck them. It was fun watching them become so angry when I turned the tables, and hurled insults and death threats at them, and they still couldn't catch me. It just made the beating that much worse when they did catch me.

After the social worker left, things were quiet for a little while. Or least until they drank again. Amos fancied himself a carpet installer and told everyone he was self-employed. Laughable. They both ended up being clerks at a liquor store up in Egleston Square. The perfect job for them. I would hang out there sometimes, and watch them work. Amos was the type of person who would take a menial task, like putting a six-pack into a brown paper bag, and make it seem like he was doing God's work. I couldn't stand looking at the man. The epitome of "white trash."

The house had returned to its normal state of "what the fuck" within a couple of weeks. I had come to learn that the only cleaning was done just before the social worker came. So, once a month or so. She didn't take any of us away, but every time she came up the stairs, I was prepared for anything.

All things were subject to change at 44 West Walnut Park. I still live by that model.

Then came the Blizzard of 78'. Holy shit! We had a working TV that winter, but still no heat. So, we knew a massive snowstorm was coming, and boy did it ever. For me, once the first blanket of snow falls, everything seems so clean, and brand new. It's beautiful! The older houses, the trees in the backyard, the old shitty cars, all suddenly became like a Norman Rockwell picture. A beautiful transformation. I loved it. School was cancelled, and off I went to play in the snow. All day. It just kept snowing and snowing.

Behind the pear tree in the backyard was a tall chain link fence that separated us from a parallel street in a completely different neighborhood. I couldn't see the house back there through the endless rhubarb and trees in the Summer. But in the winter, it was much clearer. I would climb that fence and cut through the back yards to get to school when they were out front in the morning ready to chase me again. Morons. The snow had piled up so high from the blizzard that it went almost over halfway up the fence. It was packed in and piled up so high that at one point, I could just almost step right over to make my way to school.

The one good thing about clothes being strewn all over the house was that it was easy to just grab anything that would fit and pile on the layers. What a sight I must have been. Making snowmen, snow angels, having snowball fights, and trying and failing constantly to build an igloo kept me busy during the Blizzard of 78'. What fun it was. Everything in the neighborhood seemed to shut down. The cars were snowed in, and couldn't move. Everything, I mean everything, was buried in snow.

One morning, I got the fancy idea to grab a shovel and try to make money shoveling walkways in the neighborhood with my little brother Johnny. After an exhausting day, we made a whopping $6! Not a bad haul. My mother held onto it. I don't remember ever spending it.

By this time, I started hanging out with the new kid at school, Eric. He lived in the big mysterious house behind mine and over the fence. My "Bridge to Terabithia." Navigating through the rhubarb and assorted flora brought me to the back of an auburn colonial-style house in what seemed to be a completely different neighborhood. He was the only other white kid, other than my siblings, in the area, and we became fast friends. It was also a part of the after-school program, so we spent a lot of time together.

I never saw his dad, and wasn't sure he had one, but his mom was so sweet and kind to me. I think she took pity on me for having so many mismatched layers of clothes on. It became a regular thing for me to jump the fence and join Eric and his mom for breakfast. It was the best part of the day. Their house was so clean. On weekend mornings, I would sit in Eric's living room with his mom, and we would eat cereal and watch cartoons. Eric and I would lay on the carpet on our bellies and stare up at the television with our heads propped up in our hands. It felt good. It felt normal.

Eric became my new best friend. We did almost everything together. He was more of an indoor kid, however. He also had a shitload of toys. New toys, or newish. We played indoors a lot, or in his sprawling backyard. I got close enough to the fence I could see the back of my house. Heading back there never felt as good as heading over.

For a kid the same age as me, Eric would seem to have more of a sense of style. He seemed to pay attention to his appearance. He wore nice clothing. Not things an eight-year-old would normally wear. He wore silk shirts and dark slacks with shiny wingtips. The kid was eight years old and he looked like a mini-mobster. It was hilarious. He had a full head of jet-black hair, always neatly combed. He was always dressed for success, it seemed. I, on the other hand, was a hot fucking mess! I was a total disaster. I looked like "Pigpen" from The Peanuts Gang. A perpetual cloud of dust followed me wherever I went. I'd come to notice as a little kid that when I encountered people I didn't know, they would look at me, and then look at me again. As if they were doing a double-take. I would think to myself, *what the fuck is your problem?* Not realizing that I was just a total mess. I had no idea. Makes me laugh now. Oh well. If no one else cared, why the hell should I have.

Eric was also way into music. The Bee Gees, especially. He seemed obsessed with them. He introduced me to them, and everything changed. One of the good things about growing up in a black and Puerto Rican neighborhood was the music. Someone somewhere had R&B, soul, or funk playing. At the top of the street, it was all Latin music.

At eight years old, I fell in love with funk. Wow! I liked to dance, but I was afraid of being teased, so I always did it alone. But when you hang out with black kids and you start moving a little bit, you're gonna get called out. "Let's see what you got white boy!" So, I showed them. Turns out, I was good. Really good. And dancing to the Bee Gees was my new favorite thing to do. Nothing I could do about my look, unfortunately. I didn't have anything that even came close to John Travolta's disco 70s look. I had to leave that up to Eric. He was the stylish one.

We both loved the movie *Saturday Night Fever*. He even had all the dance moves down. He would practice them at the after-school program to the delight and applause of everyone. Eric was good. This is when I started thinking Eric might be like me in that way. I didn't know what it was called at eight years old, but I knew I liked boys a lot more than girls. I remember seeing him years later. He was working in a boutique clothing store downtown Boston. Gayer than Christmas! Good Lord, the man was flaming. I didn't go up and say hello. I wished I had. He was a good friend to have. He and his mom ended up moving away. I was sad to hear the news. We never got to share a kiss. That would have been nice. *I wonder whatever became of him.*

Chapter Eight
Michelle and I

Things were progressively getting worse at home. The drinking was now a daily requirement for both Amos and Ma. We just called her Ma. The fighting continued, the arguing, and the terrifying silence before the attack still scared me half to death.

Only instead of reaching for guns, which only happened when they fought in the bedroom *(I think they just forgot they were there most of the time)*, Ma would reach for a kitchen knife. She was always too drunk to do anything with it except horrify her children. Night after fucking night, Michelle, Johnny, and I were standing there crying for them to stop to no avail. It always seemed like Amos was trying to defend himself against Ma.

I was diagnosed with PTSD a few years ago. After a little research, it started to make sense. My always being hyper-aware, always having my head on a swivel. I always know where the exits are. I don't sit in the middle of any room. I'm always near an exit or corner where no one can get behind me. This is no way to live. I'm working on it. My anxiety and blood pressure are always above normal; another reason why drinking is so appealing to me. It numbs me to it all. It takes it all away. Even if only for a little while.

I'm not sure if this is a good thing or not but one thing about getting older is that I feel indifferent to a lot of things these days. They just don't matter anymore. That life seems a thousand years ago, and yet at times it's still right there under the surface, lurking.

I'm easily startled awake by noise or touch. Brian could touch me in my sleep, and it was ok. I knew it was him by his touch, by the size of his hand, and by his breathing pattern. If someone gets too close to me when I am asleep and startles me, I freak the fuck out. I sleep on my belly in sort of a defense position. This comes from Ma, being drunk, standing in the threshold of our bedroom, smoking a cigarette, and staring at us. It was fucking scary. I could feel the malice coming off her. She always seemed to go after Johnny or Michelle. She would beat them while they were asleep, and they would wake up screaming. I was screaming. What the fuck? This is why, at 50 years old, I still sleep in defense mode. God help the one who tries to hurt me in my sleep. It will not end well for you. Another lovely parting gift brought to you by the people here at "Dysfunction Junction."

When I look back at how young we were when all of this happened, I'm amazed at the ability us three kids had to persevere, to adapt. I'm almost proud, in a way, that we wouldn't give up hope for better tomorrow. My sister Debbie, at the time, was living in East Boston. It was about an hour away by subway. This was another reason I love Michelle so much. She would grab me and just say, "Let's go." Usually, when Ma and Amos were at it again, and if it was early enough in the day. In Egleston Square, there was an elevated train—the Orange Line, or the "Terror Train" as we called it. It was one of the four branches of the MBTA that covered downtown Boston and several suburbs. We would sneak on, because we never had any money, and head to Debbie's house. I never knew how Michelle knew how to get there by train. She was ten years old at the time, I think, and I was eight, and off we went, alone on the subway.

From the Orange Line, we would transfer to the Blue Line and head East. The view from the Orange Line wasn't pretty. More project buildings, burned-out homes, burned-out cars, and trash everywhere. An aerial view of poverty. It was depressing.

East Boston was different. It was an all-Italian neighborhood. Extremely crowded, but not as poor or dirty. There were three-story walkups everywhere. With less than ten feet of space in between them. The smell of garlic and jet fumes would permeate the air, being so close to the airport.

Debbie lived on the third-floor of a walkup on Saratoga St. in a tiny two-bedroom apartment with a view of a schoolyard across the street, and a Riley's Roast Beef Sandwich Shop. A good roast beef sandwich or sub is a big deal, depending upon which neighborhood you were from. If you ever find yourself in East Boston, go to Santarpio's Pizza and Restaurant. The pizza, the sausage and peppers, and almost anything on their menu, is unbelievably good. It's the best pizza I've ever had. Santarpio's is amazing, and it's still there.

Michelle and I made frequent trips to Debbie's house, and I didn't think anything about the fact that we were so young. I honestly don't think Ma or Amos ever missed us being gone. Michelle had the timing down, anyway, as to when they would be awake or passed out back at home. We all did really. I loved escaping to "Eastie" whenever I could with Michelle. It felt like I was leaving that world behind. If only for a little while.

Back at home, things were the same. Jimmy, my older brother, was gone. To where, I wasn't sure. He may have gone to stay with my biological father, I don't know. He was just gone. He, and my older brother Butch, turned to crime. Robbing and stealing. They both spent a lot of time in jail and in prison. There is a difference between the two. They spent years at a time, in fact. They weren't in my life very much. When I would see them, one of them was either on the run, or still dealing with the court system for one crime or another. It broke my heart. They always seem to be in trouble.

Life back on West Walnut Park, my mother and Amos' drinking was getting worse. If that was even possible. The blackouts increased. Again, we could always tell by the crazed and wild look in my mother's eyes. Almost like a blank stare, but it was seething with anger. Time to run!

We would haul ass outside and on the street until she went to sleep or passed out. I remember coming in from playing one evening. The streetlights were coming on, so it was time to go in. There was a crowd of people in my doorway. There was a lot of commotion and noise and people yelling. The neighbors were there, holding my mother up. Someone was screaming, "Call an ambulance." I ran to the top of the stairs, and my mother was bleeding from both wrists.

She was incoherent, and trying to pick herself up, while people were holding onto her. There was blood everywhere, and she was trying to fight people off. Even with all of that going on, I wasn't freaked out or crying. My first thought was that this woman was in so much pain and anguish, it almost seemed to me like she was saying, "Let me go."

That was a sense I picked up from the whole event. They took her away to a hospital, I'm assuming. We had a new neighbor. A big red-headed woman. A white woman! She was always impeccably dressed. She comforted us. From her purse, she pulled out a $50 bill. Holy shit! A $50 bill. I had never seen one before. It was beautiful. Crisp, clean, and brand new. Her house looked just as rundown as all the others though. I just assumed she was poor like us. I never knew how they found my mother in the first place. She and Amos would have people over from time to time to play cards and to drink. Or play cribbage – a game I still associate with white trash and Miller Lite beer. I can only assume that she had cut her wrists while people were in the house, or that Michelle and Johnny had found her. She was gone for a few days, and then the social worker started coming around a lot more frequently. I don't remember any suicide attempts before or after that.

Sometimes, I grow tired writing about these bad memories.

For two or three days after the social worker would visit, things would be ok. There were times when my mother was at the stove, cooking, and there was an anticipation of food to come. She was a Southerner, so we ate grits and gravy, or grits and eggs for breakfast, when there was food. Her fried chicken was so good, I still compare it to everywhere else. Fried pork chops, greens, mac and cheese. It was a mostly southern diet, when there was food to be eaten. I still love southern-cooking.

Then came the Christmas morning we woke up to find the living room covered in gifts and three brand-new bicycles parked all in a row! What the hell? Was I in the right house? Ma had transformed the living room into a Christmas miracle.

There were gifts everywhere. Everywhere. I couldn't believe it. There were so many times when Johnny, Michelle, and I would gift wrap things from around the house to put under the tree, if we had one, so it looked like we had a lot more gifts than we actually did. Usually, my mother's Elvis albums, the toaster, or other random shit.

I fell in love with Christmas from the get-go. A fully decorated tree and shiny wrapping paper with pretty bows on top made me feel so good. Christmas is still my favorite holiday. I feel such joy when the season comes. I can't get enough of the music, the smell of pine, and getting lost in the Christmas spirit. Every season, every time. Christmas, during the times of sobriety at home, things seemed normal. Whatever that means. We would clean the entire house in a day or two.

Laundry was another story altogether, however. It wasn't really done all too often, and since we didn't have a washer and dryer, we would lug all of it up to Egleston Square to the laundromat. We took the place over. At least 15 to 20 black garbage bags full of clothing. It was embarrassing. People would stare at us, and others were angry that we took up all the machines. I would just wander around Egleston, going from shop to shop, killing time. Michelle was ordered to stay behind and help with laundry.

There was a little Puerto Rican bodega and a Chinese takeout next to the laundromat. The Chinese takeout had a red door in front. Inside, was a small room, and then just a hole in the wall with an old Chinese lady yelling through it. A small window actually. It's where you place your order. So strange.

A lot of the neighborhood kids would hang out at the bodega. It had a pinball machine, and I would watch the other kids, and some adults play, and they would constantly bump the machine with their hips, trying to beat the machine into giving up more points without activating the dreaded tilt mechanism.

I liked it in there because, in the back of the store, someone was always cooking. It smelled like Goya every time I went in there. The music was fantastic. Latin conga drums and horns. It was so fast. I couldn't understand a word of it, but I knew I liked it. It was so different from the soul and funk I was used to.

Ma liked country music. Old country music in fact. Western it was called, which is different from traditional Country & Western. Different timing. There was a lot of Tammy Wynette played in the house, Merle Haggard, and Loretta Lynn. And as always Elvis. Her music was fucking depressing. What do you get when you play a Country & Western record backwards? You get your house back, your wife back, your truck back. My mother's favorite song and still one of mine was called "In the Ghetto" by Elvis Presley. I still listen to it from time to time. It reminds me of my brother Jimmy, for some reason. Jimmy is still alive though.

I liked the song "Ghetto Life" by Rick James, however. Not as depressing, and a little more accurate.

My mother always played Elvis when she was sober and in a good mood, or cleaning the house. I have a fond memory of playing in the Summer sun in front of the house, and Ma calling us in for supper. I asked her what we're having, and she said fried pork chops, applesauce, and greens. It made me feel normal for a minute. It was a nice walk up the stairs that late afternoon.

Chapter Nine
Ma Died

Then came the day when my entire world was gone and replaced with a new one in the blink of an eye. My older brother Jimmy made a surprise visit, and wanted to take me to the movies downtown. That meant sneaking in. It was so good to see him again. He looked healthy and happy. No worried look on his face or anything. We watched a re-release of the movie *Grease*. It had come out the Summer before, I think. Holy shit! We watched it twice. Back then, ushers didn't kick you out in between showings, just a 15-minute pause to let people out, clean up, and let people in. John Travolta, and another amazing soundtrack. It was about slicked-back hair and the greaser look, and once again, the Bee Gees. Between *Saturday Night Fever* and *Grease*, the Gibb brothers practically own the airwaves. I loved it. I still listen to the Bee Gees quite a bit.

I don't know where Jimmy got the money from, and I didn't ask, but he treated me to popcorn, a soda pop, and some chocolate. I was in heaven. It was a fun afternoon.

We took the "Terror Train" back to Egleston Square. Jimmy stayed on the platform on the opposite side, and headed to East Boston and to

Debbie's house. I walked home. I got to the top of my street, and looked halfway down to see two fire trucks and an ambulance with a crowd of people gathered around it.

I ran down to see my house destroyed by fire. Both levels were burned out. The windows were smashed in, and the smell of wet burnt wood was everywhere. The structure was there, but that was it. It was gutted. Both houses on either side were fine. The grass-covered walkway on the right side of the house had Michelle's mattress thrown from the second story window in her bedroom, soaking wet, and burned.

The neighbors were pointing at me saying, "There's little Eddie. There's little Eddie." I ran up to the ambulance to see what was inside, but it pulled away. I didn't know what to do, so I sprinted back up to Egleston Station. Jimmy, thank God, was still there, and we both ran back down to the house. The next-door neighbor finally grabbed hold of us and told us to just wait here and that my sisters were on the way. Patty was coming from Hyde Park and Debbie from East Boston.

So, we just stood there. In front of our house. Burned down. Staring at it, and waiting for what was to come next. What that was, I had no idea. I can't exactly say why, but I didn't feel anything. This was a big deal, don't get me wrong. But I wasn't overly excited, freaked out, or even crying. I was wondering what happened to Johnny and Michelle. I wondered what happened to Amos.

That's what we were taught to do at 44 West Walnut Park. Adapt to any situation at any given moment.

As a result of these things, I feel that the clay of my nature has never solidified. Even today, it remains in the form of mercury. Ever changing and adapting. Sometimes, instantly. Going from survival mode to fight or flight, assessing a potential threat, and always being able to read the slightest of movements in people, seems second nature to me. Or reading a facial gesture. Or the subtle flash of an emotion or expression on someone's face that might show their "tell," I see it right away. Something that comes in the blink of an eye, and I see it. I've got it.

Perhaps it stems from being an empath, or from watching everything all the time. A bit of both, I think. Being able to pick up on another's energy can be extremely exhausting sometimes. I wouldn't trade it for the world, though. It was the one tool that kept me safer than not throughout all of that. Other than my precious and ever-present anger. My new companion.

The next thing I knew Jimmy and I were being whisked away to the hospital. Patty had shown up, taking us, and that would be the end of my life in Roxbury as I knew it.

Many people were gathered in the waiting room. I can't remember which hospital it was, but I can see that room in my mind's eye. It looks like every other waiting room in a major hospital.

Johnny, Michelle, and Amos were there in the waiting room. Thank God, Johnny and Michelle were ok. I couldn't care less about Amos. The only one permitted to see my mother was Patty, the oldest of the seven. She would later tell me that she didn't recognize our mother. Every part of her body was burned. She was unconscious.

The morning before the fire I remember seeing her on the passenger side of the station wagon, parked across the street from my house. She had on an orange jumpsuit, and her kerchief on her head, as always. She was sober that morning, I think. She looked happy. That is the last image I have of her alive.

What I still can't understand is how the entire house could have been completely gutted by fire when the firehouse was less than two blocks away? It was right next to where our treehouse was, and where we used to hunt snakes. Surely the Fire Department could have been there before the whole place went up in flames?

Unless the fire had been set. I can't bring myself to believe that my mother set fire to the house to kill herself. One of the neighbors said they saw her trying to get out from her bedroom window on the second floor. It faced the street. Could it be that because the house was always so cluttered and filthy than the fire spread so quickly? It didn't make sense to me.

We went into the burned-out structure days later to try and salvage any clothing or photos. Anything that would help. I'll never forget the smell of wet, burned wood. The entire interior was burned, charred. It looked like hell.

The hallway leading into the kitchen scared the hell out of me. And it always had an ominous feel to it whenever I would walk through it. In part because I didn't know what to expect once I got to the kitchen. Now, with it charred from fire, it seemed that much more terrifying. I was glad that it burned. I was tired of being afraid of it. The firemen boarded up the front door and the first-floor windows, but we blew right past that. I recall searching through piles of wet clothes looking for anything salvageable. Climbing the stairs to the second level was so dangerous. They had become frail, and a few steps were missing entirely from the fire. The basement was off limits though. Parts of the house were unstable, and we weren't allowed to go into those areas. Fine by me.

Being in a burned-out structure wasn't anything new to me really. We played in them with the Puerto Rican kids and Terry "Ain't" White all the time. Playing in a burned-out building that used to be your house is a different story, however.

With all this happening, I never felt any sense of loss. Perhaps if I did, it was for not being able to play in the neighborhood anymore. We returned to the house for several days trying to scavenge what we could. Oddly, the interior of the house seemed strangely clean. Baptized by fire.

Don't get me wrong, the place was fucking destroyed. But hadn't it always been? Perhaps it was a sense that everything bad was burned away. I don't know. All I know is that life in Roxbury was over. I was nine years old. Where to next?

Patty's house. Culture shock. After spending several hours at the hospital and realizing there was nothing that could be done, I was taken to my sister Patty's house she shared with her husband Larry and her son Tony from a previous relationship. It was in Readville, MA., to be exact, a small suburb of Hyde Park. Going from an all-black neighborhood, where fear and anxiety ran rampant, to a middle-class, all-white neighborhood freaked me the fuck out. I had never seen so many white people in one place before. I wondered if we were related in some way. No burned-out buildings, no getting chased. People looked happy. There was no sense of struggle in the air.

Patty lived in a two-bedroom single-level house with a big open-floor plan and a huge front yard. It had amber-colored shingles and resembled a little red cottage. Everything was clean, and I could bathe nightly. I had a whole tub to myself. With bubbles made from shampoo. What? Where was I? This was fantastic.

The neighborhood had tree-lined streets, clean beautiful homes, and families with both parents. There was a Lake two blocks away. More of a large pond really, but large enough to fish in. No one ever swam in it though. So, neither did I.

My first reaction to seeing kids riding bikes around the neighborhood was thinking that they had better watch out. They're gonna get their shit stolen. It took me a little while to realize that that wasn't going to happen here. This was uncharted territory for me. I was skittish and untrusting of it all at first. I took to it pretty quickly, however. The walk from the front door was a beautiful pathway made from slated stone. It was a good start to the day.

Springtime had come, and with it, lush green grass covering the lawns of the houses in the neighborhood. Everything was green. Trees were everywhere. There was a baseball diamond directly behind the house called Kelly Field, and up a grassy knoll just behind it was an outdoor MDC swimming pool.

Readville at the time was an all-Irish neighborhood. I became friends with the neighbor's kid, Danny. A chubby ginger-haired kid with freckles and a huge smile. He was a fragile kid in a way that it made me think he was bullied. He was controlled pretty much by an overbearing, "off the boat" Irish grandmother who wouldn't leave him alone for a second. I liked her accent, but that was about it. She was a curmudgeonly old bitch. I remember thinking to myself, *this kid wouldn't last a minute in Roxbury.* He would be duct-taped to a telephone pole, and spray painted. I felt protective of him.

We would play in his room or in the backyard. His house seemed old on the inside. Or at least the decor was. There was white Irish lace everywhere, faded Kelly-green tablecloths, jars with rock candy, and a fucking fruitcake. A fruitcake! Nobody ate that shit except for old ladies, I thought. For me, that solidified the notion that his grandma ran the show. I never saw his dad either. I don't know if he had one. Where the fuck were all the dads? Danny had some sort of inner conflict. He seemed browbeaten all the time. Almost like he was trying to solve a problem. Constantly. I could relate.

His grandmother had his whole life planned out for him. He had a savings account already. A savings account? What in the hell was the savings account? It blew my mind. A little 4-inch by 4-inch glossy book with credit and debit lines. It was crazy. I had never seen one before. I called him "The Professor." Mostly due to his thick coke-bottle glasses. He looked like a chubby Alfred E. Newman from *Mad Magazine.* He had a wide smile with teeth the size of piano keys, and when he laughed, he would throw his head back and cackle, maniacally. It was fantastic. I loved watching that kid laugh. I'm pretty sure he's a serial killer now. Or a mad scientist. Nothing too ordinary, I hope.

We had a lot of fun together. I think I taught him his first curse word. Fuck! Such a great word, really. So many uses for it. As a noun, 'You no good fuck!' As an interjection, "Fuck me!" An observation, "This is fucking crazy," and the ever-popular "Fuck you!" We swore a lot in Roxbury. Everybody did. The look on Danny's face the first time I cursed in front of him was priceless. His jaw dropped. He looked like he had seen a ghost. Then his massive smile opened, and again came the cackle. I was so proud of him. My first victim. I taught him all the classics: motherfucker—a favorite of mine also—cocksucker, bitch, and a few others for good measure. Each one garnering the same wide-eyed look of shock and then fascination. Ah, my student, my fledgling, my charge.

Allow me to back track a few months…Three weeks later or month or so after moving in with Patty, she sat me down the matter-of-fact tone, and said Ma is going to die. The news never hit me like a ton of bricks, nor did I suffer any kind of breakdown or loss of control. It was at the moment, just another thing. I didn't feel bowled over by the news. I had a feeling of relief in some way. Not because she was going to die, I certainly didn't want that. I didn't hate my mother. The relief came from knowing I would never have to return to the drinking and the violence. Or so I had thought. Patty, not knowing what to do, put me in child therapy. I would sit and color for an hour once a week, while being peppered with nonsensical questions about life in Roxbury.

Patty never realized how bad it had gotten because she made her escape long ago. I found therapy to be pointless, a nuisance. I never cried. I was a hypersensitive kid, and I would cry at the drop of a hat. I had a lot of reasons to. Not about this. Not a single tear fell. Again, I don't know why really. I did love my mother. She suffered greatly from the hell that is alcoholism.

Something I would come to know all too well. The despair can be almost tangible, so the only thing to do is to bury it with more booze. Vodka. Go figure.

Patty and Debbi, being the two oldest siblings, organized a road trip for the rest of us to our mother's funeral. We all piled into two cars and drove south. More adventure, more uncertainty. I was happy for it. Something new. I recall all of us staying the night at a motel somewhere in the Carolinas. It was all so exciting. For the first time in my life, all seven of us were in the same place at the same time. This is when I realized that my siblings were funny. Really funny. Constantly cracking jokes at each other's expense, telling war stories of doing time on West Walnut Park. Things that would make the average person cringe, but we found humor in it somehow.

You would never know we were on our way to a funeral. We arrived at my uncle Gus's house in Georgia. Ma had always told us that Uncle Gus was a wealthy man. He wasn't. He made a good living it seemed at whatever it was that he did. They owned a beautiful home with a lot of land, and he had a lot of toys: boats, dirt bikes, ATVs, and for some reason, a golf cart. There were so many people around. People I didn't know. It seemed like a big deal that we were there. It made me apprehensive. I went back into observation mode and stayed there.

Chapter Ten

The Funeral

G us was a boisterous man. I liked him right away. A country bubba with a shiny bald head and a big belly. He wore an overly starched white buttoned-down shirt that always seemed to have crisp $1 bills protruding from his breast pocket. Almost as if it were a part of his wardrobe. I thought he really was a rich man as Ma had said. I had never heard the "N-word" come out of a white person's mouth before. He used it all the time. Freely. He was loud and cocky. Why, I never knew? He looked like the country version of the Pillsbury Doughboy.

I had no decent formal clothing to wear to the funeral, so Patty and a handful of older women I'd never seen before took me out shopping for a suit. It was a very belittling experience. I remember the first time I read *White Fang* by the great Jack London. I was blown away. I could relate to this dog in almost every way. There is a chapter in which the author describes the protagonist as being aware that he was being made fun of, and bristling at it. Livid and boiling over with anger. I know that feeling. I remember being made to feel "less than" for being so poor. By the other kids in the neighborhood, and by Mrs. Harris at school for always being dirty, and for having shitty clothes. To this day, if I feel like I'm being clowned, I go from zero to red line. I am taken right back to my childhood. I am overcome with rage. If you try to belittle me or clown me, you do so at great risk. I was reminded of that very feeling when these women took me shopping.

Not from Patty. But these women that I didn't know, were teasing and poking fun. I was a 9-year-old ghetto rat. What did I know about picking out a suit? It was the first time I'd ever been shopping. Even at that age, I know the difference between poking fun and being mean. I can have a thick skin when I need to, but I was also a sensitive little kid and I knew the difference.

My mother's funeral what was the first one I've ever been to, and throughout the whole process leading up to her burial, I hadn't cried or felt any emotion at all. I recall Jimmy standing next to me crying his eyes out in a brown suit with a big butterfly collar. He was sobbing so hard that his shoulder seemed to be almost spasming. I just stared at him. I thought it was so strange. Hadn't he suffered the same things we did? Why was he crying? I felt no emotion. I wanted to, but nothing came. I loved my mother, and I felt like I should show some feeling of sadness, but it just wasn't there. I was too happy to be out of that situation. That was all. Patty and the therapist likened it to some sort of shock. I assure you it wasn't. Unless I had some deep-seated resentment that I'm unaware of, it just didn't hit me like it did everyone else.

Part of me was thinking that these feelings would come later in life. They never did. I can't recall ever breaking down or bawling my eyes out over it. It's been 41 years, and I still carry the feelings of anger and sorrow. For the whole thing. Having to live that way, constantly afraid of the unknown. Constantly afraid of the violence, the horrible living conditions and the anxiety. All of that, all those feelings became replaced by my new and more powerful companion, anger.

I could get so much more done using anger as motivation. It wasn't hard to summon. It still isn't. It's always right there just under the surface. My defense mechanism if you come at me unjustly. The common denominator from which all things that keep me safe is derived, pushing me to outwork you, outthink you, outrun you. Farther and faster away from my white trash beginnings and towards something better, anything…better.

Again, everything exploded in green. It was beautiful. Kelly Field had come to life behind the house. There were flowers blooming and bulbs opening, and the sweet smell of freshly cut grass was in the air. I felt so clean. It was a new world. In my mind, it was almost like The Brady Bunch. I headed to Kelly Field one morning to sprawl out on the beautiful green grass when I noticed a bunch of kids in baseball uniforms warming up. Little League! Woo hoo! I didn't know anything about organized sports, or baseball for that matter, but I knew I wanted to be a part of it. Joining all these happy looking kids would in some way get me farther away from Roxbury.

I ran back to the house to ask if I could try out for the team. I ran twice as fast back to the field and approached who I assumed to be the coach, Jim. His back was to me, and I said, "Excuse me, but I've just moved in right over there." I pointed to the back of the house. I could see part of it through the trees. "Can I try out for your team?" He turned around to see who I was, and at that moment, there was no question anymore. I preferred men over women. He was handsome, so very handsome. He looked like a young Rod Taylor, an actor from the 60s and 70s. Most famous for a film called *The Birds* by Alfred Hitchcock.

He smiled at me and said "Sure, why not?" I was in love. It was a springtime, and everything was clean and beautiful. Summer was approaching and now I had this beautiful face to admire every chance I got. I wanted to do everything I could to impress him, so that meant being the best athlete I could be. Baseball came easy to me. I could run fast, hit, throw hard, and catch. Pretty much all that's required. I played that much harder than everyone else with the hopes that Jim would notice me and be impressed. This was also my first time being around so many family units that seemed so loving and so functional. I remember wanting that badly, and then realizing that it probably wasn't going to happen. It gave me a lump in my throat. *Why not me,* I thought.

So, I did what came naturally to me. I became angry. I resented where I'd come from, and I decided that if I couldn't have what everyone else had, I would take it out on them through sports. I would outplay everyone on my team and the opposing team. If I couldn't have what you had, I was gonna channel my anger into something I could use – being better than you at sports.

Roxbury had given me a killer instinct when it came to competition and using it on the baseball diamond gave me a distinct advantage. After all, it was only Little League baseball, right? Wrong! When I realized I couldn't have what these kids had, I became bitter and resentful. Too young to be having these feelings, but there they were, and I used them to my advantage.

I started out as a third baseman, and if I scooped up a ground ball, I didn't just throw it to first. I fired it at top speed with all the strength I had. It sure as hell got me noticed by Jim, which is what I wanted most anyway. When he realized how hard I could throw, he moved me from third base to the mound. A pitcher. Woo hoo!

Not that I wanted to be a pitcher, but this meant way more time with him one-on-one because he was also the pitching coach. More so than getting to be with Jim, I came to realize what I needed most – a father. Or father figure. I didn't know what was missing until it was right in front of me. So internally, I placed Jim into the role of a father figure. Even though I knew it to be temporary, I still did it. It felt good. I felt a little more whole.

I remember being in a Catholic Church and seeing a little kid approaching the altar. The priest bent down on one knee to greet him, and placed a hand on the boy's shoulder. It seemed so loving and genuine. I remember feeling a lump in my throat and tears coming. I wouldn't let them fall. That's what I knew not having a father left a void in me. I had to search for it in other places. I placed people in that role internally. I still do this from time to time. Anyone can have a kid, but not everyone can be a parent. So, I did what I do. I assessed the situation, adapted to it, and moved on.

Game time! My first game was a starting pitcher. We were the Red Sox, naturally. I look back on that day and I laugh a little. At the time, it certainly wasn't funny. Saturday morning and I'm up early and eager with anticipation and excitement. Ready to show Jim what I could do. Again, with the hopes to impress him.

Disaster! I couldn't find my baseball pants. What the hell? No clue as to where they went. I had my Jersey but no pants. I didn't know where Patty was, so being the genius that I was, I decided to put on black dress slacks. To go play baseball. A baseball Jersey, black dress pants, and cleats. I thought I looked rather spiffy. Good Lord!

I didn't realize my blunder until I got to the field and wondered why some people were staring. I was a sensitive little kid. I picked up on that shit right away. I remember thinking, what the hell is your problem? Realizing I was being made fun of sent me into a rage. I liked the feeling. It protected me and gave me power at the same time.

Being made to feel less than because of the way I looked brought me right back to Roxbury. I remember standing on the mound, glaring at everyone. I was going to defeat them by playing harder than them. I considered them all to be the enemy. I was going to show these kids exactly how it felt to feel inadequate. So that's what I did. It wasn't difficult. They were soft little white kids. They didn't know what it was to operate from a place of anger, fear, resentment, and hurt. I threw so hard at these little fuckers. It felt good to see fear in their faces. I think the only one on my side was coach Jim. I think he felt a little sorry for me. That and he saw how hell-bent I was on winning. Mission accomplished.

That's pretty much how the season went. Banging heads with my teammates and kids from other teams. On Fridays after practice, Jim would take the team out for pizza just up the road from Kelly Field. If I was lucky, I would sit next to him and eat for an hour. On days when we didn't have a game, my nephew Tony, Patty's oldest, and I would head up to the MDC pool to swim. It was a massive outdoor pool with a diving board. It was usually packed with kids every day. It was a welcome break from the Summer heat. Tony and I became close that Summer. He was a couple of years younger than me. We did everything together except play baseball. He was too young for Little League and too old for t-ball. Since I was at odds with most of the kids in the neighborhood now, Tony and I became each other's company. He was a quiet kid at first. Always looking around as if on guard for something. He seemed nervous a lot. Anxious. Then it hit me. That's exactly how I behaved at the house in Roxbury.

Patty's husband, Larry, was an overweight, grotesque, white trash man with shitty teeth and an even shittier vocabulary. He was Tony's stepfather. A plumber of some sort, or heating and AC guy when he was working. I remember him as always being dirty. I did not like him at all. He never talked to me, though, so there was never really a problem. Until he came home drunk.

Thus, began a season of "Doing time on Maple Drive." While the scenery had changed for the better, the circumstances had not. It turns out that Larry was a violent drunk and a woman beater. I had a little bit of time off from that shit, and then it was same as it ever was. This time, it was right on top of us. The place wasn't that big, so we couldn't hide. There was no upstairs. Patty wasn't much of a drinker, nor was she a troublemaker. This was all Larry.

I hated this man. He was one of those drink after work types who would come home shitfaced. It was a long walk to the front door, so we knew by his stride if he was drunk or not. He was usually drunk on the weekends. The first time I heard him strike my sister, I'll never forget it. I heard her cry out. I wanted to kill him. They would argue a lot, usually over money. So again, the scenery had changed, but the violence and fear were almost the same. The idea of a "Brady Bunch" life quickly vanished.

The physical violence I witnessed and endured in my childhood, I believe, are the main reason for my anger. My hair trigger. Hearing Patty being hit, and the long, loud arguing has done its damage. Now, at 50 years old, I still find myself with the spirit of a nomad. I still have wanderlust, and the only time I feel genuinely happy is when I'm boarding a plane or a train to a new destination. Whether it's escapism or something deeply rooted from childhood, I don't know. But now that my Brian is gone, I intend to travel as much as possible.

We ended up leaving Readville. There was an issue with the neighbors next door. About what, I have no idea. Most likely, we were asked to leave because of the fighting and yelling. Thus began a pattern of moving every six months to a year. It seemed like just when we were getting settled, we had to move. Another issue with another neighbor.

We stayed in Hyde Park, at least. Readville was beautiful, and Hyde Park bordered it to the East. A blue-collar town, still an all-white neighborhood. I didn't hear much P-funk or soul blaring from cars driving by, but I did hear what's now considered classic rock. Oh man!

The first time I heard the band Boston, I was hooked. Foreigner, Queen, Elton John, The Who, and Zeppelin. Wow! I felt so free. I finally had a soundtrack that matched my life. I had an outlet. These musicians felt exactly the way I did. I didn't feel so alone. Foreigner and Elton and Led Zeppelin were my favorites at the time. I still listen to the same music I did back then, although bands like Slipknot,

Metallica, and Rage Against the Machine seems like more of a match for my anger.

At the end of the day, it's the singers and songwriters of the 70s that win out. So beautiful, so heart-wrenching. "River," by Joni Mitchell or Diana Krall's remake of "A Case of You" by Joni, ruin me to this day. Music is everything.

Chapter Eleven
Moving Again

Before I continue, I wanna do a real-time check-in. It's January 6th, 2020. I'm still here at St. Matthew's House Christian Regeneration Program, or "Club Jesus" as I like to call it. I'm in the fourth month of a year-long program, and the thrills just keep on coming. This place is a fucking trip. Surreal almost. Who knew that Christians could be so loud? They blare Christian music all the time, and it's usually the same five or six songs. All day, every day. I'm losing my God damned marbles. Oops, I'm sorry Jesus!

I could leave at any time, but I'm so fascinated by the staff and the leadership here with their total devotion and blind faith that I don't wanna leave just yet. I feel like I'm conducting some sort of sociological religious experiment. Seeing these people preach the word of God, and then do exactly the opposite right in front of me, is fucking delicious. Oh, the hypocrisy. Someone said to me once, "Do you know why people shy away from Christianity?" It's because they know a Christian. I get it now. Some of the behavior I witnessed I can only call sociopathic. Preaching one thing, screaming it is a little more accurate, and then moments later, literally doing the opposite just made me scratch my head in disbelief.

They would preach that homosexuality is a sin, and then the same person that was preaching that bullshit would check out my junk in the bathroom when I was taking a piss. A part of me feels bad for them. They had such anger behind their eyes. Almost as if everything they were doing and saying went against their nature. So bizarre. Religion fucks up everything in my opinion. "Do as I say, not as I do." I'm gonna hide behind this book and tell you how to live your life.

I should have done more research. I was coming down from drinking when I agreed to come here, and at that point, I just wanted out of Seattle for a little while. It's nice to see the big skies of South Florida every morning. Beautiful sunrises and sunsets every day. Again, the campus here is beautiful. Old and beautiful. It takes some of the sting out of having religion thrown in my face 24/7.

The Assistant Director of the program is a little weasel of a man. He is vindictive, spiteful, and passive aggressive. He's from Seattle. An asshole really. He speaks to the residents like they are beneath him. He's blatantly disrespectful, insulting, and rude. Some of the men here have lengthy prison records and are no strangers to violence. Mike, the weasel, is a skinny little bone-rack of a man with a big nose and bulging eyes.

He looks like he's miserable all the time. Just like the rest of them. Any one of these men could throttle this little fucker anytime they wanted to, but half of them are on probation or parole and are ordered here by the courts, so they have to eat shit from these people or go back to prison. I can only assume that this place is better than prison. Either way, Mike needs his ass kicked. I'm here voluntarily, for now. I would have no problem grabbing this little bitch by the throat and squeezing. I wouldn't ever do that, but the thought of it feels good. My resting face tends to say fuck off most of the time anyway. He and the rest of the staff seem to avoid me.

Hearing how they speak to people is infuriating, however. A lot of the residents here are young, so they still fear the authority figure. A good part of my day is spent in anger here. I could leave right now, but I want to see this thing through, I think. I know myself well, and after all these years, it's going to require an act from God himself for a miraculous transformation to take place, and for me to stay sober. So why stay?

Being away from Seattle is, for a while, a good thing. Although, I do miss wandering around my old neighborhood where Brian and I lived. Coffee houses and bars are a painful, bittersweet reminder of our time together. It's dangerous for me to visit that pain. I usually end up drinking it away. I'll return to Seattle when all of this is said and done. For how long, I don't know. Perhaps to erect a headstone for Brian at the Cemetery up on 15th Ave., about a mile from our house. In hopes that it would offer me closure. A place to visit him and to talk to him even if I know he isn't there.

As for returning to Seattle full-time, I don't think it's a good idea just yet. There's still too much pain there. I feel a weight upon me when I'm there. At least here under sunny, enormous skies I feel lighter and more hopeful in general. To what end, I have no idea. I could go back to New England and fish lobster again, see some old friends, and maybe try to catch my old feelings for home, and find out why Ipswich, Ma. is calling to me. This whole thing about being an empath and picking up energy is so strange to me. I also get what I call "flashes," which are images of people or places. Usually places. In real time. It's as if I can see what's happening there. It's so strange.

They last for a nanosecond. A flash, and then they're gone. They don't usually happen when I'm drinking. They come when I'm physically in shape and calm. When I have clarity. When there is nothing numbing my senses. I don't know what this is, and this is probably the last I'll mention it because it feels weird talking about it. Either way I'm glad it's there, whatever it is. I'm pretty sure I haven't gone crazy, yet. So, for the time being, I'll ride it out here at Club Jesus, scratching my head in wonder, and laughing at the absurdity of my situation.

I will enjoy the beautiful Florida skies, and try to learn what I can from this experience. I do know however, that this is the last rehab/regeneration/re-whatever program I will visit. Sometimes in life you just are what you are.

Life with Patty and Larry became yet another series of peaks and valleys. More fear, doubt, and insecurity, and the same scenario played out when he was drinking. Only this time, I can't remember the silence before the brawl like it was in Roxbury. Just the sound of my sister crying in pain. Tony and I would cry and scream for him to stop. Same shit as it ever was. I could feel the fear every time he hit her as if it was an electric shock to my body. Every time. The anger that started in Roxbury was now a living, festering character defect firmly attached to my identity. And at such a young age.

It's still here. Still with me, still alive and well. The thing about them fighting, and him beating her was, like all cowards, he would leave before the police would arrive. We had a working phone, so Tony or I would call the police if we were brave enough to sneak past them to get to the kitchen where it was. For years after, I had plotted to get revenge against him for hurting her. I couldn't wait to grow large and strong enough to kick the living shit out of him. It was all I thought about after every time he beat her.

They would break up. We would struggle for money, and food was tight but always there. My sister is the strongest person I know. I watched her suffer, and endure pain and hardship time after time, and she never gave up. I like to think that this is where my tenacity comes from. She is my hero. Hands down. No doubt. The fight in me, the "never say die" or the never-ending hope for a better tomorrow have all come from Roxbury, and from her. She has been more of a mother to me than anyone. A big part of who I am I owe to her. What a fighter she is. My sister. During the times when they were broken up, Patty, Tony, me, and now a son Jason, born from Larry and Patty, would move around a lot. A new apartment, a new beginning. We seemed to move all the time. Every six months or so.

Larry became a stalker, and we were afraid he would find us and hurt my sister. So we kept moving, trying to stay one step ahead of him. At first, we moved around Hyde Park, but he kept finding us. He would just appear out of nowhere, and it scared the shit out of us. Especially when he was drunk.

We played cat and mouse like this for a long time. They would get back together for a while, and things would be tense for us, but his income helped. Things were easier in that regard. I didn't trust it. I never trusted it. I knew what was coming, and I would look at Patty and think, why in the hell are you doing this? You know what's coming. And surely enough, it did. Usually within the first couple of months.

After one final, major brawl that involved the police, that piece of shit Amos and Larry, all fighting each other, we made our escape for good. We moved over to Amos's apartment in Brookline, Mass. Good Lord, Amos again. Back to the roaches. We were hiding out once again from Larry.

Amos had a girlfriend named Debbie. A lazy-eyed purely white-trash woman that shared the same values that he did—none. I grow weary of writing about shitty people and even worse circumstances. The place was destroyed, naturally. Fucking roaches everywhere, clutter, and old food left out to rot. Just like Roxbury.

Tony and I slept on a mattress on the living room floor. There's nothing worse than trying to sleep and being woken by roaches crawling on you. Clean your God damned house! I'm not anal retentive or neat freak by any means, but my house is always clean. I make the bed as soon as I get up, and before I shower so that way, even if I have a bad day, I can at least come home to a well-made bed every evening. It makes a big difference.

Brookline was an upper middle-class town. Mostly white and mostly Jewish. A lot of academics lived in beautiful old Victorian homes, along winding roads with overgrown trees on both sides that sometimes met over the top and created a canopy to walk under. The sun poking through intermittently made it even more so magical. I would stroll through, fantasizing that I lived in one of these homes, and would think to myself, how can anyone afford to live like this? But where we were staying, not so much. A row of red brick three story walkups on Cameron Street just off Route 9 and two blocks from Brookline village.

Brookline Village boasted a firehouse, movie theater, a small business park, shops, and a Carvel ice cream store. There was a baseball diamond and a basketball court next to the apartments with the MBTA trolley tracks running behind it. They ran every 10 minutes or so with people heading into the city or coming home from it. The trains would be packed with commuters. I always got a little excited when they went screaming past. They were pretty quick those things. Escapism on my part maybe.

I spent that summer playing basketball all day, every day. I also met what was to become my first real gay experience. Teddy. He lived in the walkup next to us on the 2nd floor. He was so cute. A year older than me. A little bit shorter, more stout than chubby. Reddish blonde hair, blue eyes, and thin lips. Oh man, I wanted to kiss him right away. He was kind of doughboy-ish. I was attracted to him from the start.

We played basketball a lot and we became fast friends. Suddenly Brookline didn't seem so bad. We played outside together pretty much all day. I was smitten with him even though I never let on how I felt.

For a young kid, he had a big chest and a bit of a belly. God, I love a man with a belly.

I loved looking at him and checking him out when he wasn't aware. I couldn't help myself. Teddy had a paper route around Brookline and on the weekends. I would help him lug 50 *Boston Sunday Globe* newspapers in two shopping carts around the town. It was a nightmare, but it meant that I got to have Teddy all to myself.

His home life was awful also, it turns out. His stepfather Lenny was a drunk and a woman beater. There were times when I went to Teddy's door to pick him up and he would come bursting through the door with his basketball under his arm, and say, "Let's go," in a hurried fashion. He never wanted to talk about it, but I knew that look on his face. I knew it well.

Teddy and I would have sleepovers occasionally, and often slept in the same bed. Very exciting. I never made a move, but one night during a sleepover at his house, we were wrestling on his bed, and when he was on his back, he looked up at me and said "Wanna get gay?"

Wanna get gay? Yeah! Hell yeah. We kissed a little bit, and I pulled his shirt off over him so I could get my hands on his chest and belly. His bare skin was pink and beautiful. I climbed on top of him, and began kissing his neck. It was pure heaven. I reached down under his shorts to find him fully erect. This was too much; I was losing my mind. I was so hard, I could cut glass.

I pulled his shorts down, and was about to go down on him. He never took his eyes off me. It was very erotic. I was just about there when his kid sister, Tracy, came bursting through the front door at the other end of the hallway. We panicked, and dressed in a hurry. We stood up, and I noticed the liquid stain on the front of his shorts. He had come. I missed it. Son of a bitch!

I held a grudge against Tracy for the rest of that summer. One thing was for certain though, I was in love with Teddy. We sort of played a bit of cat mouse after that first experience. I think it was more experimental for Teddy than it was for me. I was all in. We would have sleepovers or go camping, and he would pretend to be asleep while I felt him up. I guess thinking that if he pretended to be sleeping, then he wasn't responsible. Either way, I enjoy touching him. He was so beautiful to me.

I hit him up on Facebook many years later, and he never responded. He's got a couple of kids now. It didn't look like he was married. All told, we spent about a year together. I still think of him from time to time, hoping he is well.

We ended up moving again, no surprise. But this time, it was out of state. New Jersey—Trenton to be exact. To a shelter for battered women and children. I remember playing basketball with Teddy, and Patty coming down. She leaned against the fence and started to cry. Harder than I'd ever seen her cry before. Larry had found us somehow, so it was time to go. I don't think that's why she was crying so hard though. I had come to find out that she was trying to get us all down to Georgia to stay with cousins or something. But it didn't work out.

I could feel her hopelessness. It was awful. One thing about Patty though, her despair didn't last long. She would cry and look lost, and then a look of determination would come across her face. Every single time. She would take action right away. She would get things done.

So, off on a Greyhound bus we went, into the unknown. Nothing new to me. Bring it on. We got off the bus. Tony, me, Jason, and Patty in downtown Trenton, New Jersey. I can't recall how long it took us to get there. Most of the day. With a few suitcases, and a phone number, and nothing more. I remember leaning against a brick wall, watching people scurry here and there in business attire, or trying to catch a bus or taxi. City hustle and bustle. I felt indifferent to it all. I just didn't care. Patty was in a phone booth talking with someone, and when she returned, she informed us that someone would be here soon to pick us up.

Sometime later, I'm not sure how long, a woman in a brown panel station wagon pulled up and asked us if we were the family going to the shelter. Another fucking station wagon. I associate them to this day with bad memories. We piled in, and off we went. I could feel the tension coming off my sister. I could also feel her protective vibe. She wasn't fucking around. It felt good to feel protected by her. About half an hour later, we arrived at the shelter. Women and children only. I remember being led in through the kitchen, and an older woman with long grey hair standing over a big pot of something that smelled delicious. The kitchen was all white and spotless. She greeted us with a warm smile, and it put me at ease a little bit. There was no malice, no placating or tolerating. She seemed genuine. It felt good. This place was a hell of a lot better than I thought it would be. The women were very warm and welcoming to us right away.

It was a relief to know that we weren't alone. Women of all races were represented. There were children everywhere, ranging in ages from infants to pre-teens. It seemed like a close community of people. Our bedouin lifestyle seemed to come to an end. For now, anyway. I mean, how long could we stay in a shelter, I thought to myself. I learned early how to compartmentalize things so I took what I could out of the first night there, which was a delicious hot spaghetti dinner, and I put the rest of my worries down. We had shelter for the night, we were all so tired.

The most important thing for that day was watching my sister exhale and relax a little bit. It was as if she had been holding her breath for very long time. At least we were a couple of states away where Larry couldn't reach us. There was some comfort in that.

The next morning after a big breakfast and some community time with the women and kids, we, as a unit, tried to figure out a plan of action. Patty went out immediately to find work. No time to waste. Tony and I set out to explore our surroundings and look for school and potential workplaces for Patty. We were an efficient bunch. No matter where I've traveled, or attempted a geographical cure for alcoholism, finding work was never difficult for me. Usually within the first few days I was up and running with a restaurant and earning money. I'm still like that today.

Tony and I went off to explore the area and to get a lay of the land. Trenton was kind of fucked up. A little rundown and a lot of drugs. We found a park in the middle of town, and I went in to use one of the bathrooms to take a leak. Co-Ed! What the hell? At least, this one was. They were men and women in there. I didn't realize until later, after seeing people nodded out everywhere, that the park is where everyone went to shoot up. Trenton had a Roxbury kind of vibe to it. I liked it. Strangely, it felt comfortable. Tony and I explored for the first few days, but there was nothing really for us to do, no basketball court or baseball diamond. Just the park, and that was a no-go.

Behind the shelter, there was an old beat-up hoop nailed to a telephone pole, so we would spend most of our time playing ball. Shelter life wasn't so bad. We fell into a rhythm. The food was plentiful and good. The women all took turns cooking for each other and their families. A sense of routine took hold, and with it came the ever-dangerous comfort. I tried not to get too comfortable in any situation because the rug kept getting pulled out from under me. But I was tired, and I let my guard down. Consequences be damned. I just wanted to relax. Tony and I were the only two boys there that weren't toddlers. Most of the kids there were. Their moms toted them around on their hips while they went about their day.

One thing I learned about domestic violence, and the trauma that comes after, is that a lot of these women were afraid of loud sudden noises. Something slamming, or a car backfiring, and they would jump out of their skin. I could relate. I can still relate. Anytime I hear something slam, or a sudden drastic change in volume, I'm startled, and then I bristle with anger.

Chapter Twelve

...And Again

B ack at Club Jesus, the pitfalls and landmines were everywhere. Most of the kids there were coming off heroin and meth, and were bouncing off the walls. Sudden loud noises and yells were the norm there. It was torture. I spent a good part of my time there trying not to choke the living shit out of one of those little bastards. God bless them. They were so dumb. I weep for the future of this country. Those little thieves would steal the fillings out of your head if you fell asleep around them. They lacked integrity, work ethic, common sense, and worst of all, self-awareness. They acted purely on instinct and impulse. It was fascinating to witness so much stupid in one place. Club Jesus made me wanna drink.

Back to the shelter.

All told, I think we stayed there less than six months. Patty had a friend in Bergen County, New Jersey. North. A town called Midland Park, so off we went. Midland Park was a small town, residential, and mostly white. Def Leppard was all over the radio. It was pretty much everywhere. Writing strictly from memory has its limitations when one's brain is used to being addled with vodka. I try to recall as best I can.

Middle-class pre-teen angst accompanied most of the white kids in my neighborhood. Or area, I should say. We were crashing with a woman who lived on top of what I think was a shoe store. On the corner of a side street and a main road. I can't recall if she was a lesbian or not. I'm pretty sure she was. She had a friend that would come over occasionally, who was a little bit on the butch side. I think they were a couple. Then came the day when we were all taken out for a weekend in the country. Still one of the fondest and strangest memories I have of my childhood.

We spent the weekend at what I can only describe as a commune. *A commune*! This place was a trip. There were a few men, not many. It was comprised mostly of women and children. Hippies everywhere, and hairy women with guitars. The whole place smelled like weed. To me, it was a great place to run in the sunshine. There were a lot of tents, a few cabins, and a massive open field of grass to run over. I wandered over to a circle of people sitting on the grass, and asked if this was some kind of campground. One of the young girls remarked, "No, we live here man!" *Definitely a commune.*

There was a guitarist in their group, the only male. He was singing a song that is still stuck in my head to this day. The song was called, "If the sucker push the button, you can kiss your ass goodbye!" It was perfect, a little late, but perfect. Hippies man.

After about a day and a half, I could tell Patty was getting a little uncomfortable with the scene there. She may have been getting hit on, I don't know. It seemed to be a "peace and love" vibe there. I had a great time. It all happened so quickly. I know my sister well, and I caught a look on her face that read, "What the fuck am I doing here?" I knew we would be leaving in the morning. And we did. Bye bye commune.

I think of that place from time to time. I wondered how they got money for food. It didn't seem like any of them had jobs. I like to think they grew most of their food, though I don't remember seeing a garden. Oh well, it was fun while it lasted.

Back to New England we went. I was excited to be going home, wherever that was going to be. I didn't mind the nomadic lifestyle. I still don't. Traveling is when I feel most free anyway. I feel like a citizen of the planet. Even now and again, when I board a train or a boat, I feel that same excitement. I couldn't care less about the destination unless it was out of the country. The only time moving hurt was when we left an apartment in Hyde Park, right on Hyde Park Ave. —a main thoroughfare running from Cleary Square, Hyde Park all the way into Jamaica Plain. In this apartment, my bed was directly under a big picture window, and I could look up at the stars or sleep with the moon shine on my face. I liked being there. It was comfortable.

Ah, there's that word, "comfortable." That's what I get for falling into it, I thought.

I remember crying because I didn't want to leave. I had friends there. Life seemed ok. Oh well, here we go again. Strangely enough, and some 30 years later, a good friend of mine, Chaz, one of the funniest people I've ever met, moved into that very apartment. I cabbed it over after work one night to check out his new place, and I couldn't believe it. I knocked on the door, and before I crossed the threshold, I told him I lived in this apartment as a child. He didn't believe me, so I described the entire floor plan to him in detail before I ever stepped in. It was a blast from the past. Weird to be in there. It didn't look all that different from when I was there. The picture window brought back bittersweet memories. I walked up to it, looked out the window, and then looked up.

All told, I stayed about a week there with Chaz, drinking shitty wine, and listening to music. Being around so many Christians at the moment reminds me of a cabbie that dropped me off at Chaz's place one night after work. I had a bellyful of beer, and had to piss like a racehorse. The last couple of miles in that cab was torture. My cabbie was African, and a bible-thumping Christian. When I got in his cab from downtown Boston, he, after exchanging a few pleasantries with me, asked if I would like to hear the word of the Lord?

"Sure," I said. *How bad could it be?* I had at least a half a dozen beers in me, and two jugs of red wine in tow to quaff with Chaz later. "Lay it on me," I said.

He started his spiel, and I listened respectfully for 30 seconds before tuning him out altogether. Halfway to Chaz's place, I had one of those "holy shit" moments when I realized I should have taken a piss before I got in the taxi. The driver kept saying "Yes! Yes!" with me wondering what in the hell he was talking about? Apparently, I had been saying, "Oh God! Oh God, help me!" Asking the Almighty to just get me to a bathroom. The cabbie thought I was digging everything he was selling.

"Oh God I gotta pee!"

"Yes, yes, my friend!"

We pulled up in front of Chaz's place, and I thanked him. I'm yelling at this point, "Oh God, help me! I gotta pee."

The cabbie is yelling, "Yes, yes, he will help you, my friend!"

"Oh God!"

"Yes," he said.

"Praise the Lord!" he said. "He will save you, my friend!"

I bolted from the cab, blew past Chaz, and peed for about a solid 2 minutes.

It was the funniest end to a cab ride I ever had. Me thinking I'm gonna pee myself, "Oh God help me!"

The cabbie thinking he was saving my soul, "Yes! Yes! He will help you! Goodnight my friend. God will help you!"

Whew! That was close. I sat down on the couch next to Chaz and lit up a cigarette. "I think I just got saved" I said. He looked at me like I had two heads. Never mind I said. Scratching my head.

We drank the wine and listened to singers and songwriters of the 70s, describing in detail the memories of living there that came flooding back. It was a fun night. Chaz, or Charles, has been a friend of mine and partner in crime for 25 years now. I'm not kidding when I say he is one of the funniest people I've ever met. He looks like a madman when he laughs. Sometimes, I think it's his mission in life to fuck with people. A perfect match.

Chaz and I met in the mid 90s, at a bar called the Napoleon Club in the Bay Village neighborhood—a small, gay neighborhood behind the Park Plaza Hotel. Four-story brownstones, and mostly gay couples. There were small cobblestone streets with beautiful window boxes overflowing with wildflowers in the Spring. It was less than three blocks by two. The whole area. A cozy little neighborhood.

Chaz' sense of humor is ruthless, and after living in Seattle for as long as I have, with all its passive aggressiveness, it's refreshing to hear someone talk who has little or no regard for people's delicate sensibilities. He has a huge smile with a slight gap in between his two front teeth, and a maniacal laugh. Perfect! His partner, at the time, was a cocktail waiter at a bar called Club Cafe, just up the road. A hot spot for young gay professionals. It turned into a packed-out dance bar on the weekends, like everything else did.

I was at Napoleon Club with a friend drinking and dancing when I ran into Chaz' partner Tim. He introduced me to Chaz, and we sort of hit it off right away. Chaz is a big guy, larger than life, and likes to drink and smoke. A lot. The four of us danced and drank until closing. We went out to the park across the street, I smoked a joint. I'm not much of a weed smoker, so I got baked right away. It was probably part weed and mostly Chaz, but I laughed my ass off in that park. I'm lucky to call him a friend. He's also one of those friends whose occupation was never clear. He wasn't mobbed up or anything, I don't think. It was always just so vague, his explanations for what he did for a living. I stopped asking.

When we first met, he worked for Cablevision TV. We'd ride around, smoking weed in his work van on business hours, or he'd be cocktailing at whatever bar I was tending, trying to hide it from his partner. Tim would call while Chaz was drinking, and I'd rattle glasses trying to get him busted. Theirs was a volatile relationship. They fought constantly. I felt bad for Chaz. Tim was an alcoholic also, but a messy one. Overly dramatic, and a yeller. I avoided drinking with him. Sadly, their relationship went on that way for the better part of 20 years. Chaz broke free not too long ago, and is finally free of the codependency and dysfunction.

On paper Chaz and I are great match, but, in the end, to me, the friendship we have is too valuable. I don't want to lose it.

When Chaz and I first met, I was dating a cop. His name was also Tim. A chubby handsome Irish American from Peabody, MA. The sex was fantastic. Good Lord! And yes, I would make him put on the uniform from time to time before we did it. It was so hot! Tim, unfortunately, was a jealous and possessive lover. With a gun. So, when Chaz and I would get together, it was almost like it was a clandestine operation. Getting away from the Tims, and avoiding phone calls and petty arguments, almost became our mission. It made it a lot more fun also. Our hanging out.

Then came the night of the infamous "Black Fatty." Chaz had stopped by a friend's house to pick up some weed. And on his coffee table was a joint. Or mini baseball bat, I should say. With black rolling papers. It looked a little ominous. Chaz's weed dealer gave it to him, and said, "Here. Enjoy yourselves, but be careful. It's a little strong."

The "Black Fatty!" So, we smoked this thing and rode around in Chaz' work van for a while. And then it kicked in. I had never been so high in my whole life. It wasn't good. I felt like I was tripping balls. We were driving down Tremont Street at about 40 miles an hour when I decided I was too high, and tried to jump out of the van. "I gotta get the fuck outta here," I said to Chaz, and I open the door for a split second.

Chaz was screaming, "What the hell are you doing? Close the door!" We took a left, and I asked him to pull over for a minute. I almost "tucked and rolled" onto Tremont Street, over a joint. The infamous "Black Fatty." I'll never do that shit again.

Hanging out with Chaz is always good for my soul. I've never laughed so much with another human being. I wasn't terribly invested in Tim, the cop, other than for his cock. Jealousy doesn't work for me. Chaz was in it a lot deeper than I was. For me, as soon as I start to feel like a possession, it's over. I hung on a little longer with Tim selfishly for the sex. Why are all the lunatics out there so good in bed?

So, Chaz and I, and his work van would take off on daytime adventures, smoking weed, and terrorizing the public at large. It always amazed me how well he handled mixing weed and booze. I could drink like Foster Brooks, but introduce a little pot into the situation, and I'm all done. It's one or the other for me.

Chaz and I had some great adventures back then. Road trips to Montreal or out to San Francisco to see some people he knew. He was escaping from Tim, and I was just escaping. I'm grateful for our friendship. He reminds me to keep one eye on the perils of alcohol, and one eye on life. All the while reminding me not to take it all too seriously. I love him. Chaz is my best friend. The gap-toothed maniac that he is.

Being back in that apartment also brought back a memory I hadn't thought of in ages. Summer camp.

Chapter Thirteen
Summer Camp

Y.E.S. Or Camp YES. In Boston. Youth Enrichment Services it was called. A camp for inner city kids. For two weeks in the summer, Camp Y.E.S would take ghetto rats like myself out to the Berkshires to camp outside and run around in the woods, and experience life away from the brick and mortar of the projects and the inner city.

It was fantastic!

I remember boarding an old school bus with my nephew Tony on Center Street in Jamaica Plain, right across from the Woolworth's Department store. They had a soda fountain, and an old-timey ice cream bar, where everything was red, white, and checkered. If you were lucky enough to order a banana split, they would hand you an old coffee can filled with pieces of paper with different prices on it, ranging from one cent up to $0.99.

I cheated, I looked in the can, and I saw the coveted "1 cent" piece. I grabbed it, and I devoured that fucking thing. Oh baby!

The bus pulled away and off we went. Tony and I, and two other kids from Patty's best friend at the time, Mary Ann, with us. They were inseparable, her and Patty. I liked Mary Ann because Patty was happy when she was around. They smoked weed together, maybe that was why. She just seemed a lot more relaxed when they hung out together.

The Camp Y.E.S Summer Program was located in the beautiful Berkshire mountains, west of Boston by a few of hours. Not really mountains so much as they are rolling hills. Beautiful year-round, but especially in the fall. Foliage tour buses dominated the months of September and October. Summer, high summer was the perfect time to be there, though. Hot, hazy and evergreen.

Swann Lodge it was called, named after Arthur Wharton Swann., from Monterey, MA. It was just west of Springfield, and about 3 1/2 hours west of Boston. The lodge resembled a big red barn with a row of screened in windows running along the facade on the first floor. Just past the front door, it opened to a screened in dining hall. Not very big, but open and airy. This is where we ate breakfast every morning for two weeks. Huge lumberjack style breakfasts. Pancakes, always pancakes, sausage, eggs, toast, and bacon. There was so much food.

Up to the left of the lodge and behind it was a small clearing that held several fire pits and around 12 to 15 tents. This was the boys lodging area. Lying on my back, I could hear the wind dancing through the tops of the pine trees. It made a soft billowing sound that almost sounded like slowly escaping steam.

When the school bus was driving up towards the barn, we couldn't see anything on either side except for huge pine trees on either side of a long and winding gravel road. Then, it opened to the lodge and a wide-open space of green fields and wildflowers, twice the length of a football field and just as wide. Absolutely beautiful! With the barn smack dab in the middle. This was paradise for me. It was the height of Summer. The air was sticky and sweet with the smells of the forest. I was in heaven.

There was a stream on the North side of the field that collected into a natural pool, just to the right and downhill a bit from the lodge. Or the barn, as I called it. It was crystal clear, and you could even see the leaves that had fallen in it from the last Fall season. A circle of trees loomed over the pond and created a canopy. The sun broke through in different spots reflecting off the surface. It was the most beautiful thing I'd ever seen. It became my wishing well. And I had every intention of baptizing myself in that water. So that's exactly what I did.

The Polar Bear Club, they called it. This pond was famous for having freezing cold water. At the crack of dawn, the counselors would come around asking if anyone wanted to join the Polar Bear Club? That meant jumping in. Yes! Bring it on. In those early mornings, the surface of the pond was like glass, perfectly still. Steam dancing across the surface gave it a mystical quality, as if it were something out of the *Lord of the Rings* movie. It was magic to me. In I went! Son of a bitch! It was cold. It was like being stabbed with a thousand tiny needles all at once. I was shocked awake. Any bravado I showed quickly gave way to, "Get me the hell outta here!"

There were less than a handful of us brave or stupid enough to take the plunge every morning. I did it to impress the counselors. In the heat of the day, the pond warmed up nicely, and all of us would swim or fly into the center of it on a rope swing. So much fun. I spent every second that I could sitting on the bridge at the end of the pond, thinking and dreaming. It became my own personal "Bridge to Terabithia."

Out into the wide-open fields we ran like the wind, playing frisbee or flag football, and chasing fireflies at night. I knew I was making the mistake of getting comfortable, but I didn't care. Why in the hell shouldn't I? I was happy for a minute and I was determined to enjoy it.

I can't exactly say why being back in Chaz' apartment, my old home for a minute, brought back the thoughts of Camp Y.E.S., but I'm glad it did. It was a good two weeks out in the woods.

Back in Boston, we moved around a few more times and finally shed that piece of shit Larry. I guess we had officially settled in Revere this time. Debbie was living two blocks away, so I had the structure and discipline of life with Patty, and the laissez-faire way of life with Debbie. It was a nice balance.

The neighborhood in Revere was still full of guidos. I liked it. It was predictable. A lot of crime though. Home robberies and car thefts were rampant. Someone tried to break into Debbie's place, but her doors were so securely locked, there was no getting in. She was no dummy. Some of her friends were familiar with that lifestyle. Some were drug dealers, some were armed, some were strippers. She never seemed to have ordinary friends. They all seemed to be out of *Cirque de Soleil*, or they were enmeshed in something dangerous. I loved it! Anytime she threw a party, I was sure to be there. As a Go-fer mostly. I love being around so many people that seem to live the hell out of life. It was refreshing and intoxicating at the same time. Almost like Halloween every day. I did notice that after a lot of Debbie's parties, there were people passed out everywhere. A cautionary experience. I learned that that was when it was time for me to go.

So much fun, though. I miss her. Always a hopeful smile she carried. Just like Michelle. It was my favorite thing about her. I always pictured her as a child, giving her hope-filled smile to anyone and everyone. Only God and Patty know what she went through as a child. I have a bit of an idea though. Patty started dating one of Debbie's friends by the name of Bob—a big Sicilian guy from Revere. Go figure. He seemed like a nice guy. Always optimistic. That's what I liked about him. He was a great cook, and could build just about anything. He was a small-time coke dealer when I met him. This was before Patty started dating him. Debbie did coke, but I never saw Patty do any lines. Bob and Patty hit it off, and before I knew it, we were off to California. What the fuck?

All things are subject to change right? A whirlwind romance that uprooted us yet again. They married quickly. So fast.

Generally speaking, straight people piss me off when it comes to marriage. Gays had to fight so hard for the right to marry. When I hear the argument over the "sanctity of marriage" being reserved for heterosexuals, it makes me laugh. Straight people piss all over their so-called sanctity. Marriage is used for every purpose under the sun, except for the one it is truly meant to. Don't worry, gays will fuck it up too. I take marriage very seriously. The commitment to another soul is exactly that, a commitment. Sacrifice and compromise, open lines of communication, not holding onto resentments, and loving something more than yourself are to me what sanctity means. Not diving in on a whim, and then giving up when it doesn't go as you planned. Marriage is work. If you're lucky enough to find someone like minded and kindhearted, then fight for them.

I was lucky enough to have this with my Brian. I didn't always see it, and at times I took it for granted, but after an argument, we couldn't stay away from each other for more than a day. Marriage is an ongoing process, ever-changing an ever-evolving. As is any relationship. Your partner is going to know how to piss you off more than anyone on the planet, and may use that knowledge to get at you. Being aware of one's own ego and pride, and not overreacting when they get stepped on is one of the many keys one can play in an effort to find harmony and longevity in a relationship, I think. Too often people are in it for their own selfish reasons. I was, in some of my early relationships in my 20s, and I did exactly what I wanted. I wasn't able to trust people for fear of being hurt, so I never fully committed. I would only give the parts of me I was willing to give. It was selfish, but I felt I had to protect myself. And, in the process, I never experienced what a fully committed partnership felt like. I would never give my heart away. It went on that way until I met Brian.

As I see it, growing up with such a shitty, unreliable foundation, one of two things were likely to happen. Either I would continue the cycle of violence, alcoholism, and poverty, or I would become the complete opposite. Thank God, I became the opposite, except for my alcoholism. The gift and curse of anger that has helped me through the worst of times also makes me capable of becoming a fiend, if I let it. I try not to let it. That would make me just like them.

When I look back at the violence we had to endure, I think to myself, "Rank fucking amateurs." The monster that lives inside of me, the "Closet Maniac," is the reason why I never need motivation. My anger is my nuclear battery. It takes a lot of energy to burn so hot. There are times when I feel completely indifferent to it all. There is a certain freedom that comes with not giving a shit sometimes. It's almost as if I take a mental time out.

However, in these times of indifference, I have to be wary of letting this turn into bitterness. That's the sneaky thing about holding onto resentments. Sometimes, they are so deeply rooted that they become character defects we can sometimes be unaware that we have. For example, because of the white trash environment and mentality I was raised around, I find myself bristling and angry when I run into that type of person or people. I really do. But when I do, I end up hating a complete stranger. If that's not an unresolved issue, then I don't know what is.

Shedding light on these issues, and digging to the root of why I do what I do and react the way I do is why I came into treatment in the first place. All I can do is try and hope for the best. It's gonna take a shit load of work and a lot of time. I've come to understand that I may have to forgive my "parents" and others for what happened to us. That is a big fucking no! This may change in the future, I highly doubt it, however. One day at a time, right?

I carry so much anger and resentment about it that even the notion taking a look at it makes me upset. Progress not perfection, right? Fuck off!

Many, many quotes and clichés to follow.

Look, at the end of the day, Patty and Debbie did the best they could given their circumstances. My "parents," not so much. I saw Ma suffer, but I couldn't tell if it was from something other than drinking. I know her pain now. Alcoholism is a living hell that only another alcoholic can really understand. Suffering the misguided slings and arrows by the loved ones of an addict can sometimes push the addict further into their disease. Because of the resentment and shame the addict may be feeling, knowing the pain they've caused loved ones and friends.

Denial is a strong, subconscious defense mechanism. It is for me, at least. Many times, with my Brian, I had no idea I was hurting him so badly. I figured I was only hurting myself. I honestly couldn't see it. The shame I feel over this is overwhelming. I have to look at it piece by piece. It will push me to a drink. Guaranteed. My denial is powerful. The pain I feel over wronging Brian with my drinking is so acute that I instinctively want to reach for a drink to bury it. It's too much.

So, when it comes to my parents, forgiveness is going to take a miracle. That's how I feel about it at the moment, but as they say, all things are subject to change.

When I look back on my childhood and life before Patti and Debbie, I'm reminded of so much fear, pain, and insecurity. My sisters were Rock Stars, as far as I was concerned. They became mother figures right away after Ma died. The shit that happened in Roxbury, and with that piece of human garbage Larry, have molded the clay of my nature into many, many different forms. It still hasn't hardened. Thank God. My foundation has a mixture of pain and anger, sorrow and empathy, and always, always, hope. All of that, coupled with a strong will and a deep well of strength that I can draw from when I need to.

As it stands, I have left Club Jesus. I reached the point where as soon as I opened my eyes in the morning, I was boiling over with anger and frustration. I'm grateful for some of the things I learned there, but overall, it was just a lesson in frustration. Their method of shoving Jesus down your throat and up your ass twenty-four hours a day, and then condemning people for rebelling was pushing me away from my "higher power." The hypocrisy was rampant and clearly visible to anyone with half a brain. It was like a Christian boot camp. I felt as if most of the staff and residents were faking it. As if they were trying to psych themselves up into believing.

Listen, if that's how you wanna roll, then more power to you. Just don't push that shit on me. The staff literally tried to bully residents and intimidate them into a Christian lifestyle. Their approach was so wrong. Again, a lot of the men were facing prison time, and the program helped get them to get released because of their faith-based nature. So, these guys would, of course, accept a year in the country, instead of doing time.

But St. Matthew's House forces you to take either their way or the highway. I've seen hardened criminals say "Screw it," and go back to prison, instead of laying up and eating shit for year. Mind you, a lot of these men were not exactly the best that society had to offer, and a lot of them were just scumbags. Even they could feel the oppression the staff was putting down on people. Remember the saying, "Why do people not like Christians?" It's because they know a Christian. It is true. St. Matthew's House is not what I thought it was. Pharisees and false prophets, all. There were some positives that I took from the experience, but all in all, I found myself fighting for peace there.

I am not to be bullied, and I think it was just a matter of time before I exploded. Never again. Never. Go fuck yourself Club Jesus!

Chapter Fourteen
Alcohol

Back to the grey. Seattle. It feels comfortable for now. I'll continue seeking help for my disease through Alcoholics Anonymous and counseling. I don't think it will help much if I don't want it to, and the truth is, I just don't. I never really have.

That was another thing about being at St. Matt's. I felt as if they were trying to brainwash me. I suffered more mood swings in one day as a resident there than I ever did in the real world. So many peaks and valleys in a 24-hour period. I thought I was gonna lose my shit. I feel like going to a Christian rock concert and throwing punches at people. Or starting a one man mosh pit. No worries, they'll forgive me, right?

I will miss the big Florida skies, and the myriad of pastel colors at sunrise and sunset. In time, I think I will find some little hovel in the Keys or the Bahamas, and "Jimmy Buffett" the rest of my days away in Margaritaville.

While here in Seattle, I have to try and not let the depression set back in. There is still a lot of pain here. For now, I'm going to blast forward and try to stack some money, keep my body in shape, and try to dodge the minefields of the past. Losing my Brian and the pain of it are in front of me here in Seattle, and I must keep a watchful eye on how I react to it. I have to be on guard against a slip.

There's too much work to do, and if I do decide to pick up again, I don't want it to be here in Seattle. It's too easy to fall back into that darkness. It, coupled with the grey, would set me back a couple of years. I don't want that.

So off to A.A I go. It keeps me honest, at least. Sometimes, just hearing the preamble is enough to keep me sober for the day. That's not to say that I sit around, wringing my hands and sweating like some lunatic out of a Sir Arthur Conan Doyle novel, but the obsession and compulsion that acts as a precursor to my taking the first drink is a powerful thing. It is real.

Other diseases are not like the disease of addiction. No one is shunned, or cast out for having cancer. No one attaches morality to a terminal illness, but society seems to condemn the addict at every turn. We are considered weak, or lacking in character or even strength.

Strength? Recovering addicts are some of strongest people I've ever met.

Think about this, try losing everything you have ever loved in this world. People, possessions, dignity, self -respect, and all sense of selfworth. Even the will to live.

I've been to this place many, many times.

Imagine yourself crawling and fighting your way with all the strength and willpower you can muster, fighting off hopelessness, despair, guilt, and shame, all the while just to get back to the fucking starting line. Sound like fun? I've done this so many times it has become old hat.

I heard someone say in an A.A meeting once that getting sober mean that "the party's over." Party? I wanted to punch him. Life in addition is no fucking party. I can promise you that. And I hope you never have to find out. It is a living hell. Do your homework before you judge an addict.

I have heard it said that when a person is self-destructing, they're not trying to destroy themselves. They're trying to destroy something inside that doesn't belong. That's pretty spot on for me. The thing is, I also love to drink. I love it. All addiction is progressive, and I was up to about a gallon of vodka a day. Or, in a 16 to 18-hour time frame. The rest I spent passed out. It became a requirement first thing in the morning. I had to level off to stop the agony of withdrawal. I had to stop the shaking, just so I could shave without cutting my own throat. Good times.

Alcohol is the most dangerous substance to detox from. An alcoholic in active drinking, if you are as bad as me, can't just stop without medical attention, or wean off it little by little. I still try the latter. It can be fatal to the drinker if not done properly. Hence, my social membership at a few of the hospitals in Seattle.

The insidiousness of addiction will have the addict believe that things aren't so bad. That, and denial have taken many addicts to their graves. I wish that were enough to scare me. It is not. I feel confident in saying that I don't think it scares many of us.

Drinking and the restaurant business went hand in hand for me. In 1994, I was working at a gym called the Metropolitan Health Club on Columbus Ave. in the Back Bay neighborhood of Boston. The clientele was almost entirely gay. The gym was underground and located just under club cafe. A gay bar/restaurant that catered to the up-and-coming crowd in Boston. Gay urban professionals or Guppies as they were called. They seemed to stand around endlessly talking about their jobs, careers, money, and status. It was boring. I like my bars to be a little raunchier.

If I'm at a gay bar, I'm either there to get drunk, or get laid. Preferably both. If you're gonna yammer on about how important your work is, you can keep that shit to yourself. The gym itself was beautiful—80-foot ceilings, exposed brick everywhere, and state of the art equipment. And men!

It was a great pick-up spot. I enjoyed every minute of it. I worked as a personal trainer, even though I had no formal education on the matter. I was in really good shape, and I think they just assumed I knew what I was doing. It worked. I was busy, and always, always on the lookout for Mr. Right. Most of the time it ended up being Mr. Right Now. I was a bit of a man-whore in my mid 20s. Who am I kidding? I'm a bit of a man-whore now.

I loved working there. Anyway, one of my clients was the general manager of a four-star Italian restaurant called Rocco's, located in an old Greyhound bus terminal between the park Plaza Hotel and the Boston Common. He had a crush on me, and asked if I knew anyone who could tend bar. We needed staff for the restaurant. I said, "I'll do it." I had zero experience, but I always wanted to learn how to tend bar. He hired me. I think he assumed it would get him laid. It did not. He wasn't my type at all. He looked sort of Cro-Magnon, but with Coke-bottle glasses. Word at the gym was that he had a huge cock. I wasn't interested. Besides, I'm not a size Queen.

Yes, I am.

No, I'm not! I am a sucker for a cute face and a bulge though. Hairy, and in any way resembling Robin Williams or Rod Taylor, I will most likely fall in lust with you.

That season of my life was a good one. I had always wanted to live in the Back Bay. At the time, it was predominantly gay. The Brownstones were beautiful, and they lined nearly every street. Lucky for me, one of my clients, through conversation, said that he was looking for a roommate. He lived in the garden apartment of a Brownstone a few blocks from the gym. It was perfect. And fully furnished. I moved in the following month. Being a personal trainer at a gay gym, and living in a gay neighborhood was where it was at for me. I loved it. I made a lot of friends, and a lot of friends with benefits. Dare I say I was happy?

George, my client and the general manager of Rocco's, never really asked me if I had any experience. He just wanted me to work with him, I think. Rocco's was a beautiful space. Extremely high ceilings. Colors of amber, burnt orange, and straw were everywhere. The colors of Tuscany. The bar was off to the left with beautiful sconces and soft lighting hanging from wire that ran all the way down from the ceiling and stopped 10 feet over the bar.

I knew I had found what I wanted to do for living as soon as I stepped behind the stick (bar). I could feel it. I felt a surge of energy. My own personal stage, an endless menu of strangers, and alcohol. Perfect.

It was also set in a fine dining atmosphere, which meant I was moving farther away from Roxbury and my white trash beginnings. That's what I felt the most about it. I was home. On that day in 1995, I became a service industry person. Problem was, I didn't know the first thing about it. No problem. I went to the Boston Public Library on Boylston Street, across from the Trinity Church and the Copley Plaza Hotel. A beautiful Piazza with benches and a man-made waterfall. A perfect gathering spot for Brown baggers to eat their lunch in the shadow of the Hancock building. I spent a lot of time there imagining a bright future. I snatched up every book I could find on tending bar, waiting tables, and the study of wine, food and spirits.

Engaging the clientele was the best part of the job. Again, the endless menu of strangers, and the men, oh baby! Having a handsome traveler or businessman all to myself for an hour or so and plying them with liquor was a hell of a lot of fun. It's amazing what people will tell their bartender when they're drinking.

When it comes to making people feel comfortable, it is second nature to me. Anticipating their needs made me good. Being an empath has made me great at what I do, and after 25 years I still love it. Watching how people behaved, spoke, carried themselves in a fine dining atmosphere was a free education on etiquette. Watching people behave in a refined manner until the booze kicked in and then all bets were out the fucking window was hilarious. It's fascinating to watch people change when they drink. Sometimes for the better, sometimes for the worse.

There always seems to be one common denominator that people use the drink for, however. People drank to forget. For a little while. I know I sure as hell did. Alcohol is the great equalizer, as it is said. If people have worries, and they want to forget, if they're mourning the loss of a loved one, if they're celebrating, lonely, horny, or just out to have a good time, alcohol is always there.

The socially acceptable substance that has been destroying people since the beginning of time.

Watching people lose their inhibitions due to alcohol right in front of me was a trip. I did enjoy watching someone come in with a heavy burden on their heart, and for a little while forget their problems and let go. Restaurants and bars are almost recession proof for this reason. People need conviviality, a sense of belonging, mostly a fucking release.

Working in the service industry has giving me the opportunity to see so many different sides of people. I've watched people kiss, fight, break up, forget their cares and worries, get hired, get fired, laugh from the bottom of their hearts, and cry like they didn't care who was watching.

The one thing I can't forget is watching a young man fall in love with this girl right before my very eyes. There was no other way to describe it. She wasn't looking at him, he leaned toward her about half an inch and... a very subtle, but clear to me look came across his face. He blinked, and exhaled. A look that seem to say, I'm at your feet, I am all yours. I struggle to describe it exactly. How many people can say they've witnessed something like that? It was beautiful. Lucky me. I hope they're still together.

In all my experiences with people, the one thing I've noticed in everyone is that they're all so fragile. The human condition breaks my heart. At the end of the day, each one of us all want the same thing. To love and to be loved. This "Keeping up with the Joneses" bullshit is exhausting, people. I see it every day.

I love the service industry. I'll always do it. Not exactly the best job for an alcoholic. In fact, some would call it guaranteed relapse in the making.

The truth is I don't ever want to get completely sober. I enjoy drinking too much. I've just turned 50, and I feel exactly the way I did about quitting as I did after my first A.A meeting. I'm a binge drinker. I'm an all or nothing type of person. If I'm on the good foot, (sober), then there's no booze, no tobacco. I hardly ever smoked weed anyway so none of that. I exercise like crazy. No more junk food or late nights. I'm up by 6:00 a.m. and in bed by 10:00 p.m. Life is ultimately better living this way, but I'm unwilling to give up my right to drink.

Some of the people in my life can't understand why I don't just walk away from the booze once and for all. The bottom line is, I can't. What's more is I don't want to. Again, consequences be damned. Barring a miracle, this is how I'm going to be for the rest of my days. Peaks and valleys. The risks involved with this "selfish" decision are many and profound.

I risk never having a serious committed relationship again. I risk financial security, I risk being homeless again, physical destruction, bankruptcy, and even death.

Possibly not having a significant relationship is the one that may hurt the most. My most important relationship is the one I have with alcohol.

Damn. That hurts to say.

I don't mean to sound defeatist or full of doom and gloom. I feel that there are way too many variables involved to think in absolutes. One never knows.

You would think that any normal person faced with such potential ruin would do the obvious and never drink again. Ah, but addiction is like no other disease on the planet. The insidious, rapacious creditor as it says in *The Big Book of Alcoholics Anonymous* is always there.

Always waiting.

The phenomenon of craving, the subtle and even subconscious triggers that leads to an alcoholic picking up a drink after years of sobriety is fucking baffling. I've been through these back alleys and sloshed through, waded through and drowned practically many times, and at the end of the destruction, when I climb back to the starting line, beaten and destroyed, I get up, dust myself off, and begin the process of rebuilding.

All the while knowing that after a length of sobriety, I will pick up again.

Addiction, for those who know and have suffered, truly is a living hell. My disease progressed to the point where I absolutely had to have a bottle of vodka on the nightstand for when I came to, whenever that was.

Wherever that was.

Usually, a shady hotel or a bathhouse somewhere. I would have to carefully choke down half a pint in the hopes that it didn't come back on me because that liquid was a lifesaver.

I would have to so I wouldn't shake apart.

Again, just to shave without cutting my own throat. Mostly, just so I didn't have to feel the crushing guilt and shame involved with my drinking.

I just didn't want to feel anything. I still don't, but pain isn't the only trigger in my arsenal. I say arsenal because some things people may see as weaknesses, I see as strengths and motivators. Anger, rage, pain, trauma, a beautiful sunny day, a handsome face, an attractive man, money, no money, longing, loneliness, and fear are all triggers and motivating factors at the same time. The things that make me drink are also the things that make me say enough is enough.

I don't know if it's self-pity, self-loathing, or if I'm just used to things being always a little fucked up, but when I'm on the good foot (sober), I've come to realize I am untrusting of a good thing. As if it won't last so I tend to self-sabotage, whether I realize I'm doing it or not.

These ups and downs or peaks and valleys are how I have lived all my life. The constant moving when I was young has imprinted upon me the idea that nothing good ever lasts. However, trying to survive the despair I feel in the middle of a run or a bender can be a difficult thing to navigate.

Alcohol is a depressant remember, so for me, at the beginning of a run, I feel elated initially unless one of my triggers ends up being the loss of Brian. The beginning otherwise is always fun, especially the first drink the next morning to get rid of my hangover. At this time, I still have most of my motor skills. The booze takes longer to do damage because my body is usually extraordinarily strong from exercise. I love that first drink in the morning, and again only at the beginning of a run. I shower up, with music blaring. I feel happy in these moments, and then into an Uber and off I go. To God knows where.

In search of "A Moveable Feast" I suppose. Thank you, Papa Hemingway. Usually, out to do some street therapy or trying to edify someone.

Chapter Fifteen
The Restaurant Business

The fragility of the human condition to me is heartbreaking, and Seattle has more than its fair share of the homeless and addicted. Street therapy means finding someone that I can help. Not just monetarily, or with food and resources, but more importantly with time. Being marginalized by society and being made to feel invisible are feelings I never want in my life again. I know what less than nothing feels like, and when I see that look on a homeless person's face, I ask if I can sit down and hang out for a bit. Light up a smoke, or share the bottle I'm most likely carrying.

Just spending time trying to lift up another human being can mean everything to someone. One simple act of kindness can make all the difference to someone who thinks that nobody cares. I do. I care.

Some of the realest moments in my life have been just sitting on the ground talking with people. I saw a quote on social media once that read, "I'd rather sit with the broken than stand with the great." I loved it.

Addiction almost always leads to homelessness. As it stands, there are 550 thousand homeless people in the United States. Over half a million on any given day. If you think you are a strong person or are strong of will, then stop and for a second, imagine yourself in the shoes or no shoes of a homeless person you pass on the street that looks like hell and looks banged up and desperate. Could you survive in their position? Could you persevere? Sleeping outside night after night in the rain and cold? No one to care for you. Struggling to eat, stay warm and being looked at as less than human by your fellow man?

Now for fun, let's throw in addiction or mental health issues. The homeless are far stronger than you or I. Don't forget that.

I just ask that the next time you have the opportunity, and if it's safe, look someone in the eyes, and say hello. Let them know that you see them. Throw them a buck or two. People will say "Oh, they're just gonna use the money to buy more booze or dope." Maybe, maybe not.

What you've given them is not just a couple of bucks. What are you giving them is a choice now. An option they didn't have before. A lot of addicts will commit petty crimes just to get inside for a couple of days or weeks by being arrested. But if you're addicted to opiates, detoxing cold turkey in a jail cell can only be a living fucking nightmare. I can only assume.

I don't speak from experience personally with opiates, but I was in a cell with a young man, who was coming down. It was heartbreaking, watching him suffer so greatly. All I could do was pray for him.

I don't know whatever became of him. He looked to be around 25 years old, homeless, and addicted. I hope he made it. Odds are against it. Addiction, as I mentioned, almost always leads to homelessness, and once you're there, it's extremely hard to climb out. It's very hard to fight your way back.

If you look like hell, have little or no money, and haven't bathed in forever, how can you interview for a job? Especially if you're addicted. Most or all of your day is spent trying to get the funds to keep from getting dope sick or get another bottle of liquor or a pack of smokes.

The daily struggle just to get well or as in my case to get level, to have enough vodka in me first thing so I could function, is what keeps people on the street.

The thought of simply dusting oneself off, and giving it the old college try is far down the list of priorities.

Luckily for me, I have my precious anger to help pull me up by my bootstraps. I would become so hurt and so upset with myself for where I ended up that I would force myself through a detox, clean up where I could, and find a job. This was a sometimes long and painful process.

Fighting off the guilt and shame that kept me at the bottom of the bottle was the hardest part about climbing back out. Once I detoxed and started to look and think like my old self, then the ball started rolling again, and I would gather momentum very quickly.

It's funny to me that I can walk up to a gym after being on a long bender, smoke a cigarette just before I walk in, and after that initial workout, not smoke anymore.

Done. Just like that. It's part of my all or nothing personality. After properly destroying myself, I somehow find the strength to turn it all around. Once again, my precious and ever-present anger.

My stubbornness and even my ego won't let me linger in desperation for too long. I can tell myself that I'm the biggest piece of shit on the planet and then I'm just like my parents, that I'll always be a drunk and with the very next breath I will say to myself, "You are Ed fucking Cleaves. Get up, get to work, and get it done."

Compartmentalize everything, and start fighting again.

There is always hope regardless of how bad I let things get in the futile effort to bury my pain. It's as if somehow I flip a switch when I seem to be at my lowest. Enough is enough.

When that happens, I feel different, focused, and better. That part of my anger slaps me around and says let's go, let's get this shit done. It has been that way for all my life. The yin and the yang, the ups and the downs. The highs are unbelievably joyous, and the lows are a nightmare. The difficult part is that I have become so familiar with the lows that they don't scare me anymore. This needs to change. I deserve to give myself better. No more "sounds of silence." It's so weird that that would be the first song in my head when I would pick up a drink after any length of sobriety. Very strange.

I don't know if I feel self-pity when that happens? It most certainly seems ominous.

Perhaps some subconscious form of self-loathing. And then off to the races. I would slam a few drinks just to get that damned song out of my head. The beginnings of a run once I take the first drink are usually the same.

I'm good for about the first week or so, keep the same work schedule, I sleep and eat regularly. I don't exercise though, and I begin to smoke cigarettes right away. So weird. I'll buy a couple of packs of smokes at the same time I buy a bottle or two. I don't want the cigarettes when I'm sober. You never realize just how much they stink when you're smoking them. I'm surprised anyone ever kissed me.

Back to Rocco's

My first ever restaurant gig! I was learning so much in such a short amount of time about people, food, wine restaurant culture, and its lifestyle. Of which, I seemed perfectly suited for. Unfortunately, a lot of the front of the house staff at Rocco's were selfish, greedy, childish people that didn't really care about anything other than themselves and money.

So, me being as green as I was, got ridiculed a lot for not automatically knowing things a more experience server or bartender already knew. In hindsight, there were shitty people who were unwilling to share their knowledge of the business or help me or even each other to learn and to get better.

One would think that it would be a no-brainer, right? The better we all are, the better the service. The better the guest experience the more they come back to spend and tip. Not so much at Rocco's.

So, I took it personally and became hell bent on being better than all of them, and that's what I did. It took some time and hard work. I got to the point where I was fast. Really fast. If I was working the service well, (making drinks from a separate area of the bar for the dining room only), I would bang out a long list of tickets or drink orders with lightning speed, and at times, a busy server wouldn't be able to get to them quickly enough so they would die in the well (become waterlogged) from the melting ice.

I could have helped the server by running the drinks to their tables for them, but no. Fuck them! I'd rather watch them go down in flames. Petty, I know, and at the end of the day, it's the guest who suffers, but again, fuck them! I have a long memory. Don't fuck with me.

I'm not proud of that kind of behavior, but they needed to learn what it felt like when a person is out of control, busy, and no one cares enough to help. Their selfishness and unwillingness to help another person in our business is something I still haven't forgotten even after 25 years.

I now make it a priority to help anyone who is struggling in the business. 1: Because it's better for business, and 2: because it's the right thing to do.

All in all, that first step behind the bar at Rocco's changed the course of my life. For better and for worse. The initial thrill I got from stepping behind the stick is still there. The love for the industry is still there.

How many occupations are there in the world where one can take time off pretty much whenever one wants to. Write your own schedule within a year of employment in most places, or less. Have an endless menu of strangers and people from all over the world to meet and talk with? Get to feed them, create a memory for them through great service, find out about their lives and their points of view?

Getting to watch people forget about their worries for a little bit and relax it's one of the many benefits of the service industry for me. I get to enjoy all this all while making decent money. While working only 30 hours a week with very low overhead. Not a bad deal at all.

I rarely went food shopping because I ate at work all the time. For years, my freezer had ice and vodka in it. That's about it. My fridge had mixers like club soda tonic water and assorted juices. Add some garnishing fruit. Lemons, limes, oranges. And that was about it.

I usually ordered out or brought food home from work. If I did cook, it was for a dinner party or some recipe specific meal, so I only bought the ingredients I would need for that evening.

Wine however was everywhere. I always had wine on hand. Oh, and the fridge would also usually have something that used to be cheese in it.

I loved the Bohemian lifestyle so much. Not in the sense of belonging to or being involved in the arts, but more in the sense of being in the company of Raconteur. Late night throw downs at my place or pretty much any other co-workers' apartment or house is one of the best parts of being in the business early on for me.

The night didn't really begin until the restaurant closed and a handful of us would meet up at a local watering hole, usually within walking distance of work. The first time you sit down at a chair or bar stool after a long night, or God forbid a double shift, is the greatest feeling in the world. Other than the first pint going down, and trading war stories about the night with coworkers. The service industry is like no other in that respect, I think. If you find the right restaurant with the right crew, a decent, hardworking crew, then it almost becomes like a family.

The work is hard and stressful as hell, but at the end of the shift when cocktails and tobacco and weed are flowing and people are decompressing, it is so gratifying. There's nothing like it.

I felt a great sense of accomplishment, and had a job well done sort of feeling.

The restaurant business it's not exactly the best place for an addict, as I have mentioned, but at the time, my disease had progressed to where it was getting in the way, so I felt that it was the perfect place for me. There were many, many nights where we would hold court at some pub or restaurant after hours or at a coworker's flat, fearing the dreaded dawn. For me, that was when the evening ended. Sunrise.

I hated to see it come. Pre-dawn was when it was time to shut it down. It was easy to get to that point though. Quickly. If the bar closes at 1 or 2 a.m., then by the time I'm all cleaned up behind the bar and ready to go it's 2:30 or three in the morning. Wide awake from work and ready to throw down.

So, reaching the dreaded dawn really wasn't that hard to do. It just sucked because it meant the night was over.

Again, this was early in my addiction, so I could stop. I didn't want to, but I could. Besides, after crashing out until two or three p.m., it was time to get up, eat a huge breakfast somewhere, usually a big Irish fry up somewhere with a pint of Guinness, and start it all over again.

Another of the good things about the service industry is that even if you have a shitty, stressful night, by the next shift the following day, the slate is wiped clean. It all washes away, and the stage is set for another round of strangers.

If I work the lunch shift, then I had Chaz to keep me company on slow days with his four martini lunches. I'd always try to get him to five.

We had a local sportscaster from one of the major networks come in for lunch a few times a month and he would slam five martinis in about an hour and 15 minutes. And then go back to work. I'd see him on the 6:00 o'clock news and think holy shit, that guy was just getting fucked up at my bar.

Back then, I thought that was a lot of booze. Now, if I see someone drink like that, I think, amateurs. Although five good sized martinis in just over an hour is good enough to get anyone on their way.

It would shut most people down for the rest of the day.

Not me, because I had discovered cocaine! Holy hell!

Chaz had a buddy who was a dealer. The same one that gave us the "Black Fatty." He sold weed by the pound and cocaine. A lot of cocaine. I had come to find out kilos at a time. That was some serious weight. To me it was anyway.

There were times after closing the bar, take off with Chaz in his work van, and tool around the Gay bars in the Back Bay. Drinking and getting high.

I didn't like to smoke weed when I went out clubbing. It slowed me way down and made me not want to drink. In hindsight, I should have become Rastafarian. It would have saved me a lot of money.

I took to cocaine right away. I completely blew past that "party's over" thing at dawn. I would just keep going long after everyone else had gone home. I never wanted coke when I was sober. Never even thought about it, but after a few cocktails, it was all I could think about.

The night wasn't a success unless I found an 8-ball. This is where my addiction took a giant step forward. Sleepless nights, paranoia, fatigue, and just fucking anguish. I would party on school nights, and God forbid I had to open for a lunch shift and wait on the public in that condition. That was pure hell.

It was the worst feeling in the world. Standing in front of a bar full of people on their lunch hour, twitching apart, trying to hold it together. Good Lord that was awful, and even more so if I had to work a double shift that day.

Early on, I would just suffer through it, and by nightfall I was ready to go again. A few drinks and back to chasing the high. My appetite for destruction knew no bounds so I just kept getting after it and getting after it. People at work began to take notice when I would show up in that condition. So, I started making a couple of drinks for myself while

I was setting up the bar if I was opening that day. It helped take the edge off.

Not by much, but just enough to where I could face the public without shaking apart. There's nothing worse than being coked up and hung down at the same time, and waiting on people. And in daylight no less.

That was the worst part. Everyone was so fresh and ready to go, and I was there looking like fucking party monster. I needed to drink to ward off the guilt and shame. I felt like everyone knew what a piece of crap I was.

There was always an overwhelming sense of shame after. Then by nightfall, my second wind would kick in, and that was it. Cocaine is an appetite suppressant, so I lost a lot of weight early on. I didn't notice it, but my coworkers did. I shrugged it off. Work started to only exist to support my habit. At the time, an 8-ball would last two days. That was my norm for most of that winter. I was still doing a decent job at work but only when I was level, and had enough booze and blow in me to function. When I was on, I was on and could hold court with anyone from captains of industry to sailors, and everyone in between. It was easy to schmooze. It was also easy to just talk to people, anyone at my bar. I still found their lives to be so fascinating. I just had no desire at times or ability to do it when I was hurting so badly. I went on a bad tear with that shit. I got most of it through Chaz's guy, but after a while I ended up finding a guy through work that was open for business 24/7. Not good.

I started rocking and rolling all the time. I would manage my intake to get to just the right level of booze and blow to where I could function at work. Once I was there and on, making money and having a good time was easy. And so it went, night after night with fewer to no day shifts eventually. Thank God.

The hell was still there, but it was more manageable having more time to deal with it without being there in the morning. All in all, it was no way to exist. The lines on my face were getting deeper. I finally noticed the change in how I looked, shaving one afternoon, getting ready for work. I felt good that afternoon. I managed to get a few hours of sleep, so I felt ahead of the game. The face I saw staring back at me was not what I was used to seeing. I looked tired and worn out. Older than my 26 years, it seemed. But hadn't I always?

I didn't look like my usual self, however. Brimming over with vitality and strength. I didn't like what I saw. So the seed was planted, and it was time to stop. Time to get back on the good foot, and that's what I did. But not until after my vacation. I used my tax return to book a flight to Ireland to see a friend, so I didn't see the point in cleaning up my act until I returned.

Chapter Sixteen
Europe and the Lovely Ian

I had never been abroad, and I wanted to take full advantage. One of my coworkers, Craig, was an avid traveler and was headed to Amsterdam around the same time I was leaving. So, having never been, I altered my trip by a couple of days, and flew into Amsterdam with him. With the plan of making my way to Dublin after a couple of days. We landed around 8:00 a.m. and took the train from Schiphol, A.M.S into the city. Craig suggested we slam a double espresso and hit the town instead of wasting half a day sleeping. Once out of the train station, we were bombarded by kids with flyers for hotels and hostels around the city. "Hey Mr., stay here," "Hey Mr., this is the best hotel in town." They were relentless. They must have gotten a kickback for sending tourists and backpackers to their respective joints.

Craig suggested a hostel by the name of Durty Nellies 2. I would come to find that there was a Durty Nellies in Galway, Ireland. I didn't know if they were the same company.

This place was fantastically shitty. The downstairs was a pub with a long bar of about 30 stools. Dark and dingy. Not from tobacco smoke, but from age. It was perfect.

Upstairs was a second level of tables and TVs, and behind that was the actual hostel. So you had to fight through the crowds to get to your bunk. Again, perfect. I only spent a few days wandering the cobblestone streets and checking out the bars and coffee shops. It was so beautiful. I admired the gabled fronts on many of the houses.

Oddly enough, my favorite parts of the city were the tiny bridges spanning the canals that ran everywhere. I never made it to the museum district or the Van Gogh Museum. Something I would come to regret after leaving. Next time.

I enjoyed smoking a little weed and riding along the wet cobblestones late at night on an old, beat up rented bike after the city went to sleep. The coffee shops were fun. I enjoyed shopping for different kinds of weed even though I didn't know much about it.

I never understood why they were vending machines everywhere that dispensed hot food of all sorts until I smoked some hash with Craig, and we wandered around Leidseplein Square. Sort of the entertainment district. A lot of clubs and street performers. It felt so different and freeing being in Europe for the first time in my life. I felt completely anonymous, and that I had a blank canvas before me to paint on what I would.

I didn't want to go back home. I just wanted to keep traveling. On my last night there, I realized that I had no actual plan to get to Dublin to meet my friend at Shannon airport. I called him, and told him there was a change of plans. Craig was a master at traveling on the cheap, so he mapped out a pretty easy route from Amsterdam to Ireland for me. We were smoking hashish at the hostel, and I was complaining that I wasn't getting high.

We parted ways with a big hug. I really liked Craig. All he wanted to do was to travel. I would end up running into him again some 20 years later at a Smith and Wollensky's Steakhouse in Boston. He was manager there.

So, the plan he mapped out for me was a train ride from

Amsterdam to Calais, and then a ferry ride from Calais to Dover across the English Channel. And from there, another train into London. Pretty straight forward. After that, it was a quick and easy plane ride to Dublin.

We said our goodbyes and I headed to the train station. It was snowing, and I stood on a tiny canal bridge not far from the train station and watch the snowfall. It was so beautiful, so quiet. The city was going to bed, it seemed.

I watched the snow hit the stones and they glistened with the reflections of the streetlights and neon above.

The hash was kicking in. I didn't realize how high I was until I boarded the train.

It was so brightly lit and antiseptic in a whitewash that made everything abundantly clear. I was fucking high! But hashish was different than weed for me. It was an all-over body high. I was stoned and a little paranoid because the train was so packed with people and so brightly lit. I managed to find a seat with a little cubbyhole for my luggage, and I hunkered in for the ride. Driving to Calais on the E-40 would normally take about four hours, according to the locals in Amsterdam. But the train was the cheapest and the most direct route.

Arriving late to Calais, I made my way to the ferry terminal at the very last second. The ticket agent told me I got the last bunk. I made it just in time. He sold me a private room on board, so I went to store my backpack and then explore the ferry and have a few pints.

I think he tricked me because he sold me a ticket for private bunk for 75 guilders or about $42 US, and when I got to the room, there were three other people already in there. Oh well, the more the merrier. They were backpackers from South Africa. They seemed nice enough. I stored my shit, took my passport with me, and hit the upper decks.

I found the lounge and was having a pint. It was raining and windy as hell, so I decided that it would be a good idea to go out onto the top deck and check it out. In the dark. Black as pitch and raining. The only lights to be seen were coming from the ferry itself.

It was being knocked around a bit even as big as it was. I sat in the wind and rain and the dark and listened to Metallica on a little Sony CD player.

Yay alcohol! I could have slipped off that fucker and ended up at the bottom of the English Channel, and no one would ever have been the wiser. I make the best decisions when I drink! Ugh.

I was soaked to the bone and a little drunk, so I went down to my room to dry off and change clothes. My room was empty, blessedly, so I dried off and went back to the bar area.

I ended up chatting with a couple of musicians from London who were headed home from a weekend in Amsterdam. They were a lot of fun. Guitarists it turned out. Man could these guys drink. I remember looking out over the lounge area at the tables filled with travelers, all bumping to "Gangsters Paradise" by Coolio. It made me laugh.

A bunch of white kids getting their inner gangster on. It was so brightly lit inside, W.T.F? Whatever happened to my dark and seedy hideaway at Durty Nelly's? It was much better there.

The distance from Calais to Dover is only about 42 kilometers (26 miles), but it seemed to take a long time to cross. It almost seemed like an over-nighter, but it couldn't have been. I had time to drink on the upper deck outside, hang out in the lounge for hours, and even crash out in my bunk for a bit before we docked.

I just remember the P.A system on the ferry being so fucking shrill and loud that I thought I jumped out of my skin. I was hungover from the beer and tired as hell.

Upon arrival to Dover, I couldn't get to a bar to try and call my nerves with a couple of pints, so I searched for a train into London. Luckily, I found one departing within the hour. Great news. It meant I could have a pint or two on the train and maybe take a nap on the way.

It was only about two hours to London, so I opted on having pints to get my head right instead of napping. Feeling much better and having rediscovered my joy for traveling, I went out in between the train cars to have a smoke. That was one of the good things about Europe, everybody smoked.

There were a couple of Irishmen there with the same idea. We exchanged a few travel stories, and then I made my way back to my seat. The English countryside was so beautifully lush and green. I spent a lot of time just looking out the window.

I made it to London in no time, and with a fairly good buzz going. I still had no idea how I was getting to Dublin. Poor planning on my part, but I was on holiday, so I wasn't in a terrible rush.

I recall walking around the airport checking out the smartly dressed businessmen. Any airport is perfect for checking out men. There are so many cuties at any given airport it seems. Go figure. I couldn't tell if some of the men I spoke to were Gay or just British. No offense. I opted for a small airline called Ryan-Air.

The cost was about $75 US for a one way to Dublin. It took less than an hour, as I recall. I had a shot of Jameson and a beer brought to me by a stewardess with a shock of red hair and the bluest eyes. We chatted for a bit, and I told her of my travel plans or lack thereof. "Flying by the seat of the pants are ye?" she said.

God, I love the Irish brogue. In no time, I was in Dublin, and found my way to Heuston train station. My friend/lover Ian was down in Limerick, so I purchased a ticket and off I was again. I had a little bit of time, so I found a pub near the station to get a bite to eat and have a proper pint of Guinness. The train headed South past Kildare and Portaloise through Nenagh and into Limerick. "Stab City" it used to be called, I guess. There was a lot of crime at one point, according to Ian.

Once again, the countryside was amazing to look at. So very green. Only a little bit of a darker shade this time.

I met a tall, very thin bespectacled Irish man on his way to Limerick as well, and we had a few pints and a couple of smokes together on the way down. The train ride was a little over 2 1/2 hours, so I had plenty of time to kick back and relax. The perfect Irish proper Guinness in an Imperial pint is a thing of beauty! It's the only beer that I don't quaff when I order it. Mostly because it's a stout. A Budweiser or any American lager doesn't last very long around me. They are too easy to drink.

I usually just slam the first couple of pints, and from there, I tend to slow down and sip. It's like that with any liquid for me. Milk, chugged. Water, chugged. Juice, soda pop same thing. Not so much with Guinness.

I made it to Limerick and to Ian with a pretty good buzz going. Ian was the cutest thing.

We met at a bar called Luxor about two blocks away from Rocco's, right around the corner from The Napoléon Club. It was mid-week; a Wednesday, I believe. I finished my shift early, and went out looking for love.

Luxor was a regular spot for me, so I knew the bartenders well. I spotted Ian right away. What a lovely face he had. My goodness. He had reddish blonde hair, beautiful blue eyes, and thin rose-colored lips. He was stocky, hairy and humble in nature. I wanted him right away. I already had curtains picked out. He was absolutely beautiful to me.

I sent him a beer and he accepted thankfully as we were the only two sitting at the bar. It would have been a bit awkward had he refused it. He was over visiting friends in Boston and New York. I couldn't get enough of him. He was so damned cute. The combination of his brogue, the beer, and his seductive mouth made it hard for me to focus on anything but my desire to kiss him.

We chatted for a couple of hours at the bar and I asked him if he wanted to take a walk through the Public Gardens with me. About two blocks away. They're just opposite to where the Ritz Carlton and The Four Seasons hotels are. Where the famous duckpond is and the ever-popular Swan boats. It was also becoming crowded at the bar, and I wanted Ian all to myself.

The Boston Public Gardens was always one of my favorite places to hide. Cornered on Park Square and running along Charles Street past the Bull and Finch pub where the T.V show *Cheers* was inspired.

Tourists still wait in long lines every summer to get a look inside and take pictures of the facade. The Public Gardens themselves had beautiful winding pathways going here and there with a giant mounted statue of George Washington on horseback at the opening gate. It's a romantic place. A first-date kind of place.

In the springtime, tulips and lollipop flowers blossomed everywhere. Nine to fivers eating lunch, or lovers taking a stroll.

It's not as large or spread out as the Boston Common across the street. Ian and I found a bench near the pond and talked for a while longer. I was smitten. He was just so damned cute. I couldn't take it anymore. I had to kiss that ever so alluring mouth.

I asked if he minded if I kissed him, and he said no. No, he didn't mind. What I heard was "No, you may not," so I pulled away. Then he corrected me and said, "No, I don't mind at all." So, I leaned back in and gently kissed that gorgeous mouth of his. Good Lord! I dove in and we stayed under for a good 15 minutes. I, standing at full mast the whole time.

Ian mentioned something along the lines of "I don't ever really do this so soon after meeting someone," and I chuckled to myself. I sure as hell did, and especially with a face as angelic and apostolic as his. Cherubic and tinged with red, and with the bluest eyes I had ever seen up to that point. So very lovely. I dove back in for a kiss, but not before I asked him back to my place for a nightcap. He said yes!

I was taking this lovely creature home with me. By the way, nightcap in the Gay dictionary means do you wanna get naked? He did, and I had been pointing north from the very first kiss. I was ready to rock and roll.

We cut down Dartmouth Street, hooked the right onto Columbus Ave, and followed it all the way down to Wellington Street and my humble garden apartment. My roommate was not home blessedly. I had Ian all to myself, finally.

I pulled a couple of cold ones from the fridge and we sat down on the couch. I took his face into my hands, and I kissed him ever so tenderly at the edge of his lips. Ecstasy. That mouth of his had me hard as a rock once again.

I couldn't take much more, so I kinda just pounced on him. I reached for his crotch while my mouth was still firmly planted on his, and unbuttoned his pants. Button fly jeans. While I agree that button fly jeans are sexy, they're not very functional. I couldn't get to his cock fast enough.

I unbuttoned his fly to reveal bikini briefs. Irish and European men always wore bikini briefs. I didn't get it. I could see that he was just as ready to go as I was, so I pulled back his briefs and let his manhood out so I could get at it. He was sporting a tuft of red, neatly trimmed pubic hair. He was circumcised thank goodness. Uncut penises were unattractive to me back then. I'm not so picky anymore. I unbuttoned his shirt to reveal a chest and belly covered in blondish, reddish hair. It was such a turn on. I rubbed his chest and belly, running my fingers through his hair, and then we went at it.

I had what I like to call a "systems check" orgasm. So powerful and intense, I could feel it down to the ends of my limbs. Oh baby!

We laid there for a while after, and we finally cracked the two beers that were on the coffee table. We leaned back with our heads touching on the couch.

I asked him if he wanted to stay the night, and he said yes. We showered up, and I saw just how hairy he really was. From the neck down, he looked like a Wookie. With a brogue.

I gave him a white V-neck T shirt to wear and some boxers. Both a little too big, but they worked as pajamas while I washed his clothes.

He laid back on my bed in that white T and looked up at me it smiled ever so slightly.

God! Why did he have to live in Ireland, I thought.

Ian was all I wanted in that moment. I had found this lovely creature and he lives almost three thousand miles away.

We spent the night in my bedroom spooning. I was the big spoon. Ian was around five foot seven. We slept together very well. It was a great end to a wonderful evening.

He was only in town for about a week or so, and we made the most of it. He spent the rest of the week with me showing him around town, introducing him to the restaurant crowd, and drinking. He stayed at my place for the rest of his holiday, and I would have let him stay for as long as he wanted to. I was crazy about him.

I couldn't get enough. I found his beauty to be inspiring, he was my muse. All I wanted to do was to take care of him. Alas, he lived and worked in Dublin, and I in Boston. We carried on a whirlwind long-distance thing by phone and by mail, with Ian coming to Boston several more times to stay with me.

We were a good match and got along very well. And the sex was just so fucking hot.

After twenty-five years, we are still in touch. I haven't seen him in at least a decade, but we still email and chat occasionally. I still think of him fondly. It was a wonderful time in my life with the young and lovely Ian O.

On a side note, while in Dublin, I almost forgot to mention, for some reason, I decided to call Rocco's to check in. The owner, Patrick answered, and I asked how it was going. "Good for us, not so good for you" he said.

"What do you mean?" I asked.

"YOU'RE FIRED!"

"What u talkin' 'bout, Willis?"

I had it coming, and I couldn't really be mad at anyone but myself.

I had been taking liberties behind the bar, and my partying and drug use was way more evident than I thought it was. Constantly trying to get level by drinking behind the bar had taken its toll.

I said thank you for the opportunity and that I had no hard feelings. He replied in kind which made me feel good.

Patrick had always been straight up with me. He was a fucking horn-ball, that guy. And married. Banging everything in sight. Hostesses, waitresses, and I had a feeling he liked the cocaine as well. He always seemed to be in a hurry. I liked him either way. He kept me on the bar when I didn't know much about the business because he saw potential in me. I'm glad he did.

Had he not, I might not have pursued a career in the service industry. Who knows what I would have ended up doing? Having been in the game for so long now, the thought of a nine-to-five job seems like a slow death to me. No way. Surprisingly, that wasn't the first time I was fired.

Chapter Seventeen
The Restaurant Game

Being let go from Rocco's was the first time I'd ever been fired from another country. I was sad, but not surprised. I had no time to waste. Rent was due and I had little to no savings to speak of. I went back to work at the Metropolitan Health Club while I scoured the city for another restaurant gig.

I needed money fast. And in the restaurant business is the fastest money around. Back then, sending resumes online didn't really exist. No one had cell phones, so it was all done in person. Something I still do from time to time.

It's always better to sell yourself in person, I think. Eye contact and a firm handshake goes a long way in my opinion. So was looking good at a restaurant interview. First impressions and all. For the most part, I don't pay all that much attention to my appearance. As long as I'm clean. But in an interview. One must look the part.

I would usually go directly after a workout so my head would be clear, I'd be bursting with vigor and ready to go. I love the service industry. I always will. The stories are endless. The guests can provide either constant entertainment or cautionary tales of how not to behave in public. I've seen some of the craziest shit ever in my business.

I'll never forget the time I watched a woman lose her fucking mind at a Steakhouse I worked at in Seattle. It was Saturday night, prime time. 7:30 p.m. The Theater was in town at the Paramount. I think it was *The Book of Mormon* by the South Park guys. We were jam-packed. Not a seat to be had anywhere. I looked across the dining room at one of my colleagues being berated by a Karen (an entitled white woman). Reluctantly, I went over to help. She just couldn't believe that we didn't have an extra chair to bring to the table for her son's imaginary friend? I shit you not.

To quote the great Ozzy Osbourne, "I'm fucking speechless!" That was a new one on me. I felt bad for the kid. He was about 8 years old. He looked like the character "Tweak" from South Park. He was just sitting there, kind of twitching and shaking. On some sort of unnecessary medication, in my opinion. But what do I know right? Maybe meds will help guard him from his lunatic mother. Not likely, that kid is screwed.

I pulled my colleague aside and said just get through the next hour or so and you'll never have to see her again. He mentioned that she was not going to tip and that it was a large check. They had 10 people in their party, and most of them were drinking. I reminded him that on parties of eight or more, we automatically add 18% gratuity to the bill. Larger parties can tend to stay for hours, taking up a lot of real estate and minimizing your potential earnings for the night as a server. It's how a restaurant can protect its staff even if the host of the party stiffs the waiter. Which happens a lot more than you think. You don't get to come to a restaurant and treat people like shit just because you're unhappy with whatever is going on in your life. Grow the fuck up! Do not mess with people that handle your food!

I told him that he was covered by house rules and to keep pumping drinks into the other guests. They seem to be used to this woman's tirades and get through it with alcohol. Very typical behavior. Being a bartender and a waiter, we get to witness and are subjected to the worst behavior from so called adults. It's mind boggling. The idiocy and entitlement make me wonder how people go through life treating others the way they do and not getting their asses kicked. The poor waiter or bartender usually has to suffer the wrath of people, unfairly, simply because said individual is clearly unhappy with their own lives.

One of my favorite quotes is, "Do all things with kindness, you Fucker." Having been in the business for so long I can dance around "Karens" and insecure white males well enough to placate them without giving an inch into their childish, and often ridiculous, demands. All the while thinking of how nice it would be to just stomp the shit out of one of these people. Again, don't fuck with people who handle your food!

I think I may have a problem with swearing...

Also, stop taking pictures of your food. Just eat the damn thing!

I could rant about crazy customers for hours. Just a byproduct of the business.

Look, the way I see it is if you are lucky enough in this world to sit down at an expensive restaurant and have other people cook for you and bring you whatever you want, then you can at least recognize that, and show a little gratitude and humility. The homeless rate in Seattle is the third largest in the U.S behind New York and LA. When I witness a blatant lack of gratitude, it always reminds me of a song called "Pearls" by the artist Sade. One of my favorites. It offers instant perspective for me, which for those lucky enough to recognize, is a gift.

Being an empath and being able to read people so well has made me particularly good at what I do. I find it so easy to read people table side. Their body language, subtle inflections, their energy, tells me so much about them. They will usually show exactly how they're feeling or what their intentions are with the most subtle of actions, or even just a subconscious movement or glance. Being able to pick up on all of it is so strange, but if I'm honest, I wouldn't have it any other way.

My favorite people ever are the ones who are copped on to the restaurant life, or just decent human beings. Aware that what we do is not easy. A simple kind word or gesture can go a long way in this world and can turn around someone's day instantly. Being kind to your waiter or bar man can go miles. We're not used to it. Diners and drinkers that are fun and respectful are why I still love the job.

My other favorites are the long-married couples that come in to dine. They've been together so long there that there's almost no conversation. They order everything they're going to eat for the evening, and then I simply keep the drinks coming. Sometimes, sadly, the one that drinks the most is usually the angrier, or worse, the more indifferent of the two. There's not always the palpable mutual disdain; however, sometimes the couple knows each other so well that they can have a conversation without saying a word. It's good stuff. Very easy to wait on. 25% and out the door.

I like watching people relax and enjoy themselves. When the vibe is just right in the dining room. The lights are low but there's just enough to reflect off the wine glasses and the silverware. Soft music playing. Quiet conversations taking place here and there. The wine is flowing, the sounds of the glass and silverware softly clinking. This is my wheelhouse. This is what I love. And again, with an endless menu of strangers to enjoy all the while.

And once in a blue moon, my beloved Muse would come in to dine. The ever-so-elusive face that makes me freeze in my tracks. A one-in-a-thousand face that completely destroys me the moment I see it. It's so rare, this Muse I speak of, but when it comes, everything stops. I can focus on nothing else. It becomes difficult for me to concentrate on my work. Especially if he is sitting at one of my tables. I am an expert at hiding my tell, except in the presence of one of these faces.

Again, it is so rare that I see one, that at times, I can't help but be a bit flabbergasted. My Muse, as I like to call him. My elusive beauty that makes me want to be better. To not settle. My Muse makes me feel alive and inspired.

A beautiful face can be a complete and total inspiration for me. It is how I have found a lot of the things I love. I re-discovered the writings of F. Scott Fitzgerald through a Robin Williams interview. His face used to make my heart sing! I knew of the author through Hemingway, but I never tore through his body of work until after.

Through the beautiful face of an older man at an outdoor flea market in Newburyport, Massachusetts, a beautiful seaside New England town, I discovered the great Jack London. My favorite author to this day. The older gentleman had a face like Rod Taylor, the actor in *The Birds* by Alfred Hitchcock. He was reading a book with no title on it, and as soon as he put it down, I scurried over to pick it up. It was *White Fang*! The man sauntered off to the Mrs. Lucky girl. So I grabbed the book for purchase. I remember reading *To Build a Fire* when I was in grade school and enjoyed it, but that was all.

After *White Fang*, I was hooked. Part of my addictive personality, I suppose. I read everything I could get my hands on by the author. My two favorites are a toss-up between *Martin Eden*, a semi-autobiographical novel, and *The Sea-Wolf*, a tale of treachery and survival on the high seas. Fantastic!

Jack London doesn't waste a single word in his writings. He says so much with so few words. He and Anne Rice are my top two favorite authors to date.

I discovered the poetry of Lord Byron, then John Keats, and Shelly —Byron's "To A Beautiful Quaker" being my favorite—the same way I discovered most things, a lovely face at an outdoor theater, Summer stock on Boston Common, I think. The actor was so handsome, and after reciting Byron, I tore into everything he had ever written. That's how it goes for me sometimes. Well, most of the time.

A beautiful face can move me, inspire me to do just about anything. It's far more than sex. My mind takes off at light-speed, chasing a million and one scenarios of how we meet, fall madly in love, and live happily ever after. I'm a bit more of a realist in my old age, I think. These muses all tend to have the same facial features as well. Thin lips, blue eyes. As for body type, usually a bit shorter than me, stocky, or even kinda chubby. And a hairy chest and belly is such a turn on.

It's so rare that I see an actual muse, but when I do, I turn into a blithering idiot. I can usually talk to anyone about anything with a confidence that just comes naturally to me, but put me in front of the ever-elusive muse, and I am lost. I end up blurting out the dumbest shit. It's almost like I can't stop myself! My idiotic ramblings tend to snowball, run downhill, and end up in an avalanche. I can feel my blood pressure rise And I can usually tell by the expression on his face that he thinks I am insane.

"I LIKE FROGS." I blurted that out during a conversation. I don't like frogs! I don't hate them either, but why did that come flying out? Idiot!

I wish I could have recorded one of these episodes. Cringe worthy. But at least I felt completely alive. Moments like that I like to compare with jumping off a high ledge into a lake. Or going on stage when I was a kid at the Winthrop Playmakers. In Winthrop, MA, Summertime theater. It was terrifying.

Going all in on someone or something scares the shit out of me, but I never feel more alive when it happens. Especially becoming smitten by a lovely face. Now, being a bit older, I still feel the same way when these moments arrive. The edge is a little less sharp. I tend to protect myself more in the interest of self-preservation. While always keeping one eye open for a lovely face, I tend to try and stem the tide of emotions involved. It can be exhausting. I also don't jump from high places anymore into water. One of the benefits of getting older. Semi-dangerous shit I would normally do, I now look at, and think, "Nah, not gonna happen."

I've put my body through enough hell, and quite frankly, I can't believe I'm still alive. Now at 50 years old, when certain things pop up that might require a lot of physical exertion, my body says, pass. I think I'll just sit down and have a sandwich. Couldn't possibly hurt myself doing that right? Wrong!

I completely fucked myself up making one of my favorite things in life, a nice sandwich. Ham and cheese. Two slices of thick and doughy white bread. Exactly how I like my men, thick and doughy. Tomato, lettuce, salt and pepper, and an unnaturally large amount of mayo (on the sandwich, not the man). What can I say? I'm white like that.

A good sandwich can turn my whole day around. Not on this day, however. While using a ton of Canes Mayo, I spilled a bit on the floor, and unbeknownst to me, after having finished my masterpiece, I turned to make my way towards the T.V. and some *SportsCenter*. I slipped on the mayonnaise, and ended up ass over teakettle. The sandwich was flung in the air. Some of it stuck to the ceiling – I'm kinda proud of that actually – and I ended up flat on my back with sandwich makings everywhere. Good times.

Another thing about getting older was that I was in no rush to get up from this catastrophe. I just laid there. I reached over and picked a bit of cheese off the floor and popped it into my mouth. Call it a win, I said to myself. My dog was just looking at me like I was nuts. How 'bout it, Sweet Pea? She did the cleaning for me while I hopped in the shower.

So, let that be a lesson, boys and girls, a ham sandwich will fucking kill you if you're not careful!

Chapter Eighteen

Sweet Pea

Sweet Pea was a Boston terrier we got when my Brian was still able to walk early on in his battle with cancer. We already had a ton of shit on both of our plates, and having just gone through a couple of rounds of chemo, getting a new puppy would add a lot to our lives.

Brian would become so sick after chemo that all he could do was just lay down on his side and try to sleep. He was so sick from it, and there was nothing I could do except bring him what he needed when he needed it. I just let him know I was there. He was so strong. He never complained. He would just say, "I don't feel good," and lay on his side.

I used to think I was strong in life, but I've never seen anything like I witnessed with my Brian. He had such inner strength and a quiet dignity about him when he was suffering. It was amazing to me. I've never known someone so strong like that. Through temperatures of 104 degrees, chills, sweats, body aches that I'm sure he downplayed for my benefit.

I asked my sister Patty if she had any advice, and she said to keep 100% of my focus on him. Be strong in the face of it, and most importantly, remain calm. He would need my strength in the end. I would have given my life for him to have been cured. A thousand times over. I saw a side of Brian that I never knew existed. He was a stronger and better man than I could ever hope to be.

In between chemo treatments, Brian would sometimes return to normal. I liked to tell myself. He had more strength more clarity and even seemed to be a bit chipper. It was great to see him playing with Sweet Pea. She brought him hope, I think. This fucking dog was a terrorist, however. A lazy-eyed psycho!

Brian found her through a breeder in Oklahoma. On the way to pick her up, I had never seen him so giddy with anticipation. We went out and bought a doggy bed, and all kinds of toys and things we thought she would like.

On the day of her arrival, we had to pick her up from air cargo freight at SeaTac Airport. We waited there a long time for her, and I could see the anticipation building in Brian. He was nervous. I was thinking, *let's just get her and get home so we could try to acclimate two fully grown cats to a brand-new puppy*. Neighbors and friends said we were crazy taking on a new puppy, and at first, I kind of agreed. But after watching Brian get so excited in the waiting area, I didn't give a damn. He was all about it and so was I.

The clerk at the cargo hold came from the back and shouted, "Guess who's here?" We really were waiting for quite some time, so she became just as excited as Brian was. We opened her kennel, and couldn't see her at first. She was so tiny. Being mostly black with white patches on her belly, she wasn't easy to spot in the dimly lit waiting area.

Brian coaxed her out with some treats, and she ever so slowly poked her head out. She was so tiny and so scared. Brian scooped her up, and held her upside down like a newborn. Kinda what she was really. 8 weeks old, I think. The thought of a puppy not being a good idea quickly vanished. The look on Brian's face said it all. It was beautiful.

I got my chance to hold her, and I cradled this thing in my arms. She looked up at me with her lazy eye, and I was hooked. She had me. I was in love with this helpless creature. We both were.

Little did we know she would turn out to be insane! A lazy-eyed psycho. She was a lunatic. I loved it. The first couple of weeks were an adjustment, especially for the cats. They looked at her, and then back at us as if to say, "Are you fucking kidding me?" They avoided her, and as she grew, so did her boldness towards the cats. It was great. I'm not exactly what you would call a cat person. By the way, there's no point in naming a cat. Ever! They don't answer.

Sweet Pea, as Brian had named her, would bark at the cats with her high pitched yipe. Sam and Neelix were so used to running the show at home that they didn't know what to do with this little thing that invaded their territory. They couldn't hide under anything, so the only place for them to go was up. We had one of those cat jungle gyms in the living room, so they would climb to the top of it, look down, and hiss, with Sweet Pea offering her yipes and asserting her dominance every chance she could.

It wouldn't last too long, however. Those cats were gonna fuck her up! It was just a matter of time. I'd be watching T.V. and I would see Neelix, the tabby, stalking slowly towards Sweet Pea, with laser like focus. The puppy mustering all her courage to try and scare him off to no avail. Unbeknownst to Sweet Pea, Sam, the much older black cat would be flanking her. You'd think with her lazy eye she would be able to see both of them simultaneously. But no such luck. It was a thing of beauty to watch these cats hunt. Pure instinct.

I wasn't going to let them hurt her. I'm pretty sure they were just gonna teach her a lesson. I knew it was a matter of time before they caught her alone. When Brian and I were asleep is when I thought they would get her, and that is what they did. We were napping and I heard a ruckus coming from the living room. Could I describe the ruckus you asked? Why Certainly!

It started with a hiss, then another, and then an ear-piercing yelp. Followed by Sweet Pea trying to run across the hardwood floors in the living room Scooby-doo style. Sam and Neelix had her cornered behind the jungle gym, and were about to whoop her ass.

Sweet Pea was looking back and forth between the two of them. At least I think she was. I never really knew what the fuck she was looking at. Trying to be as brave as she was, she had a look about her that was somewhere between "Bring it on," and "Holy shit, I'm dead!"

I swooped in to rescue her, but I made it a point not to yell at the cats. Sweet Pea had to learn not to mess with them. I think she did learn.

Sam, the older cat, just sort of walked away and seemed to be done with it, in true cat fashion. Neelix, on the other hand, wanted to keep going. He finally walked away, slowly. He looked back a couple of times at Sweet Pea, as if to say, this shit ain't over motherfucker! I know where you live.

Sweet Pea brought a lot of joy to our lives, and a lot of work to mine. She was a never-ending bundle of energy, and as curious as all new critters to the world are, she was difficult to potty train, and would just pee where and whenever she wanted to. Usually while staring right at both Brian and I at the same time. From different parts of the room.

Sweet Pea was constantly wagging her butt and she always seemed to be smiling. She brought so much love and excitement to our household. She made Brian happy. That was all I cared about. I used to see men in our neighborhood walking these tiny dogs, and I would think, "You little bitches, get a real dog." And now I had a little dog, and I loved it.

I was now one of the homo's on Capitol Hill with a tiny dog.

As Sweet Pea grew, so did her appetite for mischief. She was a sneaky little thing. I was so proud. She also like to eat cat poop! Gross. When Sam or Neelix would do their business, Sweet Pea would make a beeline for the cat box for a fresh and tasty snack. And then want to come and lick Brian or me. So gross.

I would yell at her to stop when she was about 10 feet from the litter box. She would freeze in her tracks. I would turn my head, and she would take a couple of steps closer with one eye on me and one eye on her prize. I would look again, and she would scoot a little closer until I finally had to chase her away. If I left the room for a second, she would dash over there, grab a poop snack, and dash back to her bed. She would hold it in her mouth. She tried to convince me that she didn't have fresh cat shit in there. Again, I would look away, and she would chew. I would turn my head back, and she would stop. She was the sneakiest little thing.

We had to break her of that habit and very quickly. Chemotherapy can weaken the body's immune system, so I couldn't have little "Miss Poopy Mouth" licking Brian all over his face.

We liked to play with her on the couch or in the backyard and kind of toss her around, or play tug of war with some of her toys. I would put my hand in her tiny mouth, and roughhouse with her. She loved it.

The breeder we got Sweet Pea from told us that she had already been spayed. The vet down the street from my house had confirmed it. However, when Springtime arrived, with it came a very horny puppy. Well, with this newfound horniness, Sweet Pea began clamping her two front paws around my elbow, and then wrapping her hind legs around my wrist and her body around my forearm, and would start humping the shit out of me. I couldn't shake her off at first. She would grunt and growl and stare at me with her one good eye. Apart from being grossed out a little, it was the funniest thing ever. She was so strong. I couldn't get her off me without some serious effort.

That coupled with the fact that I was pissing myself laughing. The combination of her grunts and that one eye looking directly at me was too much. I lost it. Which in turn made it harder to pry her loose. It was so funny. We brought her to the vet again just to be sure. She was properly spayed, just a little horny!

She had grown quite a bit, but I wasn't prepared for just how strong and determined she was to hump the shit out of my arm. I remember watching T.V. one Saturday morning, Brian was still in bed, and I heard him yell for me, "Ed, help! Get her off me."

I ran into the bedroom in a panic, thinking he was hurt, and there he was lying flat on his back, with his forearm up in the air, and Sweet Pea going to town on it. She clamped on while he was sleeping, and he couldn't shake her off. I couldn't stop myself from laughing. She was grunting and humping away while staring at who knows what. I was roaring. Brian was somewhere between laughing hysterically, and screaming, "Get this fucking dog off me!" I wish I had taken a video. It was hilarious.

That was one of our favorite memories with her. She brought so much joy to our household. She was a blessing. In disguise mostly. She came on like a fucking hurricane. Our house at the time was filled with laughs and love, but always with, at least for me, and underlying fear and a sense of impending doom.

Fear of what everyone said was going to happen to Brian. The inevitable. I felt like a little kid whistling past the graveyard. But I always had hope. Always. Until the very end. So, while he was alive, I did everything I could to make sure our home and our time together was filled with fun and laughs. We had medical needs and routines that we addressed daily. Brian suffered edema in his legs as a side effect of one of his many, many medications. The medication to counteract his edema would literally make his legs bleed water from his pores. So, he needed bandages daily, and they needed constant changing. His ankles and calves would swell so badly that he couldn't walk, and when you combine that with him getting so sick every three weeks from chemo, he was unable to move on his own. My faith was strong back then, so I begged God to cure him, to give it to me, I would take it on just spare him.

We needed the morphine sulfate and liquid morphine during these times to help him with his pain. Most of the time, it would knock him out so he could sleep peacefully. Every once in a while, however, it made him a serious flight risk.

We reached the point where we needed a hospital bed in the house, so we got rid of the couch, and we put a functioning hospital bed in its place for him. I would sleep on the floor next to the bed since it was too small for the both of us. Plus, Brian didn't like to be touched right after chemo. It was so hard not being able to hold him while he suffered. I couldn't let on how much it hurt. I would sleep on the floor with one arm draped up onto the ledge of the hospital bed, so that Brian had only to feel for my arm to know that I was there.

The flight risk episode came one night after we both had a pretty normal day. He was able to eat a little and at around 11:00 p.m., and it was lights out for both of us. I administered his medications, and he complained of body aches, which were not uncommon. He wanted some liquid morphine. This stuff was serious business, I would come to find out. It was given the same way you would give cough syrup—on a teaspoon. In fact, that's what it kind of looked like, except this looked more like motor oil. I gave him a teaspoon full, and we went to bed in our customary positions.

Just across the room from the hospital bed was our T.V., and to the left of it, a computer desk. With a giant black swivel chair for Brian to sit on when he could walk. Around 2:00 a.m., I heard the familiar squeaking of the wheels under the chair. I jumped up and turned on the lights, and Brian was there with his winter coat on, unzipped, sitting in the chair, wearing nothing else! Buck naked!

He was sitting in the chair, and using his feet to try and make his way to the front door. He had the biggest grin on his face. His eyes were half closed. I don't know how he got past me, got undressed, got his coat from the closet, and sat down to make his escape. Almost completely naked, and smiling. I usually sprung up as soon as he would call for me, but I must have been out like a light. I said, "Baby, where are you going?" He said with a smile and half-closed eyes, "I've gotta go. We've gotta go!"

He was making a run for it using his feet, Flintstone style, to get himself across the room. I said, "Babe, where are we going?" He just giggled and kept trying to move forward. It was lovely.

That morphine is serious business. I hugged him, got him back into bed, and popped on the T.V. for some background noise while I rubbed his feet. It seemed to relax him so quickly, and he would fall right asleep. I stayed up and watched T.V. on the edge of the bed. I couldn't believe he got past me so easily.

So that was our routine for some time. We had highs and lows, peaks and valleys, and most of all, we had each other. We were in this together. Him and me, and Sweet Pea, and the two cats.

There would be times, even late in his battle, where he would almost return to normal and, by that, I mean he could walk with good strength and balance. Slowly. He had clarity, his mind was sharp, his timing and reflexes were good, and he even seemed happy.

It was so great. These were the times when we would go outside to return to normal for a little while. Even though nothing would ever be normal for us again.

We lived on the third floor of a building with a backyard that was beautifully landscaped, and adorned with tables for eating. It even had a couple of hammocks. The grounds were so beautiful, but very uneven and difficult for Brian to navigate. So, we would mostly just go for a stroll through the neighborhood, or to the Trader Joe's up the street. Anything to give him a sense of normalcy and anything to get him away from that hospital bed. We even managed to get to a movie once.

By the way, I don't know what's up with movie theaters, but they need to be brought before Congress for price gouging! You practically need a second mortgage just to buy popcorn and a soda.

We saw movie called *The Martian*. Matt Damon was the actor. Brian thoroughly enjoyed it. I think he was just so happy to be out in society again, and to feel like a normal person. I glanced over at him while he was watching the movie, and he looked so happy. It didn't seem to matter what was playing. In that moment, he was happy, and so was I. I reached over and held his hand.

It was my life's honor to be able to take care of him.

There were times in our fight against this that it became extremely difficult for Brian. We spent so much time in hospitals that we were on a first name basis with most of the staff. A good visit was when we heard news that chemotherapy was shrinking some of the lesions on his brain. The cancer, at this point, had metastasized to his right hip and to parts of his brain.

When we got news that the cancer hadn't spread, and that the chemo had even shrunk some of the lesions, we would take that as a win. We knew that within hours of chemo, he would become sick again, and have to spend the next several days in bed. I hated it so much. So, we had to take advantage of the little time we had before that happened. That usually meant lunch together somewhere around the hospital. There were a bunch of little restaurants and sandwich shops on Madison Street, near the hospital. We would just pick one we hadn't been to yet, and have lunch. It was a good day when Brian could eat. Getting him home after that was a priority. He would need morphine to help with the pain and sickness that was coming.

There were days that would go by when Brian couldn't eat anything at all. Many days. There was just no way around it, so I would go to the kitchen and cook anyway. Just to get the smell of food into the house with the hopes of getting him to take a bite. But mostly to keep a sense of normalcy in our home. A break in the routine of constant doses of pain medication.

Some days we were lucky, and Brian ate a few bites. But usually, a few hours after chemo, nothing. Getting him comfortable and managing his pain were the two biggest concerns.

I wasn't worried so much about weight loss as I was about his nutrition. He was on a steroid called dexamethasone. That, combined with his edema, made it look like he was gaining weight. So, getting nutrients into him was a priority and a challenge at the same time. Looking after his mental well-being was just as important.

Brian used to call me weird when he would catch me looking at him early on in our relationship. I wasn't weird, I was just smitten. He was so beautiful. I loved looking at him. Now, with all that had happened, I kept my eye on him to make sure he didn't get too stuck in his head or fall into a depression. I refused to let him feel overwhelmed, or beaten down by all of this. So I became his constant cheerleader. I tried always to be upbeat and hopeful, without being too annoying. With care not to invade his personal space when chemo stole my ability to touch him and to hold his hand.

We had a way of communicating without speaking that I think came from our being together for so long, and our love for each other. My favorite thing to say to him was, "Have I told you that I love you today?" He would playfully say "No," and I would say, "I love you, babe."

I've never loved anything more than I have loved this man.

There were times when he couldn't walk without assistance, and he couldn't make it to the bathroom on time. We had these things the nurses called "chucks," or adult diapers, that he began wearing because of his incontinence. I put some on in solidarity with Brian, and paraded around the living room with the hopes of getting a laugh. Mission accomplished.

When he did have an accident, and he needed to be cleaned up, Brian would get this awful look of shame about him. He would begin to cry. I felt so bad. I felt so bad for him, but I wouldn't let him get down on himself. When it happened, I would just put my arm around him, and say "Come on, let's go babe. I got you." Brian was about 5 foot 10 inches tall and about 260 pounds, so moving him wasn't easy, but we had a good system. My arm around his waist, and his arm around my shoulder, and we sort of clamped together, and made our way to the bathroom.

The first time he had an accident, we made it to the bathroom and closed the door, and he put his head on my shoulder and began to cry. He kept apologizing for having an accident. I held onto him, and I kissed the top of his head, and said, "Have I told you that I love you today?"

"You tell me everyday" he said. One of the greatest moments I've ever had with him. One of the greatest moments of my life.

Chapter Nineteen
Caring For My Brian

Getting a 260-pound man that can't move well into a tub, and especially out of it, was no easy task either. We had a system for getting him in, but getting out was the hard part. I never let on, but tub time with Brian was one of my favorite things throughout all of this. There is something so intimate and loving about bathing someone you love. It would make me cry. Scrubbing him all over with his loofah and washing his hair.

It was him and me. Our time together, and I loved every minute of it. Pouring water over his head to rinse away the shampoo, and watching the water rinse everything away somehow brought me even closer to this man that I already loved more than life itself. He was totally dependent upon me in those moments, and he would look at me sometimes with such innocence and hope that it would crush me. Here was this humble, kind creature that wanted nothing more than to live, and this fucking disease was robbing him of that.

IT WAS UNFAIR!

It wasn't right. Everything that I considered good in this world was now in my care, and I sure as hell wasn't going to give him up without a fight. But how do you kill an intangible enemy?

Brian's parents came out from Colorado to visit and help where they could. I felt so bad for his mother, Hollis Smith. She was a tiny frail woman, but according to Brian, a force to be reckoned with. At the time, his parents were in there 80s, and still able to move around pretty well. Hollis was a homemaker and a very good cook. Edward Smith, Brian's dad, was a tool and die man from Chicago. The Smiths hailed from Mount Prospect, Illinois.

Brian and I took a trip out, and got some neat pictures in front of his childhood home. He made me stand outside in the middle of a Chicago Winter to get into a Pizzeria Uno because had I never had a deep-dish pizza before. I froze my ass off! It was worth it, though. That fucking thing was delicious.

I was the photographer in our family, and I snuck a picture of him sitting down on the window ledge at Pizzeria Uno in his big green winter coat. He looked deep in thought. How handsome he was. I was lucky enough in life to have the love of a man who made my pulse quicken every time I looked at him.

Hollis and Ed ended up renting a condo directly across the hall from us. We knew the owner, and she knew our situation, and was glad to rent it on a month-to-month basis as needed. We were grateful. It was nice to have them so close, and I welcome the extra hands.

They seemed a bit overwhelmed at first by just how much was going on in our home. How, on some days, Brian would require around-the-clock care. That meant no sleep for me. Challenge accepted. I was used to it. They were not. They were seniors. It was difficult for them. I ended up worrying about them a lot at times also. They were parents watching their son become so sick. It was heartbreaking, seeing the looks on their faces from time to time, and seeing Brian in pain so up close.

Hollis wanted to do what any mother would, which was care for her son. So it was nice when she could sit bedside, and I could go food shopping, or if I was able, crash out for a few hours. Catching up on sleep meant I had a bit more energy than normal. I was grateful to them for this.

I think having them there helped lift Brian's spirits a bit. Not long after they arrived, we had what I called an upturn in Brian's condition, which meant the chemo had shrunk his lesions a bit more. This didn't explain his burst of energy and clarity, but we would take it when it came. He could walk, but very slowly, and with a bit of help sometimes. I never let him go alone. Even if I didn't hold him, I was close enough to grab him if he began to fall.

Brian had two sisters, Elaine and Diane, both older than him. Elaine was my favorite. She was the female version of Brian. She always had a smile. Always. Like it was a natural part of her face. Two sisters married two brothers, electricians. They all lived in Colorado, in the towns of Estes Park, Greeley and Loveland.

During this upturn in Brian's health, his sisters and their spouses loaded up an RV and drove out to Seattle for a week. They stayed at the Silver Cloud Hotel on Madison, just between our place and the hospital, Virginia Mason. The family arrived early during our morning routine, and we had coffee and pastry as I got our day started.

Everything came together one sunny warm afternoon when we all had a barbecue in the backyard. Hot dogs, hamburgers, and brats on the grill, Trader Joe's potato salad, and Brian's whole family gathered around the picnic table. Soda pop and condiments everywhere. A real family gathering.

The flora was in full bloom, the air was sweet with it, and Brian was happy. Almost back to his old self, I thought. I was so happy, snapping pictures of the event, and trying not to burn the Bratwurst. I forgot to boil them in beer first. Brian's dad swooped in and saved me. Thank God. I would have burned them.

It was a perfect afternoon. Brian was eating, everyone was chatting about the old times, about their childhood in Chicago. We all seemed to relax for a second.

Cancer wasn't welcome at this barbecue.

Having Hollis and Ed so close by meant I had a three-hour window everyday almost all to myself. Across the street and kitty corner from our house was Sound Mental Health. This is where I would go once a week for therapy when I could. I had been going for a couple of years off-and-on, and found it to be incredibly useful.

Early on, in our battle with cancer, Brian's neighbor in the building, Rick, would sit with him while I ran quick errands around the neighborhood. Or if I were lucky, hit the gym for an hour. Mostly, I used the time for therapy and a quick workout. I could do the food shopping for the entire week in about 20 minutes. I'm lightning fast as a result of being in the service industry. Unfortunately, it took just as long to check out at the local Safeway supermarket as it did to shop. Civilians, as I called them, or non-restaurant people, moved so slowly.

How do you get anything done, I would think to myself. It was maddening. I would go up and down the aisles, thinking we need a new plague. There are too many people on the planet. Not so funny anymore considering current events.

The time in therapy was so extremely helpful. L.T. was my primary therapist and C.D.C (Chemical Dependency Counselor). Louise T. was her name. She has helped me so much in my life, and continues to do so. I am forever grateful to her. There's no bullshit in her. She's straight up. I love that about her.

She would later change her name to L.T permanently. She would also credit me with the change, in part, because I called her L.T. all the time. This made me proud. She had spent some time in Boston, and when she laid on the accent, it was spot on.

Between my weekly and sometimes twice weekly visits with L.T., and with a bit of consistency at the local gym, I was able to keep my mind clear and my body strong for the most part. It made caring for

Brian a little easier. There were times when Rick was looking after my Brian, when he would call me to come home right away.

In a panic, I would fly home. During these times, I was never more than three blocks away. The morphine had a weird effect on Brian sometimes, as I had mentioned, and it would change his personality. He would call out or ask for things that made no sense. And more frightening was, at times, he would make a run for it. Kinda made me laugh a little because he wasn't "running" anywhere.

It freaked Rick out, however. He couldn't handle it when it happened, so he would call me in a panic. I would come home, and Brian would feel at ease right away. I could see that Rick was visibly upset, and would have to leave whenever Brian was like this, or whenever he was in pain, he would always call my name. I would let him know I was there with a touch or a word, and seeing him relax and feel safe again made me feel so humbled and so honored.

It crushed me at the same time it made me feel so proud to be his partner in life. Moments like that would fill my tank and strengthen my resolve.

I would simply slip my hand into his, and say, "I'm here, babe. I've got you."

About a year into our battle, maybe a little less, Brian had an upturn that lasted quite a while. Several weeks in fact. It raised our hopes for remission, but the science of it said otherwise. Chemo had shrunk everything a little bit, but the oncologist said it may be only temporary, and to enjoy the upswing. One thing I appreciated about him was that he didn't sugarcoat anything. What was coming, was coming. In his business, it didn't do any good to raise hopes.

In fact, in our first meeting with him, it was Brian, me, and Hollis in his office. The doctor was getting us up-to-speed and letting us know what to expect early on—loss of energy, nausea, fatigue, and all because of chemo. My heart was breaking for Hollis. Her voice was frail to begin with, and being in that environment with your child was so hard for her. Then came the dreaded question, "How long do you think I have doctor?" asked Brian. "Two weeks," he replied, and then dashed out of room. "I'll be right back," he said.

"Oh no the fuck you won't!" I said. I chased him down the hall, and said, "You can't just say two weeks, and dash off like that. What the fuck is wrong with you? Get back in there and explain!"

I was furious. He came back in, and said, "Without treatment, you have about two weeks."

I roared at him, "YOU DIDN'T SAY THAT! You said two weeks, and you left. Of all the irresponsible things to say!" I had to calm down because Brian and Hollis were visibly upset, and I didn't want to make the situation worse. I wanted to fucking strangle this guy.

After explaining himself, and then everything else to us, we were all a little more at ease. The guy basically blew up three lives, and walked out of the door. After that, we collected ourselves, and went home.

Hollis was making her famous fried chicken, and that was something to look forward to. It was always so good. Times like that with my Brian reminded me of a John Denver song called "Back Home Again."

I should clarify, during the first two weeks after diagnosis, Hollis came out and stayed with us for a week, and then eventually returned home to Colorado. So, during the first update in Brian's condition, it was just he and I. So again, and taking advantage of Brian's improved condition, we tried to return to a normal life as best we could. He was eating regularly. We liked to eat dinner in front of the T.V. most nights, and watch our favorite programs. *The Big Bang Theory* was a favorite of ours. *Mom*, a show about a mother and daughter living together while they are both in recovery was my favorite. I would howl with laughter at it, and Brian would just look at me like "I don't get it." *I'm glad that you don't*, I would think to myself.

I was grateful to have some normalcy return to our lives. I was able to hit the gym with more frequency and attend therapy with L.T. across the street more often. I even took a part-time job at a local French brasserie called Vivre. It had just opened. It was only two blocks away, and it was just a couple of nights a week. I explained our situation to the Chef, and he was more than happy to accommodate us.

Rick was kind enough to sit with Brian while I worked. Brian was in good form, so I wasn't terribly worried. It was, on average, around four to five hours if the restaurant was busy. Brian and Rick like to smoke weed together. But since that was out of the question for Brian, he would eat gummy bears and other THC-infused edibles. I shared one with him once in solidarity. Big mistake on my part. We ordered dinner from our favorite Thai restaurant up on 15th Ave. I ate what he gave me of an edible chocolate bar, and went to go pick up dinner. Before I ate it, I asked him if it was going to be too big of a piece. I'm a lightweight when it comes to smoking, and edibles tend to be a lot stronger.

"Nah," he said. "You'll be fine." I was not fine! I got back with our dinner, and as soon as we sat down to eat, it hit me.

"Oh no, Oh no!" I said. It was as if, all at once, my entire body was high. I was high as fuck! I said, "Babe I think you gave me too much. I'm really high."

Eating Thai food was one of my favorite things to do with Brian. It was one of our favorite foods. Here it was, all laid out before us, and I couldn't eat a bite. What the hell? I was hungry when I left to go get it.

I said "Baby, what did you do to me? I'm really high." He said, "Yeah, I know. You keep telling me. Try to lie down for a bit." So, I climbed into bed, and tried to sleep it off for a while.

I woke up a couple of hours later feeling a lot better and hungry as hell. There was still a lot of Thai food left over, so I made a mountainous plate and devoured the whole thing. We finished the night off with Trader Joe's chocolate ice cream, and *The Tonight Show with Jimmy Fallon*, another tradition in our household. It would be a while before I tried edible THC chocolates again. That shit messed me up good.

I wasn't sure how long this uptake in Brian's condition was going to last. We were starting to get lulled into a false sense of security. Brian was doing so well it seemed. We had a couple of visits to the Dr.'s with little or no spread of cancer in his lungs or his brain.

The brain cancer is what scared Brian and I the most. Anything could happen with that. He could lose any one or combination of his faculties. He could lose his memory. There was no way of telling. There were times when he and I would be having a normal conversation, and then he would say something completely out of left field, or sometimes he would just stop speaking altogether as if a light switch had shut off.

A moment would pass, and he would look around as if he didn't know where he was. It scared the hell out of me. I would just softly say, "Hey babe, how you doing?" I couldn't scare him by panicking. Most of the time he didn't even know he was drifting off or speaking incoherently. All I could do was document the frequency of these moments for the doctors, and bring him back around gently. It was the strangest thing. It was almost like he would time travel. We would be talking, and then suddenly, he was somewhere else. In his mind, he was in another place in time, it seemed.

It was so frightening and so fascinating at the same time. He would look around the room as if he were seeing it for the first time. He wasn't looking at the objects in our room, however. It was as if he were actually somewhere else. I wish I could describe it better, but just as quickly as it happened, it was gone.

It happened one night while I was at work, and Rick was sitting with Brian. He called me in a panic. He said that Brian was losing his mind, and that he was talking to people who weren't there, and saying that he was going to leave. I sprinted home in no time, and Brian was sitting in his big leather chair grinning. It kinda made me laugh. I said,

"Hey babe, I'm here." I put my arm on his shoulder, and I scratched the back of his head playfully.

Rick was visibly upset, saying that Brian was in bad shape, and that we need to take him in right away. I'm surprised he had such a hard time. He and Brian had known each other for a long time, and were even lovers for a while. Long before I met Brian. Maybe it was just too difficult for him. I think Brian checking in and out was more than Rick could handle. I got Brian settled, and went in to make dinner for us. *Let's get cooking*, I thought.

We finished our night in the usual fashion – chocolate ice cream and *The Tonight Show*. I thought about calling Rick to check in on him, then I just thought it best to leave him be. He was really freaked out.

Except for the time Brian got past me and tried to make his escape almost completely naked, his time traveling episodes all but disappeared. They were becoming more and more frequent, and then, all the sudden, they were gone. Apart from the rare episode brought on by the liquid morphine. Most of the time, it was a spoonful, or maybe two, and it was lights out. A foot rub and then oblivion.

It was nice to see him sleep. Even if it was the drugs that were doing it. There were times when his facial expression returned to how it used to be before all of this. He slept with a peaceful look on his face. Not that I watched him while he slept. That's just weird, but I always came to bed well after he did, and would kiss his forehead before sliding in next to him to spoon and put my hand into his. He always gave my hand a little squeeze before we both faded off to sleep.

I got so used to the rhythm of his breathing over the years that I would wake up if he weren't in bed with me. Little things like that became the greatest things ever. Until he got a sleep apnea machine, and then it was like sleeping next to Darth Vader.

I miss him. I miss him every day. I'll never get over losing him.

We tried so hard. We fought so hard, he and I. I and him. It's been just over four years, and I still feel his loss as if it were yesterday. I still cry. I still get a lump in my throat. I still get filled with such hurt and anger.

I still want to swim to the bottom of a bottle. But I don't. I would give anything to have him back. But that's not how it goes, does it? No, it doesn't.

Chapter Twenty
Goodbye, My Love

Hollis and Ed would come over every day to sit with Brian, and when we could, we'd have a nice family dinner together at the kitchen table. We would just move it into the living room to make it easier. I took a picture of Brian, and after looking at it, I realized for the first time just how much he had changed physically. His hair was gone, yes, but his body had grown so puffy from the steroids that at first glance of the picture, I didn't recognize him.

In my mind's eye, and in my heart, he was still Brian, but I almost didn't see him at first. That's when I knew we were losing. All the medications and the chemo had done such a job on him that it changed the way he looked. Drastically. I just couldn't see it before. It came as a shock.

Things got progressively worse for us. He wasn't bouncing back from chemo as quickly as before. He stayed in bed longer, and slept way more. Mostly due to the morphine. His pain level was increasing, and the cancer had metastasized to his right hip. He needed help walking all the time now, so I quit my job. My therapy appointments were done over the phone, if at all, and hospice care was coming once a week to refill meds and to bring supplies. Bandages and medication mostly.

Hospice people are amazing. They were like angels for us. Anything we needed, we got. We were so grateful.

I kept feeling an impending sense of doom. A foreboding. So, I kicked it into a higher gear. Anything to make me feel like we still had a fighting chance.

Again, just whistling in the dark. Brian needed a lot more morphine to help him with violent coughing fits that he was suffering. They got so bad that he would vomit. The coughing sounded like it did when we first knew something was wrong. Before we knew he had cancer.

Sitting next to me on the couch he started coughing, (I may have mentioned this already), and I said, "Baby, this is not normal." It sounded guttural. Deep, brassy and raw. Nothing like I'd ever heard from him before. A red flag went up right away, and after being screened, that's when we found out it was stage four lung cancer. Our house turned into one big hospital room. There was shit everywhere. Mostly medical supplies and pills.

Towards the end, Brian slept in the hospital bed full time because it was just easier to get him in and out of. Plus, it had safety bars that prevented him from falling out.

He slept so much more now. The peaceful look was gone when he slept. He had suffered for so long that it changed his facial expressions. He even looked like he was in pain when he slept. It was awful.

We still had some moments where he would feel a little better but nothing at all like before. Everything became laborious for him. Even when he sat up, he seemed to have a heavy weight on him.

And then came the day that we feared the most.

Our oncologist called us in for the latest results, and told us that treatment was no longer working. Nothing they could do would stop the spread of his cancer. They said he was going to die. I'll never forget that moment. What do you say to someone who's just gotten that kind of news? What do you say to your best friend and life partner? Nothing. You say nothing.

I said, "Come on, babe. We're going home." We thanked him for everything he had done, and we went home. On the silent ride back, I wondered how many times he had to say that to patients?

We sat at the kitchen table and Brian was staring out the window. I'd mentioned this much earlier. The look on my Brian's face was heartbreaking. It is hard to describe. It was disbelief, mixed with anger, mixed with sorrow, and the stone-cold realization of the news we just received. I didn't know what to do. There was nothing I could do, so I just moved my chair next to his and held his hand. We sat that way for a long time. In silence.

Then, finally, he said, "I'm tired. I want to go lie down." So, I got him over to the bed. He took some medicine and laid down. This time, I sat on the edge of the bed, and stayed with him. I was there for a long time. He slept extremely hard that night. I was grateful that he did. Maybe in his dreams he would, for a little while at least, forget that today ever happened.

It should have been me. It should have been me...

It was difficult and painful sharing the news with his family. They did not take it well. Watching people suffer is difficult. Watching good people suffer is heartbreaking. Watching your family suffer is next to impossible, especially when there's nothing you can do to stop it.

We held onto hopes for a miracle. The rest of the family came out to be with us. Elaine and Diane and their spouses. Elaine did the same thing that Hollis did when she was next to Brian. She lowered her head and cried. Her resting face was usually that of a smile. She was so positive all the time.

Not today. I tried to remind everyone to remain as upbeat as humanly possible around Brian as not to upset him too much. I think he was just happy to have everyone around him again. The ever-present Sweet Pea, darting in and out of the room, seeking attention wherever she could get it.

For me, it was still business as usual. There was always something to do in our household. With all hands on deck, it was a bit easier. I was thankful for the help. Elaine and Diane did our laundry. I was particularly grateful for that. Hollis cooked for us all, and Ed and the husbands put together some chairs we purchased so that everyone had a place to sit.

It was a busy time. Most of the visiting and family time came early in the morning with coffee and pastries. After that, his siblings and his parents would busy themselves, while Brian and I went about our routine. The nurse's visits and home appointments became more frequent towards the end.

After almost two weeks, Elaine and Diane and their husbands returned to Colorado to take care of their families and their pets. I think they needed a break from seeing all of it. I understood completely. It was hard for them seeing Brian suffer. Our house had turned into a hurricane of activity with everyone there—family, nurses, hospice, friends. It was time to quiet things down as much as possible.

Ed and Hollis returned home to Colorado with the idea that they would come back in a couple of weeks. The rent next door was getting to be a bit much. They all left at the same time. It was a busy morning in our house, packing, moving things, caring for Brian, and worst of all, the goodbyes between Brian and his family. There was a feeling in the air that this was probably the last time they would see each other. No one wanted to say that, but I could feel it.

Brian's sister Elaine and her husband lived up in the mountains not too far from Estes Park. They had a neat little cottage house on around 65 acres of land. Brian and I visited on our last trip to Estes. She liked to raise dogs. Mostly Great Danes, but she had also raised Boston terriers. Before she left us, Brian asked her to take care of Sweet Pea for him. I think he planned it all along. Before we ever even picked her up. Brian and Elaine had a connection, more so than the rest of the family. He asked me if I was alright with it.

Yes and no. It would relieve a bit of the stress of having to care for that little Tasmanian Devil for sure, but I was already in love with her. She was my kid. She was my dog!

In the long run, it was what Brian wanted, and it was best for Sweet Pea. It was hard letting her go. After everyone left for the airport, with my puppy in tow, our house was eerily quiet. The cats were self-sufficient. They all but disappeared in all the noise and craziness going on.

No scampering or yipping from Sweet Pea. That was extremely hard for me. It was so quiet.

Just quiet.

I made Brian some lunch, and placed it in front of him with some juice. Knowing he probably wouldn't eat it, but it kept a sense of normalcy and routine going. He was sitting up on the edge of the bed, and he took a deep breath, and exhaled loudly. No coughing, I thought. Sweet!

It was as if he was exhaling all the business and chaos and the emotional highs and lows of the past two weeks. He almost seemed glad to be alone again. It was so hard for everybody, especially Hollis and Elaine.

I honestly believe that Brian knew all along that he didn't have much time left, and that it would be the last time he would see his family. We didn't talk much that day. Brian seemed like he wanted to be alone with his thoughts, so I didn't pester him by asking him how he was doing every twenty minutes.

The rest of that day was pretty quiet. I gave him his meds around 8:00 p.m., and he just laid back and slept. I couldn't get a read on him, so I just let him be. It was like he crossed a threshold of some sort. Like a major task had been completed.

He closed his eyes and slept. No readable expression on his face. It was disturbing. In the last two weeks of our time together, Brian's health deteriorated quickly. He now required around-the-clock care. The morphine somehow increased his escape attempts. He had a lot more trouble with incontinence, and edema in his legs made it almost impossible for him to walk. We were holding off on hiring a nurse on an overnight basis because of the astronomical cost. Almost $3000 a week.

My sleep had dwindled down to almost zero. Brian required care every couple of hours now. Thank goodness for our neighbor Rick. He was so helpful towards the end. He shopped for us and even did laundry. I couldn't leave Brian's side for too long. The sheets needed changing and washing more frequently now.

The hospice nurses showed up more and more, as did a chaplain from hospice care at Brian's request. They all suggested a nurse come in and help. We finally gave in and hired a nurse. The first night she was there was awkward for me, having someone come in and sleep in our house. But Brian was ok with it, so I was ok with it.

This is what they do I told myself.

I laid down alone in our giant bed. I had a difficult time falling asleep initially, having gotten used to being on high alert all the time. After about an hour of listening to Brian and the nurse talk, I went out like a light. Boom! I slept hard. Very hard. I woke four hours later to the sound of Brian arguing with the nurse. He was attempting another mid-morphine escape. He was not about to go gently into that good night. I was proud of him. The nurse was such a pro. She handled it so well. I assured Brian that I was here, and I held his hand for a while. He relaxed and eventually fell back asleep.

I was so grateful to our nurse and I offered to make her something to eat. She pulled out a pre-cooked meal from her overnight bag and said "Got it." She was good. "Go back to sleep," she said to me. Three more hours of rest. More comfortable than the last four, knowing she had an eye on my Brian. She was a blessing. The nurse woke me and said it was time for her to go. I popped up, surprisingly refreshed and ready to go. I offered her thermos of coffee to go. She declined. It was her bedtime almost. See you the day after tomorrow she said.

I grabbed some coffee and sat down on the edge of the bed to rub Brian's feet. He didn't wake up. He just kind of knew I was there, and he would sort of snug himself in more and continue to sleep.

With my renewed energy, I decided to take advantage of the time while Brian slept. I cleaned the house, organized the laundry, and made a big breakfast for us, even though he probably wouldn't eat it. I asked Rick to come up and join us. He must have been very hungry. I made him a giant breakfast burrito with fig jam and a tall pint of milk. He downed the whole breakfast in no time flat. It was impressive. I thought I was the only one who could slam a pint of milk like that. *Well done*, I thought to myself.

In all the madness that became our life for the better part of two years, all the highs and lows we shared, watching my Brian cling to hope and hang on every word coming from the oncologist, hoping for good news, any news that would help us, we fought the good fight.

We fought hard.

The quiet dignity, grace and strength that Brian showed throughout all of it is something I will never forget. He was the strongest person I have ever met. Such strength wrapped in humility and innocence made me repeat my mantra that it "Just wasn't fair." Take me. Let him live.

He was everything that was good in my world, and he was slipping away. And with him, went everything I ever really loved or cared about. Including myself.

Our last day together was like most days that had come to us. Brian slept most of the day. He wouldn't eat. He just laid on his back and slept. Expressionless.

February 9th, 2016. 6:11 p.m. As I opened my story with, I turned away toward the kitchen to go work on dinner, when out of the corner of my eye, I saw Brian's chest rise as if he was taking a deep breath. A very deep breath. I turned back to him as he exhaled, and he was gone.

I knew he was gone. I don't know why I looked at the clock, but I did. My Brian passed away. I sat on the bed, buried my head in his chest, and sobbed.

We lost our battle. I climbed into the bed next to him, and just held him for a while.

I needed some time alone with him before all the necessary calls had to be made. I nuzzled my head into his neck and held his face and kissed him. "Bye bye, baby. Thank you for loving me."

I was so lucky to have him for the time that I did. A part of me felt an overwhelming sense of relief that it was over. That he was no longer suffering. I felt guilty for feeling relieved. I kissed his face a thousand times. I pulled his covers up to his chest, and I turned to make the necessary phone calls.

I called Rick downstairs first and said, "Brian is gone."

Quietly and peacefully in his sleep. He left us. He said he would call Brian's parents if I wanted. I said "Yes." I don't know why, but I did. That was a phone call that I should have made. I wasn't thinking too clearly at that point.

The hospice nurses and the funeral service people needed to be called. Brian's wish was to be cremated. He said that he had seen some awful things in his nursing career, and did not want to be buried. I knew that when I called the people to come get him, it would be the last time I ever got to see or touch him again. So I waited, and just sat on the bed next to him. Him and me. Me and him. As it always was in our home.

I kissed his lips one last time, and made the call I needed to. Rick knocked on the door just after and gave me a big hug. He sat and waited with me for the funeral people. I don't know what else to call them. I spoke with Hollis and Ed to make sure they were okay. The rest of the family were all on their way to be with them. I said that I would call in the morning. Things still had to be settled here.

Just before Rick arrived, I opened the living room window and said, "Baby, you died. You're free. Go to Heaven. You are no longer in pain." The old Danish tradition of opening a window at the time of death for the soul of a loved one to pass through came to mind. I don't know why. I think it came back to me from a reading somewhere. So, I did it to try and help my Brian along. If he was even in the room anymore.

The funeral man, as I called him, showed up about an hour later. He had a gurney with him. Brian was still in his pajamas, and still had chucks on. I asked if I should at least clean him up before you take him, and he replied that it wasn't necessary. I suppose it wasn't.

We got him onto the gurney and into a bag. A fucking body bag! I wouldn't let the funeral man zip him up completely. I wouldn't let him zip it past Brian's neck. "Leave it where it is," I said.

There was some paperwork to be filled out that was attached to a clipboard. I asked Rick to fill it out while he read the questions to me. He put the clipboard down, and we took Brian down the elevator to a waiting van outside.

It was blessedly quiet for Tuesday evening. I still wouldn't let him zip Brian up all the way. We got him into the van feet-first. The fucking clipboard had been left upstairs. I roared at them both. "Go get the damn thing," I said! I didn't feel bad about it. It was dark outside and very still. Very quiet. I sat on the tail of the van, holding Brian's head in my hands, and said my final goodbye to him.

One of my neighbors came home, saw me sitting with Brian, and said, "Oh sweetie, I'm so sorry." She was kind. Rick and a funeral man returned a few minutes later with the clipboard. I asked that he wait until I was gone to zip him up all the way. I thanked him and went upstairs with Rick. I asked to be alone and he obliged, once he knew I was going to be okay.

I got back to the living room, locked every lock on the door, sat on the bed, and cried. A mix of sorrow and relief. No more pain. No more pain for my Brian. I moved over to the open window and lit up a cigarette. I sat there in silence. Trying to feel if Brian was still in the room. I looked at the big empty chair across the room and wondered if he was in it. I smoked my cigarette and thought, *Trader Joe's is still open*. I'm going to buy every fucking bottle of vodka they have.

So that's what I did.

I had remained sober throughout most of our battle with cancer, with the help of L.T. across the street.

Chapter Twenty-One
Burying the Pain

E arly on, my body was strong, my head was clear, and I was sober. I couldn't care for Brian and drink at the same time, so I stopped altogether. I even celebrated a little over a year sober. I even went so far as to buy myself a fancy one-year coin on Amazon. It was snazzy.

Any real A.A. work came over the phone as meetings were harder to come by as Brian became sicker. I held on to my sobriety for as long as I could. White knuckling it towards the end.

The hard truth is that under the crushing weight of caring for Brian, watching him deteriorate and the mental and physical stress involved, I could feel a relapse coming. I almost welcomed it.

If I could only just hold on until Brian left me, then it wouldn't matter.

I could not.

Just before he died, I drank. I call this one an actual relapse. Most of the times in my life, after a length of sobriety, I simply chose to drink. Even though I believe my disease to be genetic, subliminal and, at times, downright insidious, I still chose to do it instead of calling another alcoholic.

It happened right before Brian died. I asked Rick to stay with Brian while I ran up to Trader Joe's for supplies. Brian was sound asleep. I got what we needed for food and proceeded to the checkout line. On the way to it, I passed the liquor section. I grabbed two big bottles of Absolut vodka without ever thinking twice about it. As if it was as natural to me as breathing. I got everything home and sent Rick on his way. Brian was still asleep. I put the groceries away, found the biggest glass we had, and made a vodka and tonic. I slammed it down and made another one right away. I felt it wash over my body and mind right away. It was like being covered in bubble wrap mentally and physically. I quickly buried the guilt and shame with another drink.

Remember, all addiction is progressive, and it doesn't retreat through any length of sobriety. You pick up where you left off, and as I had mentioned before, my appetite for destruction is insatiable. Still.

I've had a lot of practice and can drink an enormous amount without showing any real signs. I was determined to be careful and not to let this get in the way of my care for Brian. To my surprise, it didn't.

I usually drank when we were alone and at the end of the evening when Brian was already asleep.

It is said in the *Big Book of Alcoholics Anonymous* that alcohol is a rapacious creditor. I'm here to tell you that it most assuredly is.

Leaning in to kiss Brian and seeing the look of realization on his face one morning made me so ashamed. I like to think that he understood. I felt like the biggest loser on the planet. I never got shitfaced or falling down drunk. I would hold that off until the inevitable had passed, I told myself. I would just try to mask the smell with an ever-present cup of coffee when I was caring for Brian.

I still carry the shame of it to this day. Now that Brian was gone, all bets were off. It didn't matter. He was gone and so was my dog. I figured by getting as much booze and cigarettes as I could carry, I wouldn't have to leave our house for a while. So that's what happened.

I put up a "do not disturb" sign on the front door, and poured a very strong drink. One of the neighbors left a bouquet of flowers at the door. I think they came from the neighbor down the hall. An oncology nurse. Go figure. She was another blessing in our lives.

After Brian died, there was still so much to do in our house. I was mentally and physically destroyed, and all I could do was cry. Going into our bathroom and just seeing his toothbrush there would set me off. Anger would replace sorrow and I would drink at it. A pattern that would repeat itself for the next four years. I received a call from Brian's dad early one morning and he tore into me about drinking, and why I wasn't packing up the house and getting ready for it to be put on the market.

At the time, there was no inventory in the Seattle real estate market, and techies were moving in and paying way over asking price. Brian and I agreed before he died that the place would sell, and the money would be divided between his siblings, Rick, and I. It was what he wanted. I didn't care. I told him that I most likely wouldn't be able to live there without him. My plan was to go home to Boston for a while and try to recover.

The phone call from his father was difficult to say the least. He was screaming at me to get things moving. I was thinking to myself, give me a fucking break. I just got spit out of a hurricane.

Brian is gone. I am not well.

I didn't unload on him. I wanted to, but I just took it. He was in his late 80s at the time and lost his only son. The call ended on an amicable note, but how the fuck was I expected to pack up our lives when I couldn't even look at his toothbrush without losing it?

I was so tired; I was so tired.

Fuck it! I grabbed my phone and called an old coworker who I knew could get me some stimulants. He answered right away.

I told him all that it happened and all that lie ahead of me. He surprisingly came over right away. "I have a ton of shit to do and I'm dead on my feet I said. Whatta you got?" I bought a small amount of cocaine. I fucking hated the fact that there was no sleeping on that shit. I didn't care. I use the booze to check out mentally from the pain and the drugs to keep my body going. It worked initially.

I was able to get a lot done the first couple of days. It took time. I wasn't just going to throw our memories into a box without going through them. It takes a long time. All the while trying to hold it together. I became angry and bitter. The only time I left the home was to get more booze and cigarettes.

I decided against getting any more drugs to keep me going. I felt ashamed initially, but that quickly gave away to fuck everyone. Still, I didn't get any more. Probably not the best idea to be doing that shit.

I would make some headway, find something of ours, a photo or something of Brian's, lose my shit, collect myself, make a drink to buffer the pain, and press on. All the while wondering what I was going to do with the cats, where I was going to live? I had little to no money. If I go to Boston, how am I going to get all this stuff across country? I didn't have any real savings. I stopped working full-time, and then completely.

These questions would have to wait. It was all I could do to get through the day. Rick was so great throughout this part. He would run errands that required a car. I had Brian's car at my disposal. The little red rabbit. A piece of crap Volkswagen rabbit. Rust red in color. I loved that thing. For long time after he died, I would see them in traffic from time to time and my head would whip around to look. The same thing with Boston Terriers. This was a tough one. Every time I saw one on the street or on T.V. my heart sank. I missed that dog so much. Rick was great about bringing things to help me. Moving boxes, food, he even did what seemed like a metric ton of laundry. I was grateful to him.

Before Brian died, he set everything up through his will. Memorial service arrangements were already made, money, property, all of it. It made things a lot easier at that end.

Sam, the older black cat went to Rick. He's the one who gave her to Brian in the first place.

Neelix, my sometimes buddy, went to the oncology nurse down the hall. It seemed fitting, considering all she done for us. That, plus while Brian was still alive, she came banging on our door in a panic one evening. We were her favorite gays. She left the living window open with the screen up and her cat got out onto the window ledge. She tried to coax her in, and it fucking fell! Three stories down. She was inconsolable that afternoon. We felt so bad for her. I knew Neelix would have a good home with her.

My drinking progressed, but I still wasn't to the point of falling or being so drunk that I couldn't speak. In trying to return to a normal sleep schedule, I found some of my old pain medicine from heart surgery. In 2015, I think, I had open heart surgery. It was a last-minute thing. I had a completely calcified heart valve and an aneurysm on an ascending aorta. The only way I found out was that I saw my dentist, whose husband was a doctor on the other side of their office. She asked me when was the last time I had a physical? I said it's been ages. She said, pop over to see my husband. So, I did.

He listened to my heart, and said something sounded a little off, and that he wanted me to go to Swedish Hospital up on Cherry Hill. He asked me to do it that day. So I did. They listened and recommended an echocardiogram for me. I found out I had an aneurysm that was ready to burst, and a completely calcified valve requiring heart surgery. Three months to live without the surgery. I had no idea, having no family medical history to speak of. Lucky me, right?

Back to the medications. Oxycodone.

Oddly, it never really did anything for the pain. It just made me hallucinate. When I was in the hospital recovering after surgery, they would administer my dose, and about half an hour later, I would see things that I knew weren't there. Shadows would dart across the room. Those pills gave me a feeling like someone was there when they weren't. It was terrible, and all the while feeling completely lucid.

I felt sober, but up in the corners of the hospital room, I was seeing things that look like gargoyles. I had all of Brian's pills and medications at my disposal. Could have taken any one of those. I didn't. I wouldn't. It would have been wrong. Vulgar in some way. Besides, at the end of the day, I've never been a pill person. Ever. I didn't trust them.

I took the oxycodone because I thought it would help me sleep. Wrong! I would pass out, initially. But I always woke up with a start, thinking I had to look in on Brian. Only, by this time, the pills had kicked in, and I was hallucinating again. It was awful.

I didn't care about what time it was. I couldn't stay in our bed because, to me, it looked like a closet door was opening by itself. It scared the shit out of me, so I rarely slept a full night. A few hours here and there, always with a pint glass full of vodka tonic to get me on my feet again to continue packing.

Rick would drop off moving boxes, and check in on me. He knew I wasn't doing well, and asked if he could do anything? "No," I said, "I still need more time alone."

Alone was the last place I needed to be. I was swimming in a sea of vodka, pills, and anger, mixed with bitterness and sorrow to be at the end of it all without my Brian.

I was furious. Days would come when I would sleep and be like my old self again. I would try to steel my mind and heart from the pain so I could get things done. Being an "all or nothing" person is a blessing and a curse, especially if you're an alcoholic like me. My good days at the house were good. My bad days were very bad. I became more and more and morose. Everyone sucked. I hated the world. I wanted Brian back, and I blamed everyone and everything for taking him. I was losing my struggle with booze, and now these pills. Pills which did nothing for me except make me crazy. They didn't help me with pain, and they didn't help me sleep.

I was still so mentally exhausted that even when my body did get some rest, I still felt strained and stretched so thin. The final few days before I left the house for good was spent drinking and taking those god-awful pills. I had a weird sense of what I thought was clarity, but I was drinking. I can take a lot of damage, and I've proven this to myself on many occasions, but this time I felt like I really was going to die. Even though I wasn't suicidal.

My beliefs at the time was that if you kill yourself, you wouldn't get to meet your maker, and since I was convinced that my Brian was in heaven, killing myself was not an option. Besides, I'm just not that type of person. Suicide is not for me. I've been in the dark places. Many times. Despair, sorrow, and now with Brian gone, a palpable pain that wouldn't go away.

So again, I am accustomed to pain, and even in the depths of my despair, I never thought that hurting myself was an option. Fuck that. I always fight my way back.

I couldn't see just how bad of shape I was in, however. Denial is powerful. My denial is very strong. *I'm not so bad*, I thought to myself. A part of me knew I was in trouble, and a part of me didn't care.

The last night I spent in our home, I was crisp and alert. Or so I thought. I was cleaning the bathroom and listening to music, and I looked down into the drain. I saw what I thought was a big fucking snake, trying to come up through the drain. There was not. I kept staring at it. I could have sworn I saw it. It scared the shit out of me. It was not there. I was hallucinating from the oxycodone.

I called Rick and he came up and looked in the drain, and then he looked at me. "I'm really worried about you, Ed. You have to snap out of it," he said.

He went back downstairs, and I said I would call him in a bit. I made another cocktail, and I called my friend Bob. I explained what was going on. Bob knew all too well about my drinking life. He didn't know I was in such bad shape. I said, "I'm kinda worried for myself this time."

"Holy shit, really?" He had seen me in rough shape before, but I never expressed any real concern until now.

He proposed that I come spend the weekend with him at his home in Edmonds, Washington. Bob lived alone in a big, beautiful townhouse about a mile outside downtown Edmonds. Edmonds is a slice of heaven. A beautiful little seaside retirement community just North of Seattle. I always loved it there. Bob said, "Why don't you pack a bag, and I'll pick you up later in the afternoon." I said, "OK, that works, because I still had some things to do."

Chapter Twenty-Two
Self Destruction

After making another drink, I called Rick and said that I would be leaving for the weekend. I needed to get out of that space for a while. He agreed that it was a good idea. I packed the gym bag with clothes enough for the weekend, a bottle of vodka, and two packs of Marlboro Reds.

I was already feeling better knowing Bob was coming to get me. I had been alone for too long. Bob's place has always been sort of a sanctuary for me. It's wonderfully comfortable and quiet. Brown leather furniture, beautiful Northwest Native artwork, and carvings were everywhere. Colors of Amber and cherry wood and again it was quiet.

Almost eerily quiet. I loved it. He gave me the master bedroom with a giant bed adorned with bedspread that had Native Northwest artwork and patterns on it. It was warm and welcoming. I put my bag on the bed, opened it up, and took a long pull from the bottle of vodka that was in there. I left those pills behind. On purpose.

Bob like to sleep in the guest bedroom just down the hall past the laundry nook. He said the master bedroom was too big. It really was. It was beautiful. The master bath had his and her sink and a big glass encased shower. A wall length mirror hung over the sinks.

Bob's color palette in his homes always matched the Pacific Northwest. I had taken to playing a song by an artist named Phillip Phillips called "Gone, gone, gone." It was for Brian, and I would play it over and over when I was drinking. It's a beautiful song. I still listen occasionally. It's not easy to hear.

When I'm on a bender, the first thing I will do when I wake up, or come to I should say, is make a drink to take away the shakes that were definitely coming. Then, I would take a shower, cocktail in hand, all while playing music. Something that's going to break my heart or piss me off and get me moving for the day. Being in the shower did two things. In one way, it made me feel like I was being productive and or washing something away. It also gave me a place to bow my head and cry.

Between the music, the drink, and the shower, I felt like I could mourn Brian in a place all my own. My own private Idaho as Brian used to say. I could close my eyes and with a drink in hand, let the water hit me, and just cry. Bob was great about giving me my space when I first got there. He would check in on me every half hour or so. I would later come to find that he was worried that I wasn't going to make it. I assured him that I was. The pills were out of my system once and for all so it was just booze. I could manage that a lot better than the combination of the two. I thanked him for checking in on me so much, and said that I was going to shower, and that if he heard me crying, not to worry. It was just all coming out.

Bob has pulled my ass out of the fire more times then I'd like to remember. This time he was saving my life even though at the time I couldn't see it. I poured a glass of straight vodka and took along pull. I left it on the counter next to the sink and turned on the shower. But not before I put on my song to Brian.

I climbed into the water, hoping to be baptized. I bowed my head and cried. For a long time. The only thing that pulled me out of the shower was my need for another drink. I climbed out, toweled off, and reached for the glass on the counter. At least I didn't take it in with me this time. Progress? Not really. I most likely didn't want to break a glass in Bob's shower.

That would not have been cool. I switched the music over to John Denver. It helps to lighten my mood a bit. It worked. I loved his music. It always had just the right mix of melancholy, bittersweet longing, and tales of true love.

I poured another drink, and feeling lighter in spirit, got dressed. I heard Bob yell from the kitchen downstairs, "Soups on!"

Bob makes some killer chili and cornbread. I could smell it on the way down the stairs. "You ready for some chili, Mr. Cleaves?" He always called me "Mr. Cleaves." "Yes, I am," I said. "Yes, I am." Even if I probably couldn't eat it. It felt so good to feel normal again. It felt good to not be alone. I spent the weekend with Bob, eating, relaxing, driving around town and down on the waterfront watching the ferries run from Edmonds to Kingston and back.

Edmonds really is beautiful. Anything anyone could ever want from a Pacific Northwest town. At dusk, you can see the ferry boat lights getting brighter in contrast with the settings sun. They seem to come alive on the water. Absolute magic.

On Sunday evening, I got a call from Rick. He said, "I'm not really sure how to tell you this, but I've spoken with Hollis and Ed and the building superintendent, and we all agreed that it would be best if you didn't return to the apartment for a while. We're worried about your condition, and that you're going to hurt yourself." As angry as I was, I knew they were right. They were right, but that's not what I heard. I exploded! "You motherfucker! How dare you? I've been literally killing myself trying to get this stuff done. I almost died trying to keep my Brian alive, and you're telling me you all think I shouldn't come back to my home? Fuck you!"

I had never been so furious in all my life. I felt betrayed. Especially by Hollis and Ed. Thanks for doing what you did for our son. See ya!

I knew this to not be completely true, and deep down, I knew that my drinking had become a liability, but I still felt betrayed. How dare you? I was furious with them all.

Even now, I'm still grateful for all that Rick has done for Brian and I, but the truth to that story is that Rick never got over Brian. He was still in love with him. I knew it. I could see it. When things were well, the three of us rarely, if ever, hung out together. It was always he and Brian. They usually hung out together at Ricks apartment, smoking weed. I didn't mind.

I asked Brian if there was anything there, and he said no. I said, "Rick is still in love with you." He said, "Well Rick is shit out of luck." That was enough for me. I let it go. I didn't exactly look at Rick as competition. He was a hairy little fellow with a big belly and a look on his face like he constantly had to take a shit. I felt bad for him a little bit. He was always so insecure or unsure of himself it seemed. He did not like me. That was for sure. I guess he had an abusive father. To what extent, I didn't know. If it was enough to make him the way he was, then my guess is that it was bad.

For that reason, my heart went out to him. That aside, other than Brian, we had nothing in common. I can't say that I liked Rick. But again, I can certainly tell when someone doesn't like me. I picked up on that from the start. I simply tolerated it. He didn't matter that much all told. That's not to say that I wasn't grateful to him in the end.

After that phone call, I wanted to knock his fucking block off. I still kinda do. What was I going do? I had to let it go. I told myself it's not what Brian would have wanted. So I relented.

After speaking at length with Bob, he calmed me down, and urged me to look at the big picture. I refused to talk to Hollis and Ed. I didn't trust myself not to blow up on them because I was so hurt. So I communicated through Elaine. She felt stuck in the middle, and me blowing up wasn't going to help anyone, least of all me, so I held it in. I felt like an outsider, a villain for some reason. Because I relapsed.

Or maybe I was just naive, and it was planned all along. All I needed was some time to mourn his loss in our home. I let booze and I let them cut it short. I blame myself ultimately for relenting, and for letting them take over, but still, I was so angry with them.

I still carry resentment to this day over it. When I look back, and dissect the whole thing, I more than accept the fact that I was killing myself, and to them had become a liability. A liability?

It should have been handled differently. With more compassion. So I left. Part of me was almost happy to be out of that space and to have a break for once. The other part of me felt betrayed and bitter. I went back and gathered more of my clothing, what little cash I had, and I left. It was all I could do to not knock the superintendent and Rick the fuck out! They seemed so nervous and twitchy. They should have been.

Chapter Twenty-Three
Trying to Navigate

B ob offered me a place to stay while everything was being finalized through Brian's' will. He kept reminding me to think of Brian and what he would want, which was peace. So I shut up.

There was still some time before Brian's memorial service, so I hunkered down at Bob's and tried to recover. Whatever that meant?

It was good to be there. I was out of crisis mode. I tapered the drinking down. No more vodka. I would drink wine in the evenings. If at all. Eventually, I got back to a normal sleep schedule and started getting up early to read. It felt good sleeping there. I'd sleep with the bedroom window cracked and let the breeze wash over me in the morning.

Bob was in the tech world, so he worked from home all the time. He's the same as me in that if there is work or a project that needs to be done, he needs to be locked in and it needs to be quiet. He would disappear into his office for hours. I wouldn't even text him. Then, he would pop out and say, "Mr. Cleaves, Lunchtime?" We would head out to the waterfront or to Claire's Diner in Edmonds. Famous for their comfort food.

I was so grateful to him for bringing back a sense of normalcy to me.

With all my responsibilities lifted, I had more time to attend therapy and to restart doctor's appointments. Because of the blood thinners I was on, I was required to take daily medicine due to my mechanical heart valve, drinking was not an option. But it never stopped me. My Cardiologist said, "You must stop drinking." I blew past that advice. The fact of the matter is I would show up to appointments still drinking actively.

Anyway, the booze would raise my INR—International Normalized Ratio. The numbers are in relation to how long it takes my blood to clot. My average numbers are between 1.5 and 2.0. That is with me taking 12 milligrams of Coumadin daily and having no alcohol in my blood.

I could cut myself shaving and it wouldn't stop bleeding as it would for any normal person. With booze in my system, all bets were off. Which is why in the mornings, I would require a stiff drink or two to calm my nerves, so I could shave without cutting myself. Some mornings I would just skip shaving altogether. The highest level I've recorded so far for my INR was 9.5, which meant that if I cut myself, I wouldn't stop bleeding for a long time.

Well, I did just that. I had a lot of booze in me one afternoon and I was on my way to a bar called The Cuff. Professional drinkers in this place and they opened at 2:00 p.m. That was a little late for me. I usually went to Lost Lake Café just down the hill to drink as early as 6:00 a.m.

So, on my way to The Cuff, I was in a bit of a jovial mood, and I playfully threw a jab at a stop sign as I was walking past. I cut the knuckle on my middle finger and blood came shooting out. That's odd, I thought. That's a lot of blood. I put a napkin on it from my gym bag and proceeded to the bar, thinking nothing of it.

I ordered a beer and sat down all the while waiting for this thing to stop. It would not. I asked for a band aid from the bartender and went outside to put it on. Mainly because it was too dark in there, and secondly, because I wouldn't be very welcome if I bled all over the bar. I wanted to continue drinking there. I got it bandaged up well, but not well enough. I just covered it with a bunch of napkins and went back inside keeping pressure on it all the while. After about an hour, I went to the bathroom to take a leak and check it out. Still bleeding!

And almost at the same rate. Shit! I re-wrapped it as tight as I could and went back to the bar. Thinking, it's gotta stop sometime soon. Wrong!

Twelve hours straight this tiny little gash on my hand bled. I had to go to emergency care to get them to stop it. Even they had a hard time. By this point, I was pretty fucked up and they wanted to keep me overnight for observation because my INR was so high.

This would be the first of many, many hospital stays for me. On that particular night though, I didn't stay. They stopped the bleeding finally, and I had sobered up enough to know I wasn't going stay there overnight.

I took a cab back to Edmonds. What time it was, I had no idea.

And so it was for me. I enjoyed being in Edmonds and tried my best to recover from everything. Again, peaks and valleys. I wasn't exercising on a regular basis, which meant I was smoking. I just liked to smoke from time to time. I still do.

I stayed with Bob almost up until the day of Brian's memorial service. I could feel the pressure and anxiety building. I wasn't sure who all was going to be there, but more importantly, I wasn't sure if I could remain sober until then.

The night before the service I was shaking apart, so I drank some bourbon. I went to bed early, so I figured I had enough time to sober up by morning. Not likely. I woke up hurting, stressed, and shaking. I went into the bathroom to shave and couldn't do it. I swore to myself I would be sober for this. I couldn't keep my promise to Brian or myself, so I poured a tumbler of bourbon and choked it down.

I began to cry. I felt like such a loser. I wasn't going to get drunk. I knew that. But the truth was my body needed booze to function.

I drank the first one and quickly poured another. My anxiety and fear turned to resolve, bitterness, and then anger. I dressed in all black and put the darkest shades I could find on my face. I combed my hair, slammed another bourbon to crush the guilt, and I was out the door.

I made it downtown way too early for the service. Almost two hours. It was being held in a little chapel in the South Lake Union neighborhood of Seattle. I shouldn't have left so early, but I had to move. I couldn't stand myself.

There was an Italian restaurant open nearby for lunch. One of those cookie cutter jobs like Buca de Beppo or the Olive Garden. A place where you're not going to get authentic Italian food. But I wasn't there for food. I had a lot of time to kill, and I needed a drink.

I bellied up as the lunch crowd made their way in. I didn't want to be one of those douchebags that wears their shades indoors, so I pulled them off revealing the destruction on my face and in my eyes. I would love to have left them on, but it was inappropriate. I thought it best to lay off the bourbon, and I switched to vodka and tonic. When I'm in that condition, I'll usually warn the bartender that the first cocktail is going to last me no more than 10 seconds and to pour another one right away. I'd always say this in a joking sort of manner. I wasn't joking. He didn't know.

I ordered a Caprese salad and was set up for lunch even though I had no intentions of eating. There was no way. It was just a cover so I could cocktail without looking like the alcoholic that I was. Mission accomplished.

I checked my watch what seemed like every 10 minutes. Finally, with half an hour before the service, I paid my tab and left.

I put my shades back on. The bartender said, "Hey man, you look like you're about to go kill someone the way you're dressed." I smiled to myself, and walked out the door. I felt physically fine, relatively crisp, and strong enough to face this thing. I didn't realize how hard it would hit me when I walked inside. I saw big poster board with my Brian's face on it.

It was at the front of the chapel on a riser with a beautiful bouquet of flowers. I lost my shit. I sat down in the front row in front of his picture and sobbed. It all came out. I couldn't stop it. I didn't want to. After I don't know how long, Rick of all people, came over to hug me. I just let him.

I snapped out of it a little bit. I never removed my sunglasses. I felt like I needed to hide behind them. Not out of shame, but I thought it best to hide the anger that I felt. I was burning hot. It sobered me up a bit. If that was possible. That never happened before. I was mad at everything. I couldn't believe I was there, that he was gone, that I was at his memorial service.

Everyone felt like an enemy after that. I felt that way for a very long time after.

People would approach me at the service, and I would bristle. Please give me a reason to end you I would say to myself. The service was light spirited and there was laughter from friends and colleagues sharing stories of Brian and their time with him.

There was a gathering in a separate room with food and drinks and Brian's favorite candy bar, Baby Ruth.

I took one and put it in my pocket and thought, mine! He was mine. Brian was mine. I sought out the chaplain who had come to our home so many times, and I especially sought out the hospice nurses. They were angels as far as I was concerned. I thanked them for helping us in our fight to keep Brian alive. I never removed my shades.

I failed to mention that I had two friends in attendance with me for support. Chef Brad I, a lunatic Sicilian I used to work for, and a drinking buddy Brad H. – Brad and Brad. I was grateful to them for coming. They put me at ease a little bit by being there. We didn't stay long after. It was done as far as I was concerned. Those people meant nothing to me. I was done with it. I had to get out of there. The Brads offered to take me to lunch, and I accepted.

They brought me to this funky little Creole joint in Fremont called Roux. They had killer food. We ordered a shit ton of oysters and the Brads both drank beer, and I, with my ever-present tumbler of vodka. It was a nice distraction and it felt good to see them again. Especially Chef Brad. He and I were close. He's a wonderful man. A fucking lunatic, but wonderful. We had the same dark sense of humor. Maybe that's why we got along so well.

After a couple of hours and several more cocktails, Chef Brad offered to drop me off where I was staying. I accepted. The other Brad wanted to go paint the town. I did not accept his invitation. I needed to get back. I was grateful for the distraction. To be around people I trusted. I got back home, sat down on the back porch and lit up a cigarette.

I took a long pull and exhaled, grateful to be alone. I sat there for the longest time in sort of a daze. Going over the events of the day, processing everything. Remembering how awful I felt just a few short hours ago and now with this shit pumping through my veins, it was hard to believe I felt that way at all.

It's coming again, I thought to myself. I got up and poured a glass of bourbon. Not yet motherfucker, I said.

I sat back down and put on a movie. *Against All Odds* was the movie. Jeff Bridges, I think. I had seen it before. I forgot it had such a powerful song attached to it—Phil Collins' "Against all Odds." The song played at the end of the movie, and I started to cry. I called out to Brian, "Bye baby. Thank you for loving me."

I drank the rest of my drink, crushed out a cigarette, and climbed into bed. The bourbon had done its trick. I was mentally whipped. It was time to shut it down. I tried to block everything and let the sleep take me. I didn't care what time it was anymore. Only light and dark. And right now, it was dark. "I love you baby," I said to Brian. And then, blessed oblivion.

I woke the next morning feeling the same pain I did as the previous one. I had nothing to do that day, so I started my routine. I poured a glass of vodka and this time squeezed some lime into it. I went into the bathroom to shave and shower.

The glass of vodka turned into half a pint of vodka with just a tiny splash of tonic water to give it a bit of carbonation so it hits the blood faster. The first pint went down easily. I didn't gag, or even worse, vomit. That is precious booze. I can't waste it.

I played that song by Phil Collins from the movie the night before, but it was too much to bear. It was too painful, so I opted for Slipknot instead. My anger broke loose. I was crying but out of rage this time. *I need a fucking plan*, I thought to myself. I cranked up the volume as loud as it would go, and I got in the shower. Having sufficiently scrubbed myself clean, I hopped out and dried off. I liked the smell of the soap on my skin. Irish spring, usually. It made me feel clean all over. I poured a fresh drink, grabbed my phone, and went out on the back patio to smoke. The back yard was secluded by a row of very tall shrubs. No one could see in. I was thankful for that. I had grown tired of people. I sat there in the silence, listening to the wind blow through the trees. Crushed out my cigarette and picked up the phone to call Paul D.

Chapter Twenty-Four
Swampscott, MA

S wampscott is a nice little seaside community on the North Shore of Boston. Not as quaint as Marblehead, the next town over. It didn't have as much access to the ocean as Marblehead did, but it was very nice, nonetheless.

Paul lived in a big beautiful English Tudor-style house that sat on top of a hill at the top of his street. A beautiful stone wall surrounded the house at the bottom of a lush, green and perfectly manicured lawn. The house was a show-stopper and a standout in a neighborhood full of beautiful homes. Taking a left off Humphrey Street onto Kensington Lane brought you to an incline with lovely homes on either side, all adorned with flower boxes and professional landscaping.

At the top of the hill was Paul's house. It was remarkable. I had noticed it long before I even met him. Kensington Lane was also a shortcut into the heart of Swampscott and then into the city of Lynn. I always wondered who lived there. It was so beautiful. I would slow the car down to get a good look at it on my way to wherever I was going.

Paul is now and has always been a trusted friend, mentor, and in some ways a father figure to me. Although I think I placed him in that role mentally on some level, I never let on. He's one of the few people in my life that loves me without condition. I'm a lucky man. We still talk to this day. I always feel more grounded after speaking with him.

We met in the early 90s on Revere Beach, the cruising spot I spoke of. I had seen him on several occasions during rush hour heading North. I thought he was so handsome. A clean-cut Irishman, with a killer smile. I think it was 1991 when we met. We became lovers right away. Inseparable for over a year. That relationship turned into a friendship, and then into family.

I usually reached out when I sought counsel. What I loved about Paul was that he wasn't just going to tell me what I wanted to hear. I got the truth. Sometimes it hurt, but it always helped screw my head back on.

I lit up another cigarette and dialed his number. He answered as he always does, "Hey, Ed. How are you?" Always with such warmth and sincerity.

"I'm ok," I said. "I have the day to myself and thought I'd call to say hi." "How are you holding up?" he asked.

"Up and down," I replied. "Somewhere in the middle at the moment." There wasn't much we didn't know about each other's lives and having always been transparent and honest with each other made it easy to talk with him.

He also had 25 years of sobriety. He asked how the drinking was going and if I was sober. I said that I was not. I was drinking day and night, not eating enough, and burdened with guilt about it.

We talked further and he asked me if I would read the first step in the big book of A.A. I promised that I would, but I said that I would not stop drinking just yet. I told him that I started isolating myself from people. I said I needed to be alone for the most part. He warned me that the mourning process could take years or even a lifetime.

He expressed serious concerns as to the amount of booze I was drinking combined with the pain of Brian's death. "They feed on one another and you are the one who will lose." Sobering words. Temporarily.

I knew all along that drinking the pain away wouldn't work. That it would only numb me to it for a while and return once I was sober.

He said, "Why don't you come home?" He didn't say Swampscott or even Boston, but home. I felt right away that it was a good idea. I mentioned that I didn't feel done in the Pacific Northwest yet, whatever that meant. He said he understood but to just come home for a while. Summer is coming to the North Shore, and we can swim in the ocean. I hadn't done that in so long. It was suddenly all I could think about.

I booked a flight for 10 days out to save a bit of money to get my affairs in order. I was excited about returning home and especially to Swampscott and the North Shore during the Summer. I just kept thinking about jumping into the surf and washing all of this away.

Which beach to go to? Preston Beach in Swampscott was where I wanted to go. It was secluded. Mostly families or nannies taking care of kids. If you catch it on the right day, and if it's slightly overcast, the ocean takes on a mercury like quality. It's perfect. I couldn't wait.

With a renewed sense of purpose, I started gathering all my shit together for the move back. I wasn't sure how long I was going to stay. I thought at least through the Summer and part of the Fall, and then for a split second, I thought about returning home permanently. The thought didn't last. I knew I wasn't done here in Seattle, but I filed that away for later. I didn't want to lose the excitement in the anticipation of coming home.

I booked a redeye flight. It was the cheapest I could get. A few days before I left, I attempted to lay off drinking so I could arrive crisp and ready to go. Not so much.

I got to SeaTac Airport insanely early. I had vodka in my carry-on, and was hitting it on the way there. I had to get rid of it before checking obviously so I hung out in the smoking section for a bit before I went through security.

After chain smoking almost half a pack, I took a pull from the plastic Smirnoff bottle, and then threw the rest away. *What a crime*, I thought. I got myself all checked in. I should have just checked it with the rest of my luggage.

The flight didn't leave until 11:00 p.m. and luckily enough for me, there was a bar directly across from the gate. I bellied up and ordered a drink. It was 8:30 p.m. Plenty of time to relax. The plan was to get enough into my system to be able to sleep on the plane.

It was just me and one other guy at the bar. He was handsome. After a little bit I said hello. We exchanged the usual airport pleasantries. I offered to buy him a shot, and we began chatting. He was a nice enough fellow. A North Carolina native working in finance or something in Boston.

After the shots and the beers went down, I started to realize that this guy could drink just as much as I could. It made me feel a little better. I used to worry that people would judge me for drinking so quickly.

Alcoholism aside, I drank all liquids the same way. I just had to be careful with booze. I didn't need that shit hitting me like a brick wall. I liked to pace myself so I could drink longer. Unless I'm hungover. Then the first couple go down as quickly as I can get them to, to pull myself out of the hell I feel.

Jim, his name turned out to be, and I were having a good old time drinking and swapping war stories. He could certainly hold his booze. He was also extremely cute. I wanted to kiss him but that wasn't going to happen. I couldn't get a read on him, but my instinct told me that he was straight, so I just let it go.

Besides, he was excellent company, and I didn't want to interrupt that. It was time to board the plane, so I ordered two more shots for us and settled the tab. Fucking airports are so expensive.

Jim was on the same flight as me and, as it turned out, only a couple of rows behind. He suggested we sit next to each other if possible and keep the party going. Sure! I said. *Lucky me*, I thought.

By this time, I wanted to jump his bones. He was very well put together, along with a handsome face, and the always sexy tuft of chest hair sticking out from the front of his button-down shirt. Such a turn on.

The flight was full, however, and we couldn't change seats. Bummer. We exchanged info, and said goodnight. I ordered a beer and a of shot bourbon and I settled in for the flight home.

After a little while, I got up to take a leak and Jim was out cold. I chuckled and returned to my seat. I only had the one beer and put the nip of bourbon in my pocket for the morning. I knew I would need it. Boy would I ever. I fell asleep shortly after finishing my beer, and was awoken by the announcement "Ladies and gentlemen, welcome to Logan International Airport. The current temperature is…" blah blah blah, "…and raining."

Ugh. I slept the whole flight, and was now jolted awake by "The time to go" seat belt off sign. Suddenly, there were people all around me, and I was hungover as hell. I grabbed my carry on, and waited to get off the fucking plane so I could drink the bourbon in my pocket. It seemed like it took forever for people to move. It always seems that way when I needed a drink and civilians are in the way.

Again, civilians are what I call people who don't work in the service industry, and tend to move at a glacial pace. They are usually in supermarkets or large crowded areas. It makes me insane. I got off the plane, pulled the nip out of my pocket, and downed it. I didn't care who saw me. I was shaking like a leaf, and needed to stop it right away. That was all that mattered.

Besides, I was in Boston again. Nobody gave a shit. Blessedly, there was a bar not too far from my gate that was open. That never happens twice in a row. It was jam-packed. I looked at my watch and it read 8:15 a.m. Eastern Standard Time. Yep, I was home. It took almost five agonizing minutes to get a drink. The place was so busy. What the hell?

I ordered two double vodka and tonics for me and my "friend." My imaginary friend. I would need more than just the one. I found a seat at a small table in the corner and slammed the first drink to try and level up. I started in on the second one while listening to my beloved Boston accent being thrown around the bar left and right.

It made me smile. I was home. I muscled my way in for two more drinks and sat back down. I knew I couldn't stay too long.

Paul was expecting me around 10:00 a.m. or so. I called, and said I would be a little late. I didn't want to show up hungover and shaking. I feel like one big raw nerve when I'm like that. It's horrible. My motor skills are off. I can't think clearly. It's an awful state to be in. My luggage! I totally forgot.

I killed the last drink and bolted to baggage claim. All told, I was in the bar less than half an hour. There were still people collecting their bags from the flight.

Whew! I even saw Jim there. I was feeling much better as I approached him, and said hello. He was not. He looked like he was hurting badly. "Need a ride?" he asked. "No. I'm going up North, the opposite direction. Thank you though."

I think he mentioned he lived on the South Shore somewhere. We parted ways, and I mentioned something about hair of the dog.

In our previous conversation, Paul had spoken of difficulty walking and getting around on his own, so before I got on the plane, I said I would just take a cab to Swampscott. It was about $40. Not bad really, considering the distance. I got outside with my luggage to hail a taxi, and it was raining and muggy.

We don't get the mugginess in Seattle, especially when it's raining. The air is always crisp and clean. The air here was thick, heavy, and smelled like car exhaust. I just wanted to get the hell away from the business of the airport.

The air on the North Shore always smelled like the ocean. I knew it would be cleaner and cooler. I got my stuff loaded into a cab and off we went. The ride from the airport to Swampscott doesn't offer all that much to look at until you get to Revere Beach. The beach itself isn't all that pretty, but it has a lot of history being the first ever public beach in the country.

A lot of pizza joints, and hot dog and ice cream stands. The memories came flooding back.

Chapter Twenty-Five
Home Again

We drove past Garfield Ave., where I lived with Debbie as a kid. It ran parallel to the beach and two blocks in. We drove past Shirley Ave., past the famous Bianchi's pizza and the even more popular Kelly's Roast Beef. An insanely busy takeout for roast beef sandwiches and fried seafood for the late-night bar crowd. We drove past the cruising area on the beach. I smiled a little. Some good memories there. I realized I hadn't brushed my teeth yet, so I reached into my carry-on for my toothbrush, and my mini toothpaste to brush up before I got to Swampscott. It was still muggy, but even on days like this, the North Shore was always beautiful.

Not being able to brush my teeth without water was a problem, so I asked the driver to pull into a 7-11 so I could get some water. I thought I had something in my carry on, but I couldn't find it.

Besides, I could get a few small containers of white wine to put in my luggage, so I could begin the tapering off process. I knew I would drink on the day of my arrival, but I refused to the day after. A plan I stuck to. I returned to the cab with a bottle of water and six containers of Chardonnay. We still had about 20 minutes or so until we arrived at

Paul's place, so I brushed my teeth in the cab, rinsed with the bottled water, and had no way to spit, so I just swallowed it. Ick.

First time for everything. I cracked open one of the chardonnays, and sat back to enjoy the ride. We were at Lynn beach by this time and it had stopped raining, so I put my window down and took a sip of the vino.

Ah, my beloved North Shore. I let the breeze wash over me from the cab window and I stared out at the ocean. The air was much lighter with a faint smell of salt to it. It was good to be home.

I wasn't one hundred percent prepared for what I saw when I got to Paul's house. The last time I saw him he was in good shape. He could move well and was out and about all the time. After some health issues and a series of falls, I returned to find a much different version of him. He was much slower. He moved very gingerly and consciously, and always with a bit of pain. He seemed much older or to have aged very quickly since the last time I saw him. I was surprised by this and a little more than concerned.

He had coffee at the ready. He always made good coffee. I jumped on it right away to mask the smell of the previous night and the mornings adventures. Even though I had told him I would arrive with the smell of alcohol on my breath, he didn't say a word about it. I knew he knew. I felt bad. I told him tomorrow meant sobriety, and a new start.

We had coffee out back while his two Labrador Retrievers played on the grass. Olive and Tosca. Both very rambunctious. One chocolate, the other Golden. Those dogs ate very well, and grew to be about 80 lbs. apiece. They were sweethearts and a big part of what kept Paul going lately I would come to find.

Paul had fallen into a depression after his partner and he split up. They were together for the better part of 25 years, and even married when it became legal in Massachusetts.

I was invited to a beautiful ceremony they held in their living room.

A baby grand piano and a floor-to-ceiling stained glass arched window served as a backdrop. I don't think Paul ever got over the divorce. He seemed lethargic. I didn't know if it was from all the physical pain, or that he had been stuck in this rut for a very long time. I think it was a combination of both. I was determined to get him out of it. The Paul I knew was a fighter. Not this person I saw now.

Being full of piss and vinegar from my morning libations, I had the idea of getting Paul down to the beach for a swim. First, I had to unpack. Paul had moved into the downstairs den from the master bedroom upstairs. The master bedroom was huge. Three large Bay windows with view of Swampscott Harbor and Phillips Beach. An obstructed view but a view of the ocean just the same. "This is your new room," he said. "There's no way Paul, I couldn't," I said. He said, "I can't get up and down the stairs anymore without a struggle, so it's just safer for me to stay down here." He had a comfy chair that looked out over the front lawn. And a twin bed. A perfect place for reading.

The neighborhood was always so quiet. I said it would be perfectly fine for me to be in one of the smaller bedrooms, but Paul insisted so I said "OK," and moved my suitcases upstairs.

Paul said he wasn't up for a swim in the ocean just yet, so I suggested we go to lunch at the Barnacle in Marblehead at the end of Front Street and on the harbor—a tiny wooden structure that jetted out from the seawall about 60 feet and was helped up entirely by pilings. When storms would come in, waves would crash with such force that it would shoot water up and over the second story. It was crazy. They also had the best fish sandwiches and chowder on the North Shore.

We agreed lunch was in order, but it was still a bit early. Paul went back to his chair to read, and I went upstairs to unpack and set up the bedroom. It was about the same size as Bob's master bedroom except for the three large Bay windows and the ocean view.

The sun finally broke through, so I opened all the windows, put on some music, and started to unpack. I put the remaining containers of

Chardonnay in the nightstand, and held one back to drink. I didn't want to leave them out or put them in the fridge.

With the local radio station going, sporting my beloved Boston accent, the breeze wafting in and the wine in my system, I was feeling rather good. I was optimistic and even hopeful again and looking forward to the drive to Marblehead for lunch. It was a beautiful drive that cut through the heart of Swampscott and Marblehead and would spit you out on Front Street at the State Street landing in Marblehead harbor.

The homes along the drive there were just spectacular. Stately, enormous and sprawling. Especially out on Marblehead Neck. An open peninsula that split off due east from the mainland. This is where you can see some uniquely beautiful homes. Good Lord!

I remember my first time driving out on the neck with friends when I was younger. I couldn't believe it. These homes were grand, gorgeous, and some of the biggest and loveliest homes I had ever seen. Devereaux Beach is just at the beginning of the neck. A good place to swim, eat fried clams, and stare at men. The men in Marblehead are lovely. There is no shortage of my type of man and they seem to be everywhere. I love that town.

I finished up another carton of chardonnay and yelled down to Paul that I was gonna hit the shower. He said OK and that he would dress for lunch.

I scrubbed up, showered and shaved in about 20 minutes. It was nice to walk around bare-assed on the second level. There was no neighbor close enough to look in and the breeze coming off the ocean felt so good.

In that moment, I was happy. It had warmed up considerably, and the sun was out in full force, so I opted for shorts and a Navy-blue pullover. Man were my legs white! In fact, my entire body was pale white. The Seattle Grey.

I would have to remedy that and soon. I grabbed my shades and a ball cap, took a long pull of the Chardonnay and bound down the stairs and into the backyard to play with the puppies. They took to me right away. Instant pals. Paul said he would be a minute. He was on the phone. I lit up a cigarette, sat down on the edge of the back deck with the puppies running around, and I stared out at the ocean. It was wonderful to be back in New England. Wonderful indeed.

The drive to the Barnacle was just as I remembered. Absolutely lovely. The roads were still drying, and the sun felt warm on my skin. It was nice to be with Paul again. We made it there in about 15 minutes. Marblehead is close. Just the next town over. We opted for a table inside. They don't have a real patio to speak of unfortunately. Too bad because the view is just so stunning. It would be nice to sit outside and stare at the water.

The Barnacle is located right at the mouth of Marblehead Harbor, and from there on out was the open ocean. I was so happy to be back. We ordered two cups of chowder and two fish sandwiches. It came on a toasted bun, tartar sauce, and melted cheese with a mound of French fries on the side. Good stuff.

Paul had opened up to me about how difficult it had been for him these past few years. I didn't realize he was struggling so greatly. I told him I was here to help in any way possible. He began to ask about Brian and all that had happened in the last two years. I felt the old familiar lump in my throat and a pang of hurt, and said, "It's a beautiful day. Let's shelve that for now and have a great lunch." So we did just that.

I stepped away from the table, and walked up the gangplank to the bathroom and the bar. I ordered a quick double vodka and tonic and slammed it. Much better I thought to myself. I hit the bathroom and returned to Paul.

The fish sandwiches were just as good as I remembered. Fat and happy, we left the restaurant and I asked Paul if he had the strength to walk to Fort Sewall. He said sure, if we move slowly. So we took a right on Front Street and walked the 100 or so yards East.

Fort Sewall was built in the mid-1600s on a rocky headland as a defense against the French. It had an outstanding panoramic view stretching from Marblehead Neck, all the way across the harbor out to the open ocean. You could even see parts of Salem, Mass, Witch City, off to the northeast by only a couple of miles.

Marblehead really is one of my favorite places. When I met Paul, I was working in the mailroom of a financial services company downtown. It was a subsidiary of Sun Life Canada insurance called Mass Financial Services. On Boylston Street in the Back Bay. It was just behind Trinity Church and kitty corner from the John Hancock tower. It was boring menial work, but it was a steady pay check, and it had great benefits. I made a couple of lifelong friends there to boot.

Marty T, one of the funniest people I've ever met. We are still in touch. We've had some great laughs, he and I. In the early 90s, you could still smoke in the break rooms located in the corners of every floor on the building.

Marty and I were smoking on a break, and I looked out the window with a view of Trinity Church and a fresh, undisturbed blanket of snow on the sprawling lawn behind it. It was about 80 yards by 80 and people would sunbathe or eat their lunches there during spring and summer.

Marty and I, being the mature young men that we were, decided to rip a couple of boards from a pallet in the mail room and trace a giant cock over the entire surface area of the park. It just snowed and it was still pristine and untouched.

Giggling like the idiots and still on the clock, we completed our task and ran back to the break room twenty stories up to look at our handiwork. And there it was. Smack dead center for all to see. A giant cock and balls. We were never found out, thank God, and it became the talk of the building for a couple of days. We kept our secret in the mailroom. We were legends in our own minds. We were idiots. He and I still stay in touch mostly via social media. He's married with kids now, and lives up in Maine. When we do talk on the phone, it's usually to relive all the stupid shit we did together. It was great fun. He is a great friend.

After Mass Financial, I went in a completely different direction and took a job on a lobster boat out of State Street Landing in Marblehead. I loved it and I took to it right away. There was the captain, the first mate, and then me, the "master baiter" as I was called.

It was my job to bait the traps when they came on board, and reset them back into the water, making sure they landed on the surface right side up. If they didn't, then the bugs or lobsters as they were called couldn't get at the bait, and the trap was useless. That usually meant that I was in trouble, so I made damn sure not to fuck that up.

It was hard work, but not back breaking. I got to see the sunrise on the water every morning with a cup of coffee from a 40-foot open stern aluminum lobster boat steaming past Fort Sewall, and then due east around the backside of Marblehead neck.

The facades of these great homes on 'The Neck" paled in comparison to the view of them from the water. They were just unbelievable. Most had their own private beaches, colossal decks and green spaces adorned with lawn furniture and grottoes with swimming pools.

I had no idea people lived like that. Being on the water so early in the morning was a good way to start the day. Some mornings we would leave as early as 4:30 a.m. That part I didn't care for.

In Massachusetts, if you're a lobster man, you're allowed so many traps or pots and state waters and so many in federal waters. The difference being three nautical miles. When we steamed out to the captain's pots and deep water, it took longer to get there, so we would leave earlier. Sometimes, it took a couple of hours or more to steam out to the pots, so we would set up the boat, then relax and smoke cigarettes until we got there. The sunrise on the water was always so amazing to me. I felt good, I felt free.

The captain was a man named Billy N – an affable chubby little guy with a bright red face and an upbeat demeanor. I liked him right away. The first mate was a seasoned vet and I, being the greenhorn, didn't know the first thing about fishing for lobster or navigating a boat mending traps. But I was a hard worker, and I kept my mouth shut for the most part.

So they were willing to teach me, a greenhorn, how to fish properly. We were a good crew and we worked well together. One of the benefits of leaving so early in the morning was that we would return on average around lunchtime or 1 p.m., finished for the day. I loved pulling back into the landing to 'tub up' our catch for the day and sell them to the local distributors, waiting with their refrigerated trucks.

Tourist everywhere, the sun was shining, and I worked on a lobster boat in Marblehead. I was happy. I love Marblehead. I still do.

It was the opposite of everything that was Roxbury. The antithesis. This is when I started renting the in-law apartment from Paul and his partner Joe. I could bike every morning to work and back. I had steady work during the season, and I was usually done for the day by lunchtime. So I had the rest of the day to hit the gym or do whatever I wanted. First thing was first though. I had to shower and wash my work clothes. I was used to the smell, but everyone I came in contact with was not.

I learned that after going into a White Hen pantry convenience store to buy a pack of smokes, and the clerk said "Jesus boy, you stink!" "I am a lobster fisherman," I said rather proudly. "That explains it," he said. I walked outside and lit up a smoke. I felt good.

The one thing I wasn't prepared for was a thing called the 'Rollies.' After being on the water all day, you get used to the ebb and flow of the water. When you return to dry land. The movement is still there for a little while, so I could be standing on dry land and then suddenly, I would feel a wave rush over me as if I were moving up and down. The Rollies! It was a trip.

Sadly, Captain Billy died of a heart attack at 36 years old. I couldn't believe it. He seemed like he was in decent shape other than a bit of a big belly and maybe high blood pressure. He seemed so young. The sad part was that he had a wife and two young kids at home. Whatever became of them I do not know. Billy was a smart man. He had insurance for everything, so I was hopeful that he had some sort of life insurance policy in place. I sure hope so.

It happened towards the end of the season. I caught on with another boat following season, but it just wasn't the same. A much older guy. He never spoke. Ever. He just listened to old country music all day long. It was fucking depressing. It was just him and I, and we barely worked a full day most days. Part-timer. He didn't have nearly as many traps as Captain Billy did. I missed Captain Billy. He was a good man. I ended up leaving the job altogether. Not enough money, and working with this guy sucked. It would be years before I returned to fishing and even then, it didn't last long. If I'm lucky enough to retire, I'd like to do it again. Either in Marblehead or somewhere in the Florida Keys. Time will tell. It always does.

Paul and I got back to the house, let the puppies out to run, and I went upstairs to finish unpacking. Paul sat down to read. I had a feeling that he was going to nap, so I closed the bedroom door, turned on the radio, and pulled out a container of Chardonnay. I killed half of it in one pull, and began hanging up my clothes and pictures of Brian.

I stacked my books where I could, then put fresh sheets on the bed. Important to have a made bed. It didn't take all that long to put everything away and store my suitcases in the cellar. My bedroom also had a very long closet that ran three quarters of the length of one wall. I put all my suits and shoes away. It felt nice to have everything in one place and completely unpacked. I had been living out of suitcases for some time and it was starting to wear on me.

I poked my head in on Paul to find him asleep, sitting up in his chair with the Bible in his lap. Paul was Catholic. Very Catholic. It seemed to cause him conflict and inner turmoil when I first met him, being Gay and Catholic, that is.

I could tell he felt ashamed for being Gay. When we first met, Paul was very much in the closet. He kept that secret from the entire world, and fought hard to protect it. He worked for a company that managed a Howard Johnsons Hotel on Memorial Drive in Cambridge. A big hotel/restaurant right on the Charles River. Paul was always so impeccably dressed, in a well pressed suit or shirt and tie. Khaki pants. I loved him in khakis when we first met. It was so sexy.

The Paul I saw now, even though he was retired, didn't care so much for his appearance anymore. another surprise to me. He always paid well attention to how he looked, normally. Even the interior of the house seemed a bit rundown and dated. Something Paul would never normally let happen. It was still absolutely beautiful.

This is when I knew that his relationship ending had hurt him much more than he let on. A part of him seem to stop caring. I could relate. I was determined to quicken his spirit, and to restore the house back to its former glory. At least inside anyway.

Paul had always kept the landscapers on the payroll to keep the outside of the house looking as beautiful as it always had. The inside work was easy enough to take care of, but not just yet. I had to sober up first.

The thought panicked me. I knew what was coming the next morning, and I shuddered at the thought of it. Real pain. It was going to suck. For at least the first few days. But not yet, I still had booze my blood, and two big containers of wine left. I would have to nurse them until bedtime. This was gonna be tricky. But if I timed it correctly, I could take one good pull and fade off to sleep around 10:00 p.m. That was the goal anyway.

I pulled some chicken out of the freezer to thaw for dinner. Paul said he liked to eat around 6:00 p.m., so that gave me time to defrost and prep some potatoes and vegetables to go with. I went outside, lit up a smoke, and played with the puppies for a little bit while the chicken thawed in the sink.

Paul was still asleep. I closed my eyes, sat in the sunshine, and listened to the wind dance through the trees overhead. It was so quiet. So very quiet. I loved it. I thought about a nap, but decided against it. The last thing I needed was to be awake late at night and unable to sleep without any booze.

Chapter Twenty-Six
The North Shore

Detoxing that way was hell. Detoxing anytime without Librium or something to help was always hell. I usually tried to time it so that I would drink my last bit of alcohol just before bed, and then try to sleep as much of it off as possible. The morning always brought hell, but at least I would have gotten some rest and could try to begin a normal daytime routine again.

Again, I shuddered at the thought of what was coming, and lit up another smoke. I got mad at myself and said, stop being such a pussy and just get it done. That usually worked to steel my resolve, and put things back into perspective a little bit. I felt better about it. I went inside, washed up, and started prepping for dinner. Roasted chicken with Rosemary and lemon, garlic mashed potatoes, and asparagus. *Easy enough*, I thought. About an hour later or so, the smell of roasted chicken and garlic permeated the air.

That, plus the smell all the saltwater coming in from the kitchen windows made me feel good. I heard Paul call to me from the bedroom, "Ed are you there?" "I sure am Paul. Dinner will be ready soon," I said, "and I hope you're hungry?"

"Wonderful," he said. "I can't wait." Paul is a Kind Soul. I set the table and we had a great first dinner together we talked about our plans for the summer and all that we wanted to do.

All the while in the back of my head all I could think about was tomorrow morning and the hell that awaited me.

And so, it came. I woke up, or rather came to around 6:00 a.m. My instinct was to reach for a bottle to take the edge off so I could start my day. It wasn't there. No bottle!

Fuck me... Here we go.

I was dehydrated, everything ached, and I felt slightly nauseous. Good times. I promised Paul more than I promised myself that this was how it was going to have to be. Even if I didn't share this plan with him.

This was going to hurt, and it did. I got up, and went into the bathroom. I heard Paul call up to me, "Good morning Ed. Coffee is ready." Good Lord, I wasn't ready for conversation. I stuck my head under the faucet into the bathroom sink and drank like a camel for about a minute. No need to look in the mirror. I could feel what I looked like. I turned on a piping hot shower and climbed in. If I couldn't feel better, I would at least smell better, damn it.

I hopped out and brush my teeth. "I'll be right down Paul," I said. "You hungry for breakfast?" He asked. I could have hurled. The thought of food made me sick. With the amount that I drink and for as long as I drink, sometimes weeks and months straight, my hangovers aren't normal. They don't go away by the end of the first day, as it is with a lot of people. I shake apart almost. The first six to 12 hours are the worst. I'm physically sick.

Again, alcohol is the most dangerous drug to detox from if you attempt to do it cold turkey. It can cause delirium tremens, the most severe form of alcohol withdrawal. It can cause hallucinations and cardiovascular collapse. Bad idea for me to detox this way, but I did it.

I'll never do it again. I went downstairs with check book in hand to give Paul rent for a month.

He handed me a cup of coffee, and I sat down to write him a check. I couldn't do it. I had to tear up the first one because my hands were shaking so badly that I couldn't write. Normally, I would never drink coffee when I'm hurting this badly. The last thing I needed was to be even more aware of the fact that I felt like shit. I drank it to help mask the smell that was now emanating from my pores. Paul made himself a couple of eggs for breakfast and suggested that we go to stop and shop to pick up food for the house. Oh no! The general public. Something I avoided at all costs when I was feeling like this.

Human interaction was a definite no no. He already had a shopping list, so I said, "Sure, let's go." Staying busy helps keep my mind from the feeling that I'm going to die. For a split second, I thought about getting a couple of containers of wine to settle my nerves, but I said no. Suffer through it. I was punishing myself for my addiction.

It's something all addicts do. Addiction is a hell that few people can understand. I would like to share something I found on a recovery page. It goes like this:

"If you are lucky enough not to understand addiction, then good for you. I hope you never have to. I hope you never see someone you love disappear before your eyes, while standing right in front of you. I hope you never have to lie awake all night, praying the phone doesn't ring yet hoping it does at the same time. I hope you never know the feeling of doing everything you thought was right and still watching everything go wrong. I hope you never love an addict. I hope you never know what it means to live afraid of yourself. To never trust yourself. To fight a raging war inside your own mind every moment. To feel unwanted and unworthy.

To need something that you know is destroying you and to do anything for it. To trade yourself, your life, your Soul and still end up broken and alone. To give away everyone and everything you had. To have no answers. To always question. To have no choice yet have to choose to fight your battle. I hope you never have to live as an addict."

— – Author Unknown

Pile on top of that, fear, insecurity, and a physical and emotional craving that is literally tearing you apart, and you have what addicts suffer every day. What I have suffered every day in my addiction. Only to be judged and dismissed as weak or lacking any moral fortitude. What the fuck does that even mean? If you're not living in addiction, then it is hard for people to understand, and it's easy for people to judge and to call addicts weak. Wrong!

An addict, any addict trying to pull their shit together and crawl back to the starting line is a hell of a lot stronger than the average person. They must be. If they want to live. I can promise you this though, a lot of addicts, myself included, couldn't care less about living when in the throes of addiction. Remember, all addiction is progressive. The body requires more, more, more.

One's personality, appetites, traumas in life, especially traumas are all factors that contribute to relapses and can keep an addict under for years at a time. In my opinion, trauma, especially childhood trauma, violence, neglect, molestation leave such a painful thumbprint on the clay of a child's nature that only drugs, or alcohol can lift. Temporarily. To know that you're fucked up and something isn't right inside you even when everything around you seems to be ok at the moment is maddening. For me, as an adult, even when my life was ok on the outside, I could still feel my underlying issues. They are always there. I can feel the hyper-awareness, anger, and fear all the time. So even if I weren't born alcoholic—I believe I was—I would most likely have turned to it anyway. With my genetic predisposition, and two blackout drunk alcoholic parents, it was almost inevitable.

Sitting in that kitchen with Paul that morning, I still had hope that I would defeat alcoholism somehow, some way, through sheer force of will. I was tired of alienating people, and losing job after job because of drinking. Now, four years after Brian's death, I have a completely different view on the subject. I simply don't care anymore. If I can't save the relationships of the past, then, for their sakes and mine, I have to let them go.

I am completely honest and upfront with people about who and what I am now. When I'm drinking, I say I require alcohol all day every day. I will not change this for you. Hell, I won't change it for myself. I don't recommend you stay for too long, but if you do, you need to know this about me. It reminds me of a line from an old Joni Mitchell song called "A Case of You."

Some may say I am selfish in thinking this way. Maybe. I disagree, though. What was selfish on my part was keeping these people around the hurricane that was, and is, my life. Constantly worrying friends and family, financial instability, and poor health. It's better to keep everyone at arm's length than to let them in at this point.

Sure, we can be drinking buddies, acquaintances, but that's it. If something changes, then I will give this further investigation, but as of now, I'm tired of apologizing for having this disease that I can't completely control. And to be perfectly honest, I'm not sure if I really want to anymore.

The truth is, I like drinking. I always have at the start of it. It turns into a living hell every time. Every time, and it destroys all that I've worked hard for. I rebuild it back to where it was, and I tear it back down again. At this point in life, I think this is just who I am, and after a lifetime of listening to people and being judged, I'm saying in a sense "Fuck you! This is just who I am. There's the door if you don't like it. Goodbye." Part of me hopes this changes. But only a little part of me.

Alright, I'm done ranting.

Back to Swampscott.

Paul and I went to Stop and Shop for groceries. I put my shades on and a ball cap to hide the way I felt. I always felt like I would bleed to death if I didn't close my eyes, they were so bloodshot. Hence, the ever-present shades. It was pleasant to be there. It was nice and cool in the store. I grabbed a cold ginger ale and popped it open while we were shopping. Paul just looked at me. "What? I'm going to pay for it." I just needed something carbonated.

What was nice was listening to people, strangers talk to each other. Friendly gestures or a "Hey, how are you" was being thrown around in my Boston accent. It was a nice reminder that I wasn't in Seattle anymore. People said hello to each other here. All the time. "Good morning!" I loved it. That just didn't happen in Seattle. The "Seattle Freeze" is real. It's not just for people new to the city either. Seattleites do it to each other all the time. It's rude really.

If you say "Good Morning" to someone in Seattle, they just stare at you like you're bat-shit crazy. Not here, not in Boston. It was so refreshing. I practically had a 10-minute conversation with deli clerk while he was cutting lunch meats for Paul and me. It was great, it was normal. I was suddenly hungry, which was a good sign, so I planned to make sandwiches for Paul and me when we got back, with sweet pickles and potato chips.

I asked Paul how he felt about going for a swim on Preston Beach after lunch. He said sure if he felt up to it. The beach, yes! I couldn't wait. Baptism. When I was younger and living on Revere Beach, I would always jump in the ocean if I were hungover. Provided it was Summer and it was high tide. I never saw the point of going to the beach at low tide unless you were digging for clams or beach combing. There was no surf to loll in, no waves to crash on you.

Jumping in when hungover always seemed to get rid of my hangover quicker. The cold salt water I considered to be a cure all, really. I try to wash away the nausea and a headache under water, splash around a bit and lay in the sun on a beach towel. Being younger and only drinking beer may have had something to do with it being easier to get rid of also.

The amount of booze I now consume took a lot longer to get rid of. So off to the beach we went. I packed the trunk with two folding chairs, a blanket, and a mini cooler with bottled water, soda, and some fruit. It was a beautiful morning. The forecast called for 85 degrees and sunny and high tide was at 2:00 p.m. Perfect.

It was starting to become clearer to me just how difficult it was for Paul to get around. He would be okay for a bit, and then he would have to sit down for a while. He would lose his balance unexpectedly, and sort of teeter totter back and forth. It scared the shit out of me. I thought he was going to face-plant or fall backward and hit his head. He moved very slowly, and I would walk him from point A to point B.

When this happened, I suddenly became aware of a mental fatigue that would hit me. I felt like I did at the end of caring for Brian. I felt my energy drain. The truth was that Paul was in worse shape than he initially let on. He required daily help. Getting up and down the stairs and sometimes bathing. I never told him, but it was almost too much for me. Not because of the work that was required, but because my tank was empty. I was beaten up and worn down by the stress and anxiety of caring for and then losing Brian. Now, the thought of caring for another person right away was so daunting. So draining. I shelved those thoughts, and focused on getting us to the ocean for a swim.

What a day! I put the two chairs and blanket over my right shoulder and carried the cooler in my right hand. After lathering up with sunscreen that is. I had Paul on my left arm, and we walked to 50 yards or so to the beach. The sand was burning hot. I had the gear on the right-side, Paul on the left, and we were moving very slowly over the hot sand. It hurt like hell.

We got there though. It was mid-week, so all the hot, chubby dads were working. Nannies, moms, and children were scattered here in there. It wasn't terribly busy, but it was high tide! Perfect. A hazy early Summer day in New England. The surface of the ocean even had an amazing mercurial glare to it. What luck I thought. It had been years since I stepped foot in the ocean, let alone swam in it. I put both feet in the cool water and it sent a chill down my spine. I took a few more steps and dove right in. Heaven!

The shock of the cold woke me up, and I could feel it washing everything away. I burst through the surface with the sweet taste of salt in my mouth, and I laid on my back floating on the water, staring up at the sky. Absolute Heaven. I flopped around like a baby seal for the better part of an hour, stopping to float on my back while listening to the waves crash and the planes fly overhead. It was wonderful. I was still very hungover, but it felt one thousand times better. I turned towards shore to see Paul making his way gingerly towards the shoreline. It scared me. He's very stubborn and will not give up control of his movement, even at personal risk.

I could respect that, but it still scared me. I met him at the shore. We walked him to the surf to cool off. What fun he had. It was obvious he wouldn't have been able to do this alone. So instead of worrying about caring for Paul full-time, I just took the proactive approach. I mentioned getting him into physical therapy right away, finding a dietitian for him, and working out a realistic exercise regimen. His doctor wanted him to lose 40 pounds. That's a significant amount of weight.

I told him that it would help with his balance and strength, sleep, and overall well-being. This seemed to pick up his spirits. I was glad. He pulled away from me, and wanted to walk alone in the surf.

"Ok," I said. "Watch out for the waves. They're still coming in." Back under I went for a split second. It felt so good. Paul was about 10 yards away from me, and I yelled "INCOMING! WATCH YOUR 6!"

There was a wave barreling down on him. He turned to look at it in the expression on his face was priceless. Oh fuck! He tried to make his escape, but it nailed him. Paul stands about 5 foot 7 inches, so the wave caught him right at the back of his head and flattened him. Between the look on his face and getting tumbled over by the wave, I lost it. I laughed so hard, and scrambled over to pick him up.

"We gotta get you out of here," I said. He said, "Yeah, it almost fucking killed me." Paul never swore.

I laughed my ass off. I put my arm around his shoulder, his arm across my waist, and walked him back to our spot. "Fun?" I asked. "Oh yeah. That was great," he said. I love sarcasm.

I got him settled with a drink, and said I'm gonna splash around for a bit longer. He pulled out something to read, so I knew I had a little time. After a while, I returned to our spot and opened a can of ginger ale. It tasted good. Refreshing.

For a split second my body thought, hey where's the booze? That happens sometimes when I first take a sip of something. If it's not water, then I usually have booze in it. Paul and I sat in silence. He with his reading and I staring out over the horizon at the sailboats.

Whenever I see someone sailing, I think, man what a great idea. That is free therapy right there. For me, anything on or around the water is therapeutic. I feel so much calmer. Camping also. A campfire, a tent and a fishing pole and I'm good to go. It doesn't happen often enough though. Not nearly as much as it should.

We stayed at the beach for another hour or so. Sandy, salty and happy. I looked at Paul, and he was almost asleep. After a while, I touched his shoulder and said "Let's get home, get cleaned up, and I'll make us a nice dinner." "Ok," was all he said, and we made our way slowly back to the car, while I was thinking of ideas to get Paul back into shape. I was also thinking about where I wanted to work. I been here a couple of days and it was time to get a job.

The Summer season was here, and I wanted to get in on it. The tourists were coming. I hear a lot of people complain about tourists in the service industry. I love them. People from somewhere else, from far away. They are usually a lot of fun to wait on. Not always, but usually. They spend well, and are full of questions about the local food and culture. I get to play Ambassador for my city or town. It's a lot of fun.

Paul and I got home, and I settled in and started dinner. Meatloaf and mashers. Easy peasy. Paul sat down to read, and while dinner was cooking, I sat at the kitchen table to formulate a plan of attack, where to look for work. Just down the road from Paul's house was a restaurant called Mission on the Bay. Right on the beach on the Lynn, Swampscott line. It had an amazing view of Lynn Beach and Nahant, Massachusetts – another small seaside community just at the other end of Lynn Beach and down along Causeway.

Mission on the Bay used to be called Red Rock Bistro. Seafood and cocktails and live music. It was an institution on the North Shore, and it was always busy. A lot of regular diners. They ended up selling the place to a developer and the restaurant group. What they did to the space was nothing short of amazing. They tore down the original structure and replaced it with a brand-new three-story restaurant, complete with a rooftop patio and bar. The view from the rooftop was unbelievable. Water, water everywhere and in the distance, you could see Boston and the city skyline.

It was a money-maker. I wanted in. I dropped a resume asking to speak with the General Manager. I usually skip past most Restaurant Managers. A lot of managers will put you off a day or two before they want to interview you, or sometimes, they just don't feel like it, so I go directly to the GM. It's a little risky because they may just say why didn't you just go to the hiring manager?

Doing it this way gives me the opportunity to sell myself to the boss and to let him know I'm here to get shit done. It has worked for me more often than not. The GM at Mission on the Bay as it is now called took my resume. He seemed surprised that I went directly to his office. I let him know that I lived two blocks away and I was ready to rock and roll. He said great, I'll check out your resume, and I'll call you in 24 hours with a decision.

"That's all I can ask for," I said. A firm handshake and eye contact. It was good to be back home. I went to the roof-top deck to check it out. It was packed, mid-week! There had to be at least 150 people up there, and the view was stunning.

I stayed for a couple of minutes, and then got the hell out of there lest I be tempted to drink. I walked North to this Italian Barber shop Paul told me about. I needed a haircut. Something I normally would have done before I applied for a job, but they were busy beforehand, so I couldn't get in. Rosa Brothers Barbers they were called. On Humphrey St. A father and son actually. Old school East Coast barbers. He offered me a glass of vino right away. I regretfully declined. It was so tempting. He did a great job.

The aftershave they used was called Clubman Pinaud, I think. Don't quote me on that. It smelled so good. So masculine and clean. I felt like quite the dandy. I walked the beach most of the way back to Paul's house. Feeling a lot better than I did yesterday. The swim in the ocean really helped me to recover faster. As soon as I got to the door my phone rang. My phone never rings. That's what I liked about it most.

It was the GM of Mission on the Bay. Already? It had been less than an hour and a half. Had to be good news, right? I said, "Hey boss, what's the good word? When do you want me to start?"

"Ed! My man. Good news and bad news. Bad news is I can't use you. We're all full up. I want you on my team though. You obviously got the skills, and I like that you showed the balls to come right to my office first. The fact is I'm completely full here at Mission on the Bay. If someone quits, I'm calling you right away. The good news is, if you're interested, a friend of mine runs a place called Turner Seafood on Church Street in Salem."

I knew the place. High-end, expensive seafood joint. Good check averages.

I said "Yeah man, I'm in. I'll head over first thing tomorrow morning with the resume." He said, "I've already spoken to the GM. She's expecting you tomorrow between lunch and dinner break. Around 3:00 p.m."

I thanked him a couple of times, and said that I'll be in for a drink soon.

I would not be.

Chapter Twenty-Seven

A New Job

The lunch crowd was just dwindling down at Turners when I arrived. Paul drove me and he parked in the lot across the street to wait for me. He just pulled out a book and began reading. The man read all the time. I envied his discipline. It was nice to be in a real restaurant again, an East Coast restaurant.

Even though it was slowing down, there was still a lot of hustle and bustle going on. I was right in my wheelhouse. I was shown to a table on the fine dining side of the restaurant. One side was the bar and pub style service, the other fine dining. After 15 minutes or so, a woman approached me with two other men in tow. They were all very well dressed.

"Edward?" she said.

"That's me," I replied. I stood to greet them before they got to the table. It was her, the GM, her assistant GM, and the dining room manager. Rarely do you ever get all three at once. It usually takes a couple of days to interview individually. I don't know why. They interviewed me for the better part of an hour. Kind of a long interview, but not unheard of.

Then came the question. "What brings you back to New England?"

I said, "Quite frankly, my partner passed away recently from cancer, and I couldn't stay in our home any longer." It was a very candid answer. I didn't elaborate. I just said that I needed to be home. I'm surprised I shared that information. I could have told them anything.

Then the craziest thing happened. The GM began to cry. She put her hand on mine, and said "I'm so sorry." This woman's heart was breaking for me, and I just thought, *what is going on here*? Come to find out, she had recently lost someone very close to her to cancer, and her wound was still fresh. I could relate. I never had an experience like that before at a job interview. We most certainly bonded through that interview. It was different, that was for sure.

She took a deep breath and said, "Well, that was fun." I liked her. There was no lying in her. She asked my availability, and I said "Anytime, Any day." She smiled a little, and said, "Let me just check your references, and I'll give you a call tomorrow morning." It was just a formality, she said. I was fairly sure I had the job. I didn't take it though.

On the way back to Paul's, we drove past the place called Rockafellas Restaurant on Essex St., just down the street from Turner's. "Pull over," I said to Paul. I knew one of the owners, Kevin, from a bar in Marblehead I used to work at. Rockafellas was not fine dining. What it was, however, was unbelievably busy. All the time, and especially in season. From Spring, all the way through Halloween. After all, it is Salem, Massachusetts. Witch city. The town went bat shit crazy with people for the entire month of October. Summer was busy, but October was ridiculous, and the streets were closed to car traffic. Everyone was in costume, and the line to get into Rockafellas usually stretched about a block down. Every day.

How could I forget about this place? I ran in with a copy of my resume, and Kevin was at the host. "Kev!" I said. "Fucking Cleaves?" he replied.

"Yeah man, I just got back to town. I think I just got hired at Turner's, but I'd much rather be here. You need a guy?" He said "Yeah, I need a part-time bartender and a full-time waiter. You in?" "Hell yeah, I'm in!"

And just like that, I started working at Rockafellas. The next morning in fact. It was comfort food, seafood, and a lot of it. Every sandwich you could think of hot and cold. Fifteen appetizers and a dozen or so entrees ranging from pasta to steak. They weren't getting any calls from *Food and Wine* magazine anytime soon, but the place was busy. All the time. They did have an excellent clam chowder, also. It's kind of a must if you own a joint on the North Shore. Or the South Shore for that matter. Out west who gives a shit? Nobody eats chowder in the Berkshires.

Rockafellas was famous for their cocktail menu. Strong drinks and at least 30 specialty drinks are what got people in the door. That and live music. The food seemed to almost be secondary.

Kevin was a regular at a bar I worked at Marblehead called the Sandbar. A small joint. Jimmy Buffett music and good wings. It was busy on weekends but that was it. Kevin knew I had the chops, so I started training the next morning. I felt bad about Turner's, but I called her when I left Rockefellers, and thanked her for her time and her sincerity. I shared the news with Paul. He was excited for me.

"Let's celebrate," he said. Then he said something funny. "Wait," he said, "How do two ex-drunks celebrate such an occasion?" I laughed. "With ice cream," I said. We pigged out on rocky road and butter pecan ice cream. That ended up being our dinner. Neither of us ate anything after that. It was a good day. I had to be there at 9:30 a.m. for training the next morning. Paul insisted on driving me. I think it gave him a reason to get out of the house. I was grateful. Black slacks, black shoes, and a Rockafellas polo shirt was the uniform. I slept surprisingly well, and with coffee in hand, I walked in for my first shift.

Kevin was there with his wife Terry. He greeted me with a smile. He was in work mode already, so I got in work mode. He and his wife ran the place with a partner and his wife. Kevin was very hands-on. I liked it. He ran the kitchen and his wife waited tables and managed the staff. The young staff.

An embryonic young man approached me and said, "Hey. I'm Chris. I'll be training you today." *Are you sure?* I thought to myself. He was so young. They all were. "When the fuck did I get old," I said to Kevin? He just laughed. "Yeah," he said, "That happens."

Chris was an affable young kid. He knew the menu and he knew the point-of-sale system. Diner-ware it was called. I knew it well. I just had to study the menu a bit and I was ready to go. The good thing about Rockafellas, and most restaurants on the East coast for that matter, was that you got your tips at the end of the night. So if you were low on money, and I was, it was a good way to save cash quickly.

I trained for a total of two days, and Kevin said "OK, that's enough. Wanna start making some money?" "Yes," I said, "Yes, I do." It felt good to be back in the game. Salem had changed a lot since last time I was back. It became very hip, bohemian, and funky. It was always sort of a blue-collar town. Good pubs and live music almost every night of the week. But it was sleepy during the week. Now, there were restaurants everywhere. Good restaurants and about a dozen bars I had never heard of before, and to my surprise, rainbow flags everywhere. Unlike Marblehead and Swampscott, which tended to be more conservative, Salem was liberal, and had sort of a "live and let live" vibe to it. I felt lucky to land where I did.

First day of training was typical. Menu study, tasting food, and learning where things are in the POS. I also got to meet the cast of lunatics I would be working with. All young kids, except for a couple of bartenders. One of the things I love about service industry people is that we all, especially early in our careers, end up burning the candle at both ends. Partying way too much and coming in hungover. Especially if one had to work a lunch shift. Ugh. The service industry seems to attract a certain breed of people. Lost sheep, lunatics, and escapees from the island of misfit toys. In every joint I've ever worked, the characters were almost always the same. The drinkers, which meant all of us, the drama queens, the coke-heads, the weed dealers, and the disgruntled old timer that's been waiting tables for way too long – *ahem* – the manager that's banging the barely-legal hostess, the chef that's banging everybody, and every once in a while, you'd come across a white rhino, a dodo bird, the rare individual that doesn't drink or smoke or even swear.

I would think to myself, *what the fuck are you doing here? You'll be eaten alive by this industry.* This is a misfits-only club. After a few weeks or even months on the floor of a busy joint, you could see the change begin to happen. You could see the anger and frustration building in these new people. I felt like the evil Emperor from Star Wars. Yes, yes let the hatred flow through you! Poor souls. This industry is not for the faint-of-heart. It will chew you up and spit you out if you are brittle. And for me, there's nothing like it. When a restaurant is packed out on a Friday night and everyone is busy as fuck, you're making money, and people are happy. It is fantastic!

However, when it goes sideways, it can be a complete nightmare. The service industry is one of the most stressful gigs on the planet. Hence, the need for so many to self-medicate after a long night of running around like a chicken with your head cut off. All that physical and mental stress manifests into drinking or smoking a little weed to calm down and to let that stress wash away.

The "one-drink-after-work" didn't work for me. It takes way more than that to wash the stress away from a professional service industry person. One of my favorite memories from Rocco's Italian was heading to the pub up the street with coworkers to have a few drinks and eat something. The song "Pressure" by Queen with David Bowie is like a service industry anthem for me. It always seemed to be playing.

Back to Rockafellas. The daytime crew started rolling in, and they were also young. Jesus! Here everyone worked double shifts except for the bartenders. Unless they wanted to. I was game. Bring it on. I needed the money. More than that though, what I needed was some normalcy. I needed a routine. Making money, working, getting to chat up strangers in the sunshine was so therapeutic. Exactly what I needed. Chris and I set up the outside patio for the lunch rush.

There was a lot of work, but the sun was shining, and tourists were everywhere. In that moment, I was happy. Then the lunch rush hit. Boom! The place turned into a shit-show. There were people everywhere. They were like hungry locust. I ran back up for Chris, which made things easier for him, having an old-timer more than twice his age at his disposal. The thing about waiting tables at a busy tourist spot is that you can walk away from your section for two minutes and come back and find it completely full of people. Four, five, and even six tables. "Flat sat" it is called. You'd better get on your bike.

"Sell 'em all booze, I said to Chris." "But it's lunchtime," he said. "Not everyone drinks at lunch." "Paduan," I said. "Everyone drinks and they use your invitation as an excuse to catch a buzz at 11:30 in the morning. No one gets out alive!" He was a good kid. I was determined to turn him into a selling machine. "Make sure you get cocktails and oysters on every table," I said. "After that, who cares if they order lunch, so long as they are drinking." I'd rather have a table slam four rounds of drinks and a few dozen oysters and be on their way to see the sights then have a table of lolly-gaggers. "They're tourists," I said. "They're on vacation. They're gonna drink." I took two tables in his section. "We're gonna get you to two thousand in sales today," I said. "At lunch? No way," he said. "Just watch, young Jedi. We can do this shit."

There was a steady line down the street, all tourists. Waiting to enjoy Northeastern seafood in the sunshine. This place was a moneymaker. At 3:30 p.m. the rush was over, and I asked Chris how he thought he did in sales. "I don't know," he said, "but it's gotta be good."

$1,920! Almost two grand on the lunch shift. That's pretty good no matter where you are. Especially considering lunch entrees and sandwiches top off at $15.

"Holy shit," he said. "I've never sold that much at lunch before." "We'll get him next time kid. Remember no one gets out alive." He made just under $400 on a lunch shift. "I've still gotta work a dinner shift," he said. "Go for a personal record young blood," I said.

I got on my feet in no time working doubles and having cash at the end of the night was always something to look forward to. I made a lot of money quickly. I would usually just bundle up the cash, throw it in my sock drawer, and count it at the end of the month. I never go by my nightly take. Monthly and quarterly is how I looked at it. It was easy money.

The stress was crazy, but I was sober and enjoying myself. In between shifts, if you worked a double, you usually had about an hour to yourself, maybe an hour and a half. Not here. It was chaos come high season, so there were days when you would work straight through. Highly, highly profitable.

I usually ate a big breakfast before a double shift. When we got rocked, there was no time to eat anything. Service industry people are used to eating on the fly, which meant gobbling up whatever you could, as fast as you could, and always while standing up. I got used to it a long time ago.

My schedule was full, and I was working all the time. I thought about joining the YMCA just up the road. It would have to wait. Summer was here and Salem was alive with people. It was so great. I was sober and life was getting better. I still smoked cigarettes though. I wasn't giving that up yet. Not until I had time to work out on regular basis.

Triggers for an alcoholic can be many. Some are blatant like a resentment towards someone after an argument, and some are subtle and subliminal. Even though things were going well in the outside, inside I was still very much a mess. I was still mourning Brian, and I could feel the weight of it all day, every day.

When you're with someone for a long time, you tend to develop habits in your relationship. One of mine was calling Brian as soon as I finished my shift. Like clockwork. I would leave the restaurant, go outside, and I have a smoke and call Brian. I had been at Rockafellas a while now and after work I went out onto Essex St. and lit up a cigarette. I picked up the phone and tried to call Brian. It ruined me.

It came completely out of the blue. The pain in that moment was too much. Brian was gone. I started to cry. I became so angry at life that I just said fuck it. I took a right on to Essex and walked to a place called Opus. Professional craft bartenders, great food and a good atmosphere.

I was there for only one reason. The pain in that moment was so great that it triggered a defense mechanism in me.

Stop the pain by any means necessary.

So that's what I did. I bellied up, and ordered a Ketel One martini, up with olives. I was angry. The bartenders at Opus are the real deal. I'm a good bartender, but I'm built for speed. These guys were artists for fucks sake. Watching them work was a pleasure. Real professionals. I introduced myself and mentioned that I worked at Rockafellas. He looked at the emblem on my shirt. "Nice to meet you Ed. Welcome." I slammed the first martini and ordered another one right away. "Rough day?" he asked.

"No," I said. "Just thirsty." I ordered some appetizers and this time I intended to eat them. The food was delicious. Regional American cuisine with Japanese influences. The food arrived and with it another martini. I ordered a couple of sushi rolls, some seaweed salad, and some edamame. The presentation was on point, the bar was beautiful.

My beloved accent was everywhere. I suddenly felt a bit better. I decided to make a night of it.

I called Paul and said not to wait up that I would be late. I was off the next day. I was off to the races also. I stayed at Opus for almost three hours, chatting with people at the bar and trying their specialty cocktails. So much went into a single drink. I had at least four martinis in me, so I was in no rush. Half of the fun was watching the bartender make the drinks.

Two hundred dollars later, I cashed out and decided to go on a pub crawl and look for live music. No problem there. Salem was chock-a-block full of live music. Little hole in the wall joints with a three-piece band or even just a guitar and stand-up bass. I walked into this little spot for a beer and a shot when the band was just setting up. "How long before you guys go on," I asked? "About 15 minutes," he said. "The drummer is late again." I grabbed a seat at the end of the bar and waited for the band to begin. That's when I was introduced to "Bam the drummer." A force of nature this guy was. He came barreling through the door like a Tasmanian devil and said "I'm here, I'm here."

The bar was mostly empty, mostly locals. This was definitely a "local's only" bar.

They finished setting up and opened with "Immigrant Song" from Led Zeppelin. This guy was fucking amazing. I had never seen his style of drumming before. He was about 6 foot 2 inches tall, ripped to shreds, with a giant mop of shoulder length curly blonde hair. Bam the drummer. They were a cover band, so a lot of their set was familiar to me. I just couldn't stop watching this guy play. He wasn't my type. I wasn't attracted to him in that way. It was all in his drumming and his personality. Apparently, he was a legend on the North Shore and played pickup gigs with a lot of different bands. It was around 9:00 p.m. and I thought to myself, *this is as good a place as any to close the night.* So that's what I did.

Alcohol, the great equalizer. It took my pain away for the night. I had no fear of the morning hell to come because I wasn't going to let it. I hit a package just before I bellied up to this place, so I had booze for the morning. I felt a pang of shame when I purchased it and quickly booted that feeling out. Nope! Not welcome here.

The bartender handed me a menu and asked if I was hungry. From where I was sitting, I could see inside their tiny kitchen. Oh, hell no! I thought to myself. That kitchen was a fucking disaster. Besides, I had already eaten. I bought the band a round of drinks in between sets and introduced myself.

That's what is so great about the East Coast. People actually talk to each other. Once they realize you're not a psycho that is. Turns out that Bam has played with some Boston heavy-hitters in the music scene. He seemed like a good guy. He was also a personal trainer I had come to find out, and was hitting me up for business. I just raised my glass and said, "I'm all good, brother."

They started playing again when a couple of our staff from Rockafellas came rolling in. "Hey, Ed! You're finally out for a drink man." I had been turning down their offers for drinks after work for some time now, so I assume they thought I just didn't drink. Wrong!

We had a great time. Swapping war stories about nightmare guests at the restaurant, decompressing, slamming shots, and smoking cigarettes. Same as it ever was in our business and I loved it. Every minute of it. One of the bartenders was feeling no pain, and I could see her sizing me up. She was a little drunk and the look on her face said, "I'm gonna make a move."

It was all I could do not to bust a gut laughing. Not because of her attempt. I was flattered, but because she was absolutely barking up the wrong tree.

2:00 a.m.! Ugh. That came quickly. I said my goodbyes to the band and the Rockafellas crew while we all smoked outside the bar. I waited for a cab. It was a fun night and I was tired. A long day. I got home in about 15 minutes. Salem is so close to Swampscott. I checked in on

Paul. He was fast asleep. As were the dogs. They weren't barkers, thank goodness.

I didn't want them to wake him up. I grabbed some tonic water from the fridge and went upstairs to my bedroom. It was far enough away from Paul's room that I didn't have to worry too much about noise. I was always quiet, anyway. I poured a nightcap and jumped in the shower to wash the day away.

I hated climbing into clean sheets with a dirty body. Fresh from the shower and with Brian on my heart, I sat on the edge of the bed and let the ocean breeze wash over me. I felt clean. Like a toddler just getting out of the tub. I sat there in the silence. The world was asleep. I looked at some pictures of Brian and finished my drink. It was too painful. I shut it down and climbed into bed. It felt so good to stretch my tired body across the cool sheets. I could feel sleep coming. No interruptions, no bad dreams, just sleep is what I hoped for.

The lights went out and so did I. I slept hard until 9 a.m. I heard Paul calling out to me. "Ed? Coffee!" "Ok," I said. "I'll be down after shower." I felt surprisingly refreshed. Rested even. I'll take it.

The pictures of Brian and I were still scattered on the foot of the bed. The pang came back. The ever-present pang. I made a drink and took my phone into the bathroom. I put on some Joni Mitchell and climbed into the shower. A quick one. I shaved and dressed quickly for the day. Shorts and a tee, I finished my drink and went downstairs for coffee. Paul had plans with his sister for the day. That meant I had the day all to myself. I planned on taking advantage of it.

Chapter Twenty-Eight
Salem, MA

I t was beautiful outside. The idea was to get in the cab, head to Salem, and go down to the waterfront. Do some people-watching, maybe go sailing and stroll around. Discovering all the changes that had happened in Salem. I started out at a restaurant called Captains Bar and Grill. Go figure.

It has since closed unfortunately. A tourist trap but it still had its fair share of regulars. I just wanted to people-watch. It was a good jumping point if I decided to go sailing. This place had the best big belly fried clams I recalled. I ordered a plate. It was noon and by this time, the place was packed out. I sat at the bar with a view of the water and the bevy of tourists with their maps making plans for the day.

They always seem so excited. I used to drink here at Captains back in the day, and I knew some of the staff and a couple of the regulars. They must have moved on or weren't working that day. The plate of clams arrived and suddenly I got the urge to go.

It was beautiful out and I wanted to stroll around town. I had no intention of eating a full plate of clams anyway. I just ordered them for the nostalgia. I did eat a few though. As good as they ever were. I asked for a "to go" box with the intention of feeding them to the seagulls. The gulls on the North Shore ate very well. They were huge. You've got to be careful or they'll fly away with your fucking kids.

Feeling no pain, I strolled back to the center of town, past Rockafellas, quickly. They were rocking and rolling, and I didn't wanna get sucked in on my day off. Day-and-a-half off, actually. I wasn't back in until the following evening. Sweet!

I ran into a place I used to drink at called the Lobster Shanty. How could I forget this place? It was a kind of an outdoor, indoor dive on Front Street. Kind of on a cobblestone thorough way in between main street. They did a brisk business. Lobsters and beer. No air conditioning. It was hot as balls in the summertime.

They had a nice patio space, however. The writing on their sandwich board outside was the best. It said, The Lobster Shanty, warm beer, lousy food, surly waitresses, rude bartenders, rough regulars and cranky cooks. Funny.

That pretty much summed it up. It was also late night hang out for service industry people getting off work. I bellied up in order to beer. Lager. It was getting hot outside. They used to have a bartender that worked there in the early 2000s. Billy I think his name was. A stocky Irish guy. He always wore rayon shorts with no underwear. He left little to the imagination. Let's just say that.

Every time I saw him behind the bar, I would end up staying way longer than I intended to. He was so cute, and he was packing! I don't think he ever caught me staring, but boy, I would have jumped on him in a heartbeat. He was very sexy. I was hoping he was still working there. No such luck. I suddenly realized that I was horny. Oh well, barring a miracle, I wasn't going to run into any afternoon delight unless I went into Boston, and I wasn't going to do that.

Today was all about roaming the North Shore in the sunshine. And that's what I did. After a couple of beers, I decided to cab it over to

Marblehead and to go to the landing restaurant. They had a great view of the harbor from their patio.

Lobster, seafood, great chowder and good-looking men. Marblehead was a drinking town. The old joke was that it was a drinking town with a fishing problem. Instead of the opposite. I always saw so many handsome men. They were everywhere. Clean-cut dough boys or older men with cute faces and nice bulges.

This day was no exception. I scored a corner table on the patio with a view of the water and a view of the tourists. Perfect. I knew my waitress; Jade was her name. It was nice to see somebody I used to work with. We worked at the Sandbar together. She was a Goth chick with jet black everything and bright red lipstick. She had ivory-white skin, and she stuck out like a sore thumb amongst all the Swedish Aupair and conservative Martha Stewart-types. I liked her. She had a fuck you attitude about most things. I think she was treated like shit by all the "Stepford" wives in town. She said, "What the hell are you up to? When did you get back to town?"

I filled her in on everything, where I was working, and I told her about Brian. She and I were close for a while when we worked together. We sort of both had the "outsider looking in" thing going on.

I said, "Listen, I'm gonna camp out here at your table, and people watch. I've come to spend money and stare at men. What's good?"

"Dom Perignon," she said, "$80.00 a bottle." "Get the fuck outta here," I said. "Really?" "Yep," she said. "Don't know why, but that's the price." "Bring that shit on," I said. I had no idea why it was so inexpensive, but I wasn't gonna argue. "Bring two glasses," I said. "We need to toast."

It turned out to be a fun afternoon. I ordered some oysters from Jade, sat back and stared out at the harbor, took it all in. State Street Landing is where the restaurant was and where I would leave to fish lobster with Captain Billy. A bit of nostalgia crept in.

It was nice to see the boats going in and out. Guys dropping off their catch for the day, tourists and their kids asking questions to the fishermen, the restaurants were busy, and it was a good time.

I looked out across the Harbor at the Corinthian Yacht Club and its sprawling deck. It was a good distance away, but I could see that it was packed with people also. The view from the patio of the Corinthian is so beautiful. Absolute magic. Everything you could ever ask for from a New England town. From Marblehead neck looking back across the harbor the view was spectacular. I worked a couple of weddings there as a hired gun. Marblehead is an old money town and people spared no expense to have their weddings at the Corinthian. The space was beautiful. The grand ballroom, the dining room and the lounge were all encircled by a wraparound deck large enough for at least 500 people. Working weddings at this place with some of the best times I had as a bartender.

Everybody drank. Including me. One for you, one for me was how it went during weddings. The old money New England blue bloods weren't exactly known for being good tippers, but this was a different generation. They tipped very well. And the eye candy was everywhere. I was in heaven. They were all straight and usually married which made them even more attractive to me. Forbidden fruit I suppose. The combination of handsome men, the beauty of the harbor of this little New England town was so appealing to me.

At the time it seemed like everything I ever wanted. It seemed like the farthest away from Roxbury I could ever get. I decided to finish up at The Landing and head over for a visit.

The good thing about being in a boating community was that there was always someone willing to give you a lift across the water. The Corinthian had a couple of skiffs at their disposal for transporting members back to the mainland they had too much to drink. Or didn't live on the neck. They were always running, and they pulled right up to The Landing.

I settled up with Jade and we made plans to have a drink in town after her shift. I walked down the gangway or plank and down onto the dock. One of the Corinthian skiffs was pulling up, and I said, "Hey, can you take me over?" "Sure, no problem." Marblehead was cool like that. It was a short ride; less than five minutes And I was the only one on the skiff headed over.

Walking up the stairs to the Corinthian was always a treat for me. It was like a different world. Everything was so clean and beautiful. Flowers were everywhere. It was an enormous Sea Gray structure built upon a jetty. 240-degree views of the harbor and points East.

Weekly races every Wednesday night. Friendly competition with the other yacht clubs on the harbor. Annual Regattas such as Marblehead race week and the Corinthian classic yacht regatta were honored traditions there. More than sailing it offered tennis, swimming, and sailing lessons for members and guests. There were two types of memberships. A social membership for those who didn't sail and a yachting membership. They both offered the same amenities with the except exception of a mooring for yachting members.

I was almost never there but I knew the catering director and one of the chefs. So, it was easy to pop in for a drink or two and shoot the breeze. Today was no exception.

Feeling fine I walked up to the main deck, turned around to take in the view and took a big breath of air. As it is at most private clubs, you don't use cash for anything. Dinner, drinks and snacks were all signed for. I poked my head into the kitchen and found who I was looking for right away – a psychotic 5-foot Thai woman, loud as hell, with the thickest accent and broken English, and an ever-present glass of Merlot.

"Shorty!" I yelled to her. Her real name was Pat. "Holy Shit, Cleaves! What the fuck are you doing here? I thought you died, motherfucker!" I loved her. She gave no fucks.

"I came over to have a drink," I said. She cracked me up. When we worked weddings together, regardless of the time of day I would say

"Hey Pat, you want a glass of Merlot?" Her response was always the same. "Sure, I have a glass of Merlot." I love working with her. She was a pistol. She was a hard worker, lightning fast and she pulled no punches. She always talked about killing her husband, jokingly. I think. One of these days I gonna kill that fat bastard she would say, and then stare off into space as if she was planning it in her head.

It made me roar with laughter. I believed her. "Have a seat at the bar," she said. "I be right out. Order a drink, anything you want." She was very gracious. So, I did. She came out a few minutes later yelling something in Thai back to the kitchen. She climbed up the bar stool next to me and sat down. "Fucking white people!" she said. Another belly laugh from me. "Where the hell have you been," she asked?

I filled her in on everything over the past couple of years, and I told her I was at Rockafellas for the season. "Oh, good money there," she said. "Yeah, it was fun," I said. "I could always use you for a wedding here and there if you want to pick up some extra cash." "Sure," I said. "If I'm free, I'm all yours."

"You remember the last wedding we work together," she asked me? "I sure as hell do," I said. It was the Summer of 2000, I think. A massive 500-person wedding was booked at the Corinthian. The entire event lasted the whole weekend. The wedding itself was on a Sunday but the catering and waitstaff were there all weekend setting up. myself included. It took the whole weekend just to get the place ready. Tables, chairs, the four bars, the dance floor, the Flowers and the rest. Everything was in white. It was gorgeous.

They were relatives of the Commodore at the time, I think. They sure spend a lot of money on this wedding. On the night of the event everything was perfect, we busted our asses making it so. The candles were lit, it was sunset, and the tables were adorned with Calla Lillies and Dendrobium Orchids. Sparkling glassware and Crystal champagne glasses. Perfect.

I had the main bar at the end of the ballroom with a view of the harbor in front of me and the illuminated swimming pool out the windows behind me. A perfect spot to take it all in. The groom had requested Dark and Stormy's as his specialty drink for the event.

Goslings Rum and ginger beer. Sort of a sailor's drink. The wife went with a Vesper. Nice choice. Didn't see that coming. They were all big drinkers.

The sun was setting, the water took on my coveted mercurial tone, the tables were sparkling, and the bride and groom were introduced. It was party time. Holy shit! Could these people ever drink! I was slammed right away. No problem. And no shortage of handsome men to enjoy.

As was tradition, the first rounds were Dark and Stormy's and Vespers to honor the bride and groom. After that, anything goes. Mostly vodka or beer. One for you, one for me. We were slammed busy. I was in my wheelhouse and loving every minute of it.

Pat would send word from the kitchen every half hour or so. "Hit me" was the message from her carried by one of the wait staff. That meant four fingers of bourbon in a paper cup. Then people began to dance.

I had a view of it all. Usually at conservative weddings, people didn't really let loose and dance. People were self-conscious and sometimes kept a drink in hand as sort of a security blanket. Not these people. They were dancing! Throwing down in fact. It was fun to watch.

The band played some old school P-funk, Rick James, The Commodores, and even some Reggae. Occasionally, I'd catch one of the groomsmen giving a heads up to one of his cohorts. A little secret nod of the head or a hint saying let's go. Off to the bathroom to do some blow. It was so obvious. It made me laugh. Eight guys walking out of a bathroom at the same time looking around to see if anyone noticed. They didn't.

At least three generations were represented at this event. I loved the sense of tradition.

The sense of family and the closeness they all seem to share was lovely. It was wonderful to see. I envied it. Then came the first dance. Everyone was seated so I had about 20 minutes to myself to take a leak and smoke a cigarette.

I did something completely different, however. I made a dark and stormy and went out back by the pool to smoke. The lights were off at the time and it was completely dark. It had been a hot day and I had been moving fast and hard for the last several hours. I thought, man a swim would feel so good right now. So that's what I did. I stripped down and jumped in. Completely naked.

I treaded water, nude, in the dark and watched the wedding guest dance. I felt like such a rebel. It was fantastic. I didn't have all that long so after only a couple of minutes I hopped out and got dressed. Feeling completely refreshed. I hustled back to my bar just in time for the end of the father daughter dance then just in time to hear one of the waiters say, Pat says "Hit me!"

I poured two shots of bourbon one for her one for me. What a splendid evening.

So I said to Pat, "Yeah, that was one hell of a night." We shot the breeze for a while and she said she had to get back to work. She sent out a plate of enormous shrimp cocktail. How could I refuse?

I ate a few and stared out at the water. It was around 4:00 p.m. when I got a text from Jade saying she would be done soon and was I still up for a drink downtown?

"On my way to you," I said, and headed towards the skiff. I left the bartender a bunch of cash as a thank you. They never get cash at the Corinthian. Everything is signed for. He was surprised. The sun was still out in full force. Walking down toward the waiting skiff I thought, this is the life for me. How can I swing this on the service industry salary? With the right gig, it's not that hard actually.

The ride back was just as lovely. Seeing all the activity at The Landing, the color of the sea, the people buzzing back and forth. I caught sight of Jade right away. All jet-black hair, clothing and nails. With her pale skin and bright red lipstick smoking a cigarette leaning against the railing. She stuck out like a sore thumb. She had a look on her face that said, "I wanna kill all these fucking people." I just laughed. I liked Jade.

I walked up the Gangplank to meet her. "How was the Corinthian?" she asked. "Lovely as ever," I said. She knew I was a ghetto rat and had an affinity for the place. "I need a stiff drink," she said. "Let's get out of here."

I laughed. "Right behind you!" I lit up a smoke as we walked a block to her car. It wasn't cool to smoke on the skiff over. I could have, but it's considered "bad form," so I waited. "Where do you wanna go?" I asked. "The Riptide," she said. Perfect.

Chapter Twenty-Nine

Back to Seattle

The Riptide was a dive bar if Marblehead ever had one. It was on Pleasant Street downtown near a place called Five Corners. Kind of the center of Marblehead. It was called that because it was a giant intersection with five corners instead of four. Pizza shops, a couple of restaurants and a bank.

I said, "What? You don't wanna go to the sandbar?" "Fuck no," she said. We both sort of hated that place after working there. The Riptide was for professional drinkers. Fishermen, landscapers and construction guys. All the blue-collar people in town. It was always dark in there. I loved that place. Even if it was a beautiful and sunny day, once inside the 'Tide', darkness. And it smelled like a bar. It didn't stink but it smelled like liquor. It had one pool table and a jukebox filled with classic rock. Good stuff. A handful of tables scattered opposite the bar.

They had a full menu, mostly burgers and fries. Comfort food. But people came here to drink. Jade and I took over the corner of the bar, it being L shaped. I asked her to switch seats with me. Why?

I nodded my head to the right. Hotty alert I said. She just laughed.

Man whore! A fisherman I think he was. Just a beautiful face, nothing more.

The good thing about the Riptide was that they were known for pouring strong drinks. Even for me. I took a sip of my vodka tonic and said holy shit! I remember now! Gotta be careful at this place. The Riptide was always busy. Today was no exception. Guys fresh from a day of fishing or mending traps, carpenters, masons, all locals and they all came to drink. I was having a good time staring at the fellas and catching up with Jade.

I did have to be a little careful I have been going at it most of the day and it was starting to catch up with me. I would nurse and the next one I thought. Jade and I were catching up and splitting an order of fries when I heard someone yell from across the bar "Is that you Cleaves? Eddie fucking Cleaves!" It made me laugh.

Why was everyone addressing me this way? I must have forgotten something. "Tom!" I said. "What the hell, man? It's been forever." Tommy Monaghan was a very handsome, stocky Irish bartender. We work together at Flemings steakhouse in the Back Bay of Boston. I knew of him first from the landing restaurant. He was a bar man there.

What a looker he was. "You back in town for good?" he asked. "I'm in Swampscott at my old place," I said. "Damn good to see you. pal." He stood in between Jade and I at the corner of the bar so he could talk to us both at the same time. I put my arm around his waist. I didn't care. He knew I was gay, and he didn't mind. I think he liked the attention. I think his image of a gay man was that of a frail effeminate man with swishy gestures.

I blew that notion completely out of the water for him. I always thought he was a bit curious. All that aside, Tom was a good man. A stand-up guy. He always did the right thing and it was a damn good bartender.

He always kept his cool no matter how busy it got. I wished I could do the same. Every once in a while, I would blow a gasket if I was working the service well at Flemings. Not Tom, cool as a cucumber he was. It was about 5:00pm by this time so I set up a deadline at 7:00pm to be home and showered up. I would need some rest before starting work the next day. I figured I may as well have supper here, so I ordered a bunch of wings and some burgers for us to munch on. Better to try and soak up some of this vodka then to keep going at the rate I was. I never liked getting wasted. That cut the evening short and it meant I had to stop drinking. I didn't want to be forced to stop. That was amateur.

The food would help. It took quite some time to arrive as the bartender was also the cook. Not the best idea. There weren't as many people at the riptide this night. Lunchtime was always packed though.

The nostalgia began to wear off, and it was time for me to go home.

I suddenly grow weary of writing about my escapades under the influence.

I will say a bit more about my time with Paul and Swampscott and then onto my return to Seattle and the coming season in hell.

My time with Paul that summer and early Fall was sorely needed. Work continued and so did my drinking. On a maintenance level mostly. No black outs, no face plants. I never got drunk at work although I drank at work. There was a liquor store next to the post office on Essex St. and they opened early.

I would grab two pints of vodka to get through the shift. I would drink it just to get ready to want to talk to people. Between my anger, the vodka, and my newfound righteous indignation, I had all the fuel that I needed to feign a smile and make some money.

And so it went for the next several weeks. I had a heavy workload at Rockafellas and a heavy workload at home. Paul's condition would ebb and flow. Some days he could move, some days not so much at all. There were times when he couldn't get to the bathroom without help. It was my pleasure to help, that was automatic. But every time I did, I came to the realization that my tank was empty. He wasn't incontinent thank God, but he needed a lot of help. Again, I felt the feeling like my energy was draining out of me. I simply had nothing left. The thought of caring for someone on a full-time basis, and working a restaurant job made me not only angry, but bitter. I was tapped out. It had nothing to do with Paul. He is family. That's what you do for family, and under normal circumstances I would have easily assumed the role of his caretaker. He needed help. I needed help. I already knew I would be returning to Seattle after the Halloween season, but I wouldn't leave until Paul had the proper care that he needed. He contacted senior services. He was able to set up visits by nurses just about every day.

Paul is a proud man and he tends to refuse help at almost every turn. Except from me. His doctors wanted him to walk with a cane. He refused. He would fall down a lot. He still does. Stubborn Irishman.

I admire him for it. But it is worrisome. Paul is a formidable character to say the least. He'll fight you tooth and nail for what he believes is right. The man won't give an inch. No quarter. I'm proud of him for that. We had similar childhoods, he and I. Paul D. is no pushover, that's for sure. His stubbornness, however, has gotten in the way of his self-care. The stairs leading up to the side of the house, his most used entrance, are concrete and one good fall could take him out. Throw in rain, snow, and ice and those stairs were bad news.

Still, he refused to use a cane. It scared the hell out of me. *Just use the fucking cane,* I would say to myself. Any ability or willingness to be a primary caretaker again was gone. I would reach down deep, but the truth was that I was done. Halloween month was in full swing, I was working like crazy, self-medicating with booze ,and trying to keep it all together.

I missed Brian and I wasn't done mourning him from Seattle. The pull to return was strong. I would miss Paul.

With his now daily nurses' visits, Paul had a little more strength. We hit a good stride the last four weeks I was there. I'd get up, make a drink, shower, bound down the stairs for coffee with Paul, and then out the door to work another double shift most likely.

This was pretty much the entire month of October. I knew I would miss Paul. A part of me knew that he would feel abandoned. That simply wasn't the case. There was nothing I could do about it. I told him that I needed to be back in Seattle. I left a well-paying job and a lovely home for the uncertainty of what lie ahead back in Seattle. I didn't care. I needed to be closer to Brian and that meant returning.

I wanted to be in the area where Brian and I lived. I couldn't explain it. I could tell Paul was hurt. And concerned. I think he thought that I was going to drink myself to death if I didn't stop going the way that I was and get some grief counseling or get back into A.A. or both.

I was fine with grief counseling, but I wasn't going back to A.A.. Not yet. Paul said, "With the amount you're drinking, it looks like you're trying to kill yourself Ed." He was genuinely concerned. I was not suicidal; I was in pain. Remember, my appetite for booze tends to surpass that of the average addict.

The pain I felt would not go away. More pain, more booze.

Salem had turned into an all-day all-night celebration of Halloween. You couldn't move on any given street in the center of town without bumping into people. It was a zoo. I didn't end up working the actual Halloween night, however. I left the restaurant a couple of days before that.

Rockafellas had reached capacity or full occupancy every day and night for the previous 14 days. 130-ish people jammed shoulder to shoulder drinking and trying to eat. It was almost impossible to move, let alone wait tables. The only free space in the whole joint was either behind the bar or in the kitchen.

By this point, I was done. I had been burning the candle at both ends for over two months. I spent the actual Halloween night at home drinking vino and handing out candy to the neighborhood kids. I hadn't been home on Halloween night in years and I had a blast. Paul wanted no part of it. He stayed in his room and read. He could see the front staircase from his chair in the window. I knew he was enjoying watching the trick-or-treaters climbing up the stairs in anticipation of chocolates and candy.

Paul's house was the biggest and most beautiful on the street. We couldn't disappoint, and we did not. We had a shit load of candy and chocolate for the kids. It was a lot of fun. Afterward, when the last trick or treaters were gone, I brought my glass of wine out to the back deck to smoke cigarette. I kept it in a coffee cup out of respect. Although I was drinking, I wasn't going to flaunt it in front of Paul. I sat down, lit up a smoke, and took a long drag.

For the first time, I could feel a real chill in the air. It felt ominous almost. Winter was coming to the North Shore. It was coming to Seattle too. I told Paul I would return in the Spring and I meant it. It was easier to leave knowing that he had proper care in place. I boarded my flight a few days later and was on my way back. To what I really didn't know. I was glad to be returning. After collecting my luggage, I went out to the smoking section at SeaTac and lit up a smoke.

It tasted good after a long flight. It felt so comforting to be back in the Seattle Grey. It wasn't raining, but everything was wet. And the cloud level was low on that day. It hadn't dropped yet but it was nice and grey. Blanketing the city.

My chef buddy and former boss Brad picked me up at the airport. He offered me a place to crash for a few days. I was grateful. I planned on staying with Bob for a while, but he was away on business. I had no real plan to speak of other than getting a job somewhere. But not right away. Somehow being back in Seattle put me at ease. I felt like I was closer to Brian again. Like he was still here. I was grateful for the grey.

Brad, being a chef and a Sicilian, always had wine on hand. An endless supply it seemed. Back at his place, he put on some music on an old turntable. LPs? No one played actual records anymore. The sound the needle made hitting the record brought back memories and a rush of excitement. Brad loved music as much as I did. Maybe more. He had a huge collection of records and CDs. At least several hundred of each. It took up an entire room at his restaurant, The Swingside Cafe —one of the craziest and most wonderful places I've ever worked.

Brad cracked a bottle of red. A big Oregon Pinot Noir. Perfect for the weather. We lit up a couple of smokes and went out to his porch. Leonard Cohen was playing. *Nice selection*, I thought. Brad was an old beat poet and hippie/mystic from way back. He was able to see things from many angles like I could. And naturally. I think that's why I liked him so much. We were close for a few years.

I met Brad in 2006, I think. He owned this small, funky, bohemian joint call The Swing Side Cafe in Fremont, Washington, right across from the Buckaroo Tavern. A New Yorickan buddy of mine, Anthony, was working there, and I went in to pick him up after his shift one night.

I didn't know much about the place. It was small, but not too small. A total of 11 tables divided into two rooms with what was most definitely a tiny kitchen. Barely enough room for two people. Brad and I hit it off right away. His pulse was always on the one. He could see, like I could.

The name "Swingside" had two meanings: one was baseball. Brad was a fanatic. He was from Monessen, Pennsylvania. Monongahela to be exact or Mon-city as the locals called it. He was also a musician, and on the weekends, or at any given time really, he would pull out a corner table in the dining room, and a band would play. Usually a two piece. Stand-up bass and guitar. A lot of solo acts like Jim page or Orville Johnson would play. Really good stuff.

The walls of the restaurant were adorned with pictures of old baseball players and old musicians mixed in with a lot of Catholic iconographies. Brad was a Catholic, and like a lot of Catholics, he had a lot of love and a lot of anger. I would watch him give the shirt off his back to a stranger and then threatened bloody murder to someone he loved. Fucking hot-blooded Sicilian.

The Swingside had many, many regulars and one of my favorite things about working there was when after a busy night, Brad would make a big family meal for us all. We would open some vino and the staff would all dine together, smoke and talk shit about the night or just unwind.

People from all over would wander in to see Brad, drink some wine, and shoot the breeze. All different walks of life. And pretty much on a nightly basis this would happen. It was fun watching Brad hold court on many different subjects. The Raconteur that he was.

Invariably someone would break out the blow, and the party would kick up a notch. Late night and early morning chinwags or heated debates about everything from politics to religion to music to fucking whatever would ensue. Sometimes very heated passionate debates. Almost actual fights. It very rarely came to that. Then great oaths were sworn, hugs exchanged, and conversations resumed.

I worked for Brad for a few years off and on. I had a wonderful time at the Swingside, and the time I got to spend with Brad, I'll never forget it.

After 25 years, he decided to sell the place. He was ready to move on to something else. Visitors, requests and reservations came pouring in. It was sad to see it go. An institution was closing its doors. Captain or "Cap" as I called him was moving on. He sold it, the land and the house above the restaurant to a developer who quickly demolished it and put up one of those cookie cutter- ant farms I like to call them. Overpriced almost prefab apartments that took over the Seattle landscape.

They were popping up everywhere. Old Seattle institutions were being torn down to build these flavorless structures to support the huge influx of people moving to Seattle for tech jobs. Thousands and thousands of people. Seattle was growing exponentially.

While it was good for business, especially mine, the city's infrastructure and housing rental market was unprepared. The techies snatched up everything that was available. The rents sky-rocketed, inventory was depleted, and the average Joe was forced to look further and further outside the city for affordable housing. Same old story.

Shit, as of June 2020, a one bedroom in Seattle starts at about $1700 a month. If you're not a techie or making at least $80,000 a year, you're not going to get ahead monetarily. You're not going to be able to save money. You will work simply to pay rent and buy food.

Look, change is inevitable, and I certainly welcomed it to Seattle. The city grew so big and so quickly and right before my very eyes. The South Lake Union area was pretty much bought up by Paul Allen, and office buildings went up left and right. Amazon moved in and gobbled up a bunch of office space and just like that. South Lake Union was its own thing. All tech business. A slew of new restaurants opened to feed all the new faces they even had their own trolley. The South Lake Union Transit, or S.L.U.T. Ride, the slut T-shirt started popping up everywhere. Hilarious. The transit folks were not amused.

It always amazed me how people could miss the obvious joke staring them right in the face. S.L.U.T!

There is a Senior Living center called Senior Housing Assistance Group or S.H.A.G for short. Their advertising always cracked me up. Showing active seniors playing tennis or drinking wine. Come down to SHAG! I guess they didn't know that shag was British for let's fuck. Whenever I see ads for senior living, it always seems to me like they're saying, "Come live here. You ain't dead yet, motherfucker! We have wine!"

The entire city of Seattle, not just South Lake Union, was peppered with new restaurants. Mostly upstarts or mom and pop joints. The thing about these new places was that they were good. This new generation of Chefs and Restaurateurs were doing their homework.

Scratch and craft cocktails were taking off. Breweries in artisanal beers were everywhere, even distilleries were making a name for this themselves in the city. It was great to see such fire and passion in the latest generation of restaurant people. Not only did it open new places to work with new things to learn but it gave us all new places to hang out and enjoy new takes on cuisine.

One thing that is great about Seattle is happy hour, and reverse happy hour period a lot of places ran it twice a day. 3- 5:00 p.m. or 4-6:00 p.m., and then usually 10 or 11:00 p.m. to close. You could get good stuff on the cheap. Happy hour in Seattle became huge. It still is.

Brad and I hung out for a few days. We went out to eat, and caught up on old times. For some reason, on our last night together, Bob Seger popped into my head, and I remembered the song, "Still the Same." It was a good feeling. It was good to see Brad again.

Chapter Thirty

First Rehab

February 5th, 2017

The night before my first ever rehab. I was at a Comfort Inn Hotel in Edmonds, Washington. By the grace of my friend Bob, I was here for the weekend to relax and to get ready for day one at Sea Mar Adult Rehab Facility in Seattle.

Twenty-eight days to freedom, right? Bob was kind enough to put me up until Monday. I had little money. I drank it all away. But I was sober when I checked in, and I was hopeful. Three nights in a very comfortable room with a giant tub and a flat screen T.V.

I was determined to stay sober, and I did. Bob gave me $100 for emergencies and food. On paper, this would have been a perfect opportunity to get drunk. A nice room, some money, and the Super Bowl! What the hell? The Patriots were playing the Falcons in Super Bowl 51. I must be a fucking masochist.

The perfect opportunity to get shitfaced and root for the Patriots. There always seems to be some big event about to happen right before I attempted sobriety. It was annoying. I did it though. I held fast and stayed sober. I knew I would. If I had reservations or didn't want rehab, I'd have gotten fucked up the minute I checked in. But I wanted this for me and for Brian. I took the time I had to rest and to catch up on some real sleep. There's a big difference between passing out and getting quality sleep. So that's what I did. There was a Safeway supermarket across the road. I went there to load up on provisions for the weekend. Cold cuts, hot pockets, and other assorted garbage.

Things I would never normally eat. Except for cold cuts. A good ham sandwich, right? I got a giant bag of fun size Snickers bars as a treat for the Super Bowl. I still can't believe I watched that game sober. What a game! Like everyone else, I thought it was over when Atlanta scored a touchdown to open the second half making it 28 to 3.

When the Patriots began their improbable comeback, I was in nervous wreck. I'm a huge Pats fan, and this was history in the making. I started eating those little Snickers bars and by the time the Patriots tied it up and sent it into overtime, I was scarfing them down one after another.

I couldn't believe it. The Patriots had all the momentum. I said to myself, if the Patriots get the ball first in overtime, this shit is over. I had to say it to myself because I had a mouthful of Snickers.

Atlanta's defense was exhausted, and I could just feel it. The Pats were going to score. James White's rush just barely over the line, and it was over. The biggest comeback in Super Bowl history! And I watched it sober. I ended up sick to my stomach from all the chocolates I inhaled in 18 minutes. I ate the whole bag. I felt on top of the world though. That was the greatest Patriots game I had ever seen. Never give up right? Isn't that how it goes?

I took a shower to try and relax. My hands were covered in chocolate , I was all hyped up from the sugar, and I had just seen the greatest game of my life. I was bouncing off the walls, but I was sober. I booked a cab before the game started to pick me up Monday morning at 7:00 a.m., and I wanted to be up early and showered and ready for it.

After my shower, I climbed onto the bed and messed around on my phone.

I waited for sleep to come. It wasn't always easy in early sobriety. It usually took a week to 10 days for my sleep to return to normal. I called Bob to assure them that I was ok and in no danger of drinking. I wasn't going to self-sabotage. I wanted this.

Besides, I have this uncanny ability to just shut it off when something big is on the horizon. It usually only lasted long enough to get done what I needed. I wish I could have used it for long term sobriety. I called Patty and said my goodbyes for the next 28 days and climbed under the covers with the T.V. remote in hand. By some miracle, I could feel sleep coming. Thank you. I turned over to sleep on my belly as I always do, and I belched a little bit. Snickers. Ugh. I almost hurled.

I thought about what was to come in the next month. I asked Brian for the courage to see me through this. I felt the familiar lump in my throat. And then I felt nothing. Blessed sleep had taken me. I was grateful, and sober.

My alarm went off at 5:30 a.m. I wanted a little bit of alone time with my thoughts and the hotel coffee before the taxi came to get me. I wanted to take one last shit in peace before I went in. I didn't know what to expect, but I suspected that this would be my last opportunity to take a crap undisturbed. I was correct.

I packed up the night before, so I was ready to go. I checked out at 6:30 a.m., and sat in the lobby of the hotel and waited for my ride. Right on time. "Let's do this," I said to myself.

All jacked up on coffee, I piled my shit into the trunk of the cab and jumped in the backseat. "Where to?" he said. I had given the destination to the dispatch yesterday, but the cabbie I got never received it. "Sea-Mar Rehab Center," I said. He just stared at me for a second.

"What Motherfucker?" I thought to myself. I was a little on edge.

A little touchy. I was heading into the unknown, and I was nervous. We made it there in no time, of course. When you're in a rush, it takes forever. When it's somewhere you don't wanna go, fucking presto! You're there in a flash.

My check-in time wasn't until 8:30 a.m., I think, and I wasn't going in one minute before. Even though this was something I wanted. I went and got another coffee. I still had almost a full pack of smokes, and I wondered how many I could smoke in an hour. Let's find out.

I sat on the bench across the street from this place and chain smoked like a lunatic for an hour. Then, with five minutes left, I crushed out the last cigarette I would have for a month. I thought about throwing the half pack I had left away, but I decided against it. I was still homeless technically and had a feeling I would need them when I got out. I would.

I walked across the street to the intake entrance. I started to cry. I felt like a failure in life. All I wanted was Brian in that moment. I felt so alone. It made me angry. My beloved anger stepped in and saved me. I bristled. I strengthened my resolve, wiped my face, and pulled the door open. "Here we go, babe, wish me luck," I said to Brian.

Intake was pretty much what I expected it to be. A ton of questions. They plied me with more coffee. I was so jacked up on caffeine that I could see around corners. I'm glad I stayed sober the weekend. A young girl came in for intake while I was still in the process. She was fucked up on something and was supposed to be admitted for treatment that morning. They told her no. She was refused. She was told to go back to detox and then to reapply for a bed.

Sea Mar wouldn't take you if you were on your drug of choice. I didn't know that. I'm glad I arrived sober. What would I have learned if I showed up there while still drinking? Nothing. I would have taken several days to clear my head so that I could learn something. I had no intention of showing up there drunk. I most likely wouldn't have gone at all.

Intake took a long time. Almost three hours. It should have only taken about 90 minutes but there seemed to be one crisis after another. Some alarm was going off here, another over there. *What the fuck did I get myself into?* I thought. I just kept drinking coffee and going to the bathroom.

The intake lady was a kind person. I was grateful. She could see that I meant business and I was there to learn. We finally finished around 11:30 a.m., and she asked me if I was hungry. I was. I needed something to soak up all the caffeine before I began fucking time traveling. I was wired!

"Lunch is about to start," she said. You can get something to eat and then rest for a bit. You're allowed to stay in your room for the first night without participating in any groups right away. I welcomed that opportunity. It had already been a stressful morning and all the caffeine didn't help.

She showed me to my room, and to which bed was mine. I had a roommate it looked like. He wasn't there, so I had yet to see who it was. I put my stuff on my bed, and after a thorough search of my property and my person, she led me to the kitchen area where lunch was being served.

But not before taking my phone, lighter, and cigarettes. I was wondering when that was going to happen. I would have turned them in if she missed them. I was there to learn how to be sober, and I didn't need the distraction nor the temptation. Besides, if you were caught smoking or with a cell phone, it was an automatic discharge. It was a no-brainer really. Just do the right thing.

We walked into the kitchen to see the staff handing out what seemed like a shitload of food. Potato salad, bug juice (Kool-Aid), and sandwiches. Ham sandwiches! Go figure. I felt a little better inside.

I'm not going to cover this ground again except to say that the hardest part of the whole thing was being in treatment on the first anniversary of Brian's passing. Thursday, February 9th 6:11 p.m., I stared at the clock radio they provided and cried. It hurts so badly. I wanted to die in that moment.

Then the craziest thing happened, I was sitting on the edge of the bed with my head in my hands, miserable, lonely, angry, and in pain when a song called "Happy" by the artist Pharrell came on. It was Brian's favorite song. I couldn't believe that it was a mere coincidence. Maybe I just didn't want to. Either way, I took it as a sign from Brian that he was okay.

The pain shifted. It went from sorrow to bittersweet relief. I felt that he was okay. I took a deep breath and exhaled loudly. I felt closer to him. Once again, I wiped my face and strengthened my resolve. Now I was ready to get this done.

As I mentioned, the rest of my stay there was spent with lunatic kids bouncing off the walls all day, every day. I think they were all on Adderall or some shit. Little fuckers. I hated them. The one good thing that came out of that place was an introduction to a program called FareStart. I didn't know it at the time, but that program would change the course of my life for the next couple of years.

FareStart is a nonprofit organization in Seattle that helps people to escape the traps of poverty, addiction, homelessness and hunger. I could almost literally go on forever about and sing the praises of this program. A representative from FareStart came to the rehab and spent a couple of hours telling us all that the program has done to help change people's lives. And it was free! All one had to do was show up, be willing to work hard, and learn. I was all in.

As were several of my fellow inpatients. A bunch of us planned to make it to this program and see it through. I was the only one that showed up. FareStart begins to the individual as a restaurant industry job training program for the homeless and the disadvantaged. They do so much more, but that's the training part of it.

A three-phased program stretching over a four-month period. The days were long, and the classes were tough. You hit the ground running here. What they also provided was free therapy, group counseling, and support on so many levels. I couldn't believe it at first.

They even provided shelter while you were in the program and working hard. Everything from renewing identification and Social Security cards to transportation vouchers and clothing and toiletries were provided. They helped with it all and at the end of the grueling four months, they even helped with job placement.

FareStart is a big deal in Seattle. It gives hope to people who feel hopeless. It adds to and reminds a soul of its worth in this world. Hundreds of people who give a shit about those who struggle. During his visit to the rehab, I peppered their representative with questions about this and that. You mean you guys really offer all that you say? I couldn't believe it. How had I not heard of this organization before? I had been in Seattle the better part of 20 years and I was clueless as to its existence. After his visit, I kept two copies of the pamphlets he handed out in case I lost one. That whole experience made my day. It gave me something to look forward to. I now had a plan. I now had a little more hope for the immediate future.

As I mentioned before, Sea Mar's lesson plan for recovery lasted only 21 days, and so for the last week, we just repeated week one. Way to go guys! I had checked out mentally halfway through anyway.

The place was a zoo, and I had to fight the noise and constant distractions to try and hear something that might help me to stay sober once I got out. You would think they would have a plan that would cover the 28 days a patient was in. Not so much. By the final week, I was a walking time bomb and ready to strangle those little bastards. They were all so young, and from the looks of it, had many more relapses to look forward to. Sad but true. Especially considering what these young people were up against. Methamphetamine, fentanyl, and heroin.

The odds were stacked way against them and a lot of them are not going to make it out alive. One of the two people I swapped phone numbers with overdosed on his drug of choice and died not too long after he left. The sad truth is that not many people get and stay clean and sober after their first visit, or ever for that matter. It takes a shit ton of hard work, surrender, willingness, and at times, a miracle for people to escape their addiction.

Addiction is no joke.

In a way, I'm almost lucky to only have an addiction to alcohol. With my insatiable appetite, I think I would have been dead a long time ago from the needle. I'm sure of it. I mean alcoholism is a living hell all its own and again it's the most dangerous drug to detox from without medical help. Fucking sweating, dry heaving so hard that you burst the blood vessels in your eyes and face, delirium tremens, seizures, and death. Not to mention shaking apart the whole damn time. Fun, right?

So why do addicts keep going back time and time and time again? All with the idea of expecting a different result. This time will be different we tell ourselves.

The definition of insanity as it says in A.A. is doing the same thing over that over and over and expecting different results.

The non-addict will never understand the phenomenon of craving. Merriam Webster defines it as

"an intense or abnormal desire or longing for something." But research by Cognitive Behavioral Psychologists and Scientists indicate that craving is a "complex multi-dimensional process involving high order mental functions. It is both behavioral and physical and involves many parts of our brain and biology and therefore it can't just be shut off like a light switch."

— – Purdue University Psychology Professor Stephen
T. Tiffany

For me, when the craving comes, it's all I can think about. I even feel physically different. It hijacks my mind and becomes an obsession. And sometimes, it's not even trigger based. I could be having a perfectly normal day at work or at home. No stressors to speak of. No subliminal childhood pain rearing its ugly head once again. And then, out of nowhere, it hits me. And it's terrifying. Especially if I've been working hard at staying sober and trying to rebuild.

If I don't counteract it with something right away, I am doomed to drink. When it comes to my sobriety, "Eternal vigilance is the price of Liberty" – Thomas Jefferson.

I know I will always have to be on guard against my disease, and for the rest of my days, if I am to live them happily and productively and for the most part, with steady work, I am able to live happy, joyous and free, albeit with a very cautious eye. But when the craving, comes it's a different story.

I find myself in a fight. Panic, sweat, shortness of breath and stone-cold fear are what I feel. I almost feel like I'm looking at the world through a charcoal screen. I can see the players and witness what's happening around me, but I feel like I'm trying to hide from a monster.

All of that, provided I even put up a fight. The times when I didn't fight it, it was like I was thinking consequences be damned. It's as if a switch is flipped internally and I am almost a different person altogether. As if there's some subliminal hypnotic word or phrase mentioned and all I want is a drink.

It's almost as if the choice has been made for me. This is the hardest part to explain to people. When the question of why did you pick up again comes, I can't always answer it.

With alcohol being socially acceptable, the alcoholic is considered weak and without moral fortitude. This is just not the case with so many of us. After a relapse, an alcoholic can easily find himself or herself destroyed after a run only to bang their heads against the wall saying, how could this have happened? Everything was fine and now here I am again.

No one is harder on themselves than an addict. So attacking the one that has relapsed could push them further into their addiction. That's how it is for me. I already feel like a piece of shit when I drink after a length of sobriety. Knowing that I may disappoint friends, loved ones, my significant other, I may end up on a run and lose my job, my home, or all the above.

That is the insanity they speak of in the big book of A.A. If the addict knows these things are on the line, then why in the world would they risk it? Let alone time and time again? That's the insidiousness of addiction. We, as addicts, fight an intangible enemy. We fight a disease of the mind, body, and spirit. We fight ourselves, and the worst part is, we fight everyone else, too. We are stigmatized, labeled as weak, selfish and uncaring of our loved ones and those in our lives.

It's just not so. At least not for this alcoholic anyway. The guilt and shame over drinking again is so intensely painful the next day that I can't bear it.

Now, throw in verbal attacks from people you love and respect, and it pushes me even further in. It's a hell I don't wish on anybody. So, if you know an addict, and you can't help them, at the very least, don't hurt them. They may just be on their last leg.

Chapter Thirty-One
Shelter and Shame

After an orientation with a guy that looked like Quentin Tarantino, I was accepted and was due to start day one the following week. Orientation for FareStart is every Tuesday. I had a little under a week to kill and I was still homeless technically. This began my first stay at a homeless shelter in Seattle. The William Booth Center it was called. Shelter for homeless Veterans on Maynard Street just South of Chinatown. It was run by the Salvation Army of Washington state. FareStart rented an entire wing to house their homeless students throughout the duration of the program.

My case manager Richard at FareStart secured a bed for me, and I made my way over not knowing what to expect. I was on edge and I felt like I had to be ready for anything. I'm glad I prepared myself.

Pioneer Square and Chinatown had its fair share of homeless people camped out or passed out here and there, and I just kind of followed the trail of homeless and addicted that led me to the Booth center. There were men out front smoking. Some in fatigues, some with injuries, and just about all of them looked like they were coming off or still on one thing or another.

I hit the buzzer at the front gate and told them my name. They buzzed me through the first gate, which led me to a small courtyard with a picnic table, some free weights, and a staircase that led up to a second level. They were small apartments or rooms up there you could rent if you were sober for a length of time. I walked past the picnic table with a couple of guys rolling cigarettes. I raise my hand to say hello. They just stared at me. *Fuck you*, I thought to myself. *Pricks.*

I was buzzed through the main door that led into a hall with the intake desk on my right. A stocky man with glasses and head-to-toe fatigues looked me up and down and said, "Have a seat on the bench behind you. I'll be doing your intake. I'm Mike."

"Ed," I said. "Thank you." I sat down. He seemed okay. The cast of characters that paraded by almost made me run out the door. I couldn't, though. I would have lost this opportunity at FareStart. By this point, I was so pissed off at the world, and at myself for being in this position that I just glared at anyone and everyone who walked by. Fuck them.

The residents here all had one thing in common. They were rife with indignation. All of them practically. They mostly behaved as if the world owed them something that they were cheated out of. It was constant, and it was everywhere.

The Booth Center had two main rooms. The FareStart wing, and the main room with the Vets and other homeless. All were military-style bunk beds stacked two high, and they seemed to go on forever. It was thoroughly depressing. *Where the fuck am I?* I said to myself.

Intake was done one on one in a private room behind the front desk. Mike asked me a series of questions, gave me a cup to pee in, and said bring this right back. You had to be clean and sober every day to stay there. They had a breathalyzer at the front desk, and no matter how many times you went in or out, you had to blow. It never worked. If they caught you, out you went. Men were kicked out every day with new men coming in right behind them. I assumed this place was transitional setting for men trying to get back on their feet. Short term.

I was wrong. Most of the men here didn't work for some reason or another. And the ones that did would come back from day labor acting like they just cured cancer.

It was the lack of gratitude I saw and heard that pissed me off the most. *Be happy you are sleeping inside,* I would think. Mike showed me to my bunk. After the paperwork part of intake, they took my photo, and put it on a key card for me to go in and out. I took the piss test, and then had to shower and give them all my clothes to be treated for lice. Standard procedure for any homeless shelter.

I was given pajama tops and sweatpants to wear, along with flip flops. The flip flops were extremely valuable I realized after stepping into their showers for the first time. Mike said always wear your flip-flops in the shower. It was awful. What I could only hope was soap scum covered the shower floor, along with hair and God knows what else.

I was afraid to touch anything. Most of the men here had been homeless for a long time, and hygiene was not a priority for half of them. Neither was flushing the toilet. I walked in so many times on toilets full of shit, and usually, the first thing in the morning. That was no way to start your day. *Good God, flush the fucking toilet!* I was given a locker assignment at a key for it to put my clothes in which were still being fumigated, so all I had was what I was wearing, my cigarettes, and my cell phone, along with my key card.

We would be lining up for dinner soon in about 20 minutes. "Okay," I said, and I went outside to smoke a cigarette. The men were loitering around. They all seem so angry. All of them. I got it; I could relate.

I spotted one of the guys from orientation at FareStart. Marcus was his name. A friendly enough, chubby black dude that had a look on his face that matched my sentiments exactly.

It seemed to say, what the hell am I doing here? I nodded at him, and he waved me over. Cool, somebody to talk to, I thought. He was a good guy. He lost a lot through alcoholism and shitty circumstances. We smoked, talked about FareStart, and what we were hoping to get out of it. He didn't seem angry like everybody else. Just a little lost. So was I.

I said, "I'm going to get some dinner wanna go?" I didn't mind sitting alone in this place at all, but it could have used a little conversation at that point. He agreed, and we walked in to get in line for dinner. The first time I could remember ever being in a chow line. I felt like such a loser. *What have I become?*

Brian was gone. Everything I loved was gone, and I was in a chow line. I felt so low. I kept telling myself, this is a means to a better end, Ed. *"Get through this"* became my mantra. A place of my own also became my mantra. The thought of it took over. A place of my own!

Somewhere I could lock the door behind me and shut the world out. No roommates, no one else. I would picture myself locking the door to my new place, sitting down, and exhaling the breath I've been holding for awfully long time.

Merle was the lead cook in the kitchen at "The Booth." A big, loud biker-type of guy with a Fu-Manchu and tattoos everywhere. He looked to be in his mid-50s, if I had to guess, and he looked like a bit of an ass-kicker in his day. He ran a tight ship and suffered no fools in the chow line.

"You guys are new," he said to Marcus and I. "Yeah, got here today." "Welcome," he said. I introduced myself and said that I had worked in restaurants, and I would be glad to volunteer to help with anything he needed. "You can sweep and mop the dining room after dinner, take out the trash, and wipe down the tables." "I'd be happy to," I said. It would serve as a distraction for me, plus I wanted to earn the meal I was about to eat. Meatloaf, mashed potatoes and gravy, and green beans. With bread and butter and bug juice. 150 men all yammering away and making a mess.

With all the noise in the chaos and general shittiness going on, there was one thing I notice about the place—the floors were clean. It didn't hit me until I sat down across from Marcus to eat dinner. Whoever cleaned the floors did a damn good job. Challenge accepted.

After dinner, Merle stepped out and yelled across the dining room for all to hear, "Who wants to help clean the dining room?" My hand shut up. "I do." I thought he had forgotten about me. He pointed at me without looking at my direction. He didn't forget. Only two more hands went up out of 150. I was happy because that meant I would most likely be able to clean up after every meal of the day. At least until school started.

FareStart didn't want their students working full-time. Even part-time was discouraged because the days were so grueling. They were right. The days were long and busy. Standing all day, learning how to use a knife at first, taking life-skills classes and learning about all that could happen through hard work and dedication with the program.

It was almost 40 hours a week with at least two to three Saturdays thrown in every month to bring food to the other shelters in Seattle. Seeing some of the other shelters made me feel a little bit better about being at the Booth Center, as shitty as it was. Some of these other shelters were downright awful. Filthy, bedbug ridden, and depressing. It offered instant perspective. It could always be worse I would say after doing a shelter run, as they were called.

Richard, my case manager at FareStart knew I was a worker, and when I pushed him for at least a part-time job, he didn't fight it too hard. Just wait until you get used to the pace here first, and then get a job. It was good advice.

Although the place was cleaner than just about every other shelter in Seattle, the shelter life still sucked. In every way. The men were loud, dirty, selfish, and mean to each other. And these were just the ones without mental health issues.

I'm not without empathy for anyone who suffers, but it is awfully hard to sleep when your bunkmate next to you is face down on the floor screaming at God knows what at 3:00 a.m. It does not make for a good night's sleep. There were men that suffered all sorts of PTSD, night terrors, screaming, and walking around at all hours of the night, and it made it difficult. I try to see the good in everyone if possible or put myself in their shoes for a split second before I judge, but there are simply just shitty people in this world. That's all.

People that will take advantage, steal, beat women, and fuck you over given the first opportunity. The Booth Center had its fair share of these types of men. I would bristle every time one came near or just walked by me. White trash, brown trash, it didn't matter. If you sucked, I knew it, and I didn't want you anywhere near me. I was constantly on edge in that place.

The only positives I took from it were FareStart and being hired by Merle to work in the kitchen. I could spend as much time in there as I wanted. Prepping lunches for the men and helping to prepare meals. There was always something to do and the dining room was locked in between meals because the residents couldn't clean up after themselves, so it became off limits. Which meant, if I had a break, I could do my homework from FareStart, or read quietly.

It was my oasis, and I was grateful for it. Richard gave me a lot to look forward to. He helped me keep things in perspective and reminded me to stay focused on the finish line. He also gave me a heads up about a severely discounted gym membership at the YMCA downtown if you were a student and living in a shelter. $12.00 a month for a full membership! I couldn't believe it. I'll never forget Richard, and all that he has done for me. He is a good man.

I took advantage of the membership right away. The first day back at the gym was tough but good. I walked up to the Y, crushed out my last cigarette and got to work. I was out of shape, but like always, the first workout after a long layoff does wonders for my overall well-being.

My hopes skyrocketed. I saw more clearly, and I was calmer. For a while anyway. At least until I returned to the shelter. I now had a full schedule. Between school, the gym, kitchen work at the Booth, and a new part time job at a Sports Grille called The Lodge in Pioneer Square, I was constantly moving. It made sleeping at the shelter a bit easier because I was so tired by lights out.

I changed bunks to a corner bed, so I had walls on two sides of me and I could see the entire room. It made me feel better, knowing I could better fend off an attack from any one of the lunatics roaming the halls. With my schedule completely full, time started to fly. Richard said to me during our first meeting that it was going to go by quickly so try to enjoy what you can from this experience, and I did.

Marcus became a pal and we did a lot of our homework together. He was a funny guy. I was grateful. Having him around made schoolwork a lot of fun, and it made shelter life a little more bearable. Phase one and two flew by. I couldn't believe it. I only had five weeks left until graduation. Richard was right. It was flying by. I was working hard saving money from my part time job waiting tables at tending bar. The possibility of finally getting my own place were starting to look real. My body was getting stronger, and I was riding a pretty good wave. *A light at the end of the tunnel,* I thought.

Halfway through Phase two, FareStart moved me to a "better" shelter called the Compass Center in Pioneer Square. It was considered better because the residents could have their own room. It was supposed to be a lot quieter, and the bathrooms were said to be cleaner. They were. Thank God.

You don't get your own room, though. It's more like an office cubicle with high walls. No door, but it did have a big comfy bed with a light socket and the lamp at the head of it. A big standing wooden locker and plenty of storage space for clothing. It was considered to be a step up from the Booth Center. And in many ways, it was. It was noticeably quiet. Thank God.

The Compass Center consisted of several floors and the longer you stayed, the higher up you went. Supposedly the amenities were better. The residents were not, however. The same bunch of scum bags were littered throughout the building and outside. I could see them walking around just looking for something to steal. From a shelter! If you're gonna steal from someone in a shelter who's trying to get their life together, then to me, you're a piece of shit. If you have to steal, at least do it from someone whose cup runneth over. Go shoplift from a Safeway or something. So, with all the upgrades, the Compass Center offered, it was still littered with dirt bags. Fuck 'em!

There were many homeless people camped out in front of the Compass and under the viaduct where it was located. Unlike the Booth Center, it was not a place to hang out and smoke. On my very first day there, I was outside with all my gear waiting for intake, when a homeless guy walked past me about 20 feet, dropped his pants, and took a shit on the sidewalk. He just dropped a fucking deuce, pulled his pants up, and kept going. Like it was nothing. Welcome to the Compass Center. The front door was secured, so you needed a keycard to get into a hallway, which led to an elevator that required a keycard to activate.

Then, it went up two floors to the main intake area and housing for new residents. This is where I stayed. Occasionally, one of the crazies got into the lobby and would crap on the floor. Always right in front of the elevator. Why?! God, it pissed me off.

It was obviously intentional. Welcome to shelter life. Still, I was grateful for the quiet once inside. I could take a hot shower in a clean bathroom. The men on my floor took pride in keeping a clean house. We all took turns cleaning the kitchen and the bathrooms. Once inside, I could focus on homework and reading if I wasn't working a shift at The Lodge.

Chapter Thirty-Two

FareStart

The Sports Grille was located near CenturyLink Field where the Seahawks played, and on game day, it was a zoo. We would get crushed by fans before and after the game. I made decent money for a part-time job.

Other than dodging the homeless and the lunatics outside of the Compass twice a day, things were rolling along nicely.

Friday had come, and with it, graduation from Phase two. I traded in my ball cap for an actual chefs hat. On Monday, I would begin Phase three. A five-week fast-paced, intense phase that would see me cooking meals for the public.

FareStart owned the restaurant on the first level of the building on the facade of Virginia street. It was open for lunch only, and in Phase three, students did all the cooking. Under the watchful eye of chef trainers. They were known to be very tough on students during the last phase of training. They were tough on us during phase one and two also. I didn't know how much harder they could be on us, but I was ready. Chefs have a reputation for being dicks anyway, so I was used to it. The Chef trainers were super strict during this phase.

Trying to train people fresh off the street or straight out of prison wasn't easy. They had to be strict to install a sense of order and discipline to those who weren't used to it. Especially if you're going to work in a professional kitchen after graduation. There was so much to learn in a relatively short period of time. Hence the intensity of the program. I thrived on it. But then again, I had 20 years under my belt. A lifetime compared to someone walking into a professional kitchen for the first time ever.

It was trial by fire from the very first day. FareStart doesn't fuck around. I left school that Friday with my new Chefs hat feeling proud. I got a 98% on my final exam. The sun was shining, I had the day off from the gym and I was headed into work for Friday night shift.

I had a pay check at work for the last two weeks. Hourly pay without tips. It was better than I expected. $600. I'll take it. I had a little time before my shift, so I went to the bank to deposit my pay check. On the way there, I received a phone call from the attorneys charged with executing Brian's will. They had a check waiting for me for $5,000.

It was a partial payment from the money Brian had bequeathed to me from the sale of our home. It hit me pretty hard. I was once again reminded that he was gone.

The lump in my throat and the pang in my chest returned. They asked if I could come by and sign for it. I said yes. Their office was a few blocks away on 5th Ave. I still had time enough before work. It was a non-game night, so we weren't going to be that busy.

The check was made out to my name from the Estate of Brian E Smith. The Estate of…

I began to cry. I left the building and walked back towards work to deposit it into my account. I felt different. I was angry again. I was hurt, and I was angry. I left the bank and headed to work thinking of Brian and thinking of Phase three on Monday. I would not make it to Phase three…

That night at work was as I suspected it would be. Slow. No game in town meant only locals and commuters leaving from King Street Station. Commuter trains bringing people home to points North and South. Amtrak also had a train leaving several times a day up to Vancouver, British Columbia. Every day, I would walk through King Street Station and look at departure times for the train to Canada. I wanted so badly to just leave everything behind. Start again. Away from all of this. Every single time I saw the monitor with departure times, I would get excited. Vancouver.

I knew I would go. It was just a question of when. I finished my shift early and made my way back to the Compass Center to shower up and read in bed. I bought a few slices of pizza for dinner to eat in my room, even though it was against the rules. No one would bother me. On a quiet floor, my corner was almost without noise. I showered, ate dinner, and laid back to read. I felt, at first, I wasn't sure what I felt, honestly. The familiar pain of thinking about Brian had lessened a little bit.

I was angry sure, but wasn't I always?

What I was feeling was disdain, indifference. Even though I had all this momentum behind me, and things were progressing, something happened when I received that phone call from Brian's attorney. The chip on my shoulder grew larger. *Fuck everyone,* I thought. I fell asleep with a book on my chest. I woke up sometime during the night to take a leak and then crawled under the covers. Out like a light.

The next morning, I woke feeling rested and strong. I had the whole weekend to myself. Just a bit of homework relating to the beginning of Phase three on Monday. I dressed quietly for a run down to the gym.

I could feel a good one coming on. And it was. I tore it up. I left the gym feeling strong. Like I was getting back to my old self again. Except for this underlying anger I now had. I blamed everything for

Brian's death. I was bitter. I felt robbed. Despite having so many positives going my way.

On my way to get something to eat, I bumped into an old acquaintance of mine, Steven. He was off to have a bite to eat and was headed to the Owl and Thistle—an Irish pub just off Pioneer Square in Post Alley. I knew the place well. It was owned by a New Englander from Newburyport, Massachusetts, by way of Dublin, Ireland. I used to spend a lot of time there when I drank. It's a small place, a true Irish pub. Good food, and great Guinness. The last place I should be, but after three months of feeling like I had no control, it felt good to say fuck it, I'm gonna do what I want to do.

I didn't plan on drinking. At all. We ordered a couple of sandwiches, Steven ordered a Guinness, and just like that, the last few months of struggle never happened. I ordered an Imperial pint of Guinness, and marveled at the beauty of it as it cascaded down from the sides of the glass. With half of my sandwich eaten, I all but drank the entire pint at once. It seemed to me as natural as anything else in the world.

Any fears or reservations were gone. I was off till Monday morning, money in my pocket, and a handsome face to look at. Steven was a good-looking man. Irish, ginger. Extremely easy on the eyes. We stayed for a couple of hours. It was only 11:30 a.m. when we got there. They had just opened.

Steven could drink like I could. I didn't tell him that I was an alcoholic who just relapsed and was living in a shelter two blocks away. I just sidestepped his questions and lied about where I was living. On paper, I guess I didn't look homeless. And in that moment, I didn't feel it either. I didn't feel anything but the alcohol doing its job. It felt good. Incredibly good.

That began to run that lasted several months and cost several thousand dollars. All on alcohol. Steven and I said our goodbyes with plans to meet up again soon.

I stepped out into Post Alley and into the sunshine. The one thing I liked about the Owl and Thistle was that it was always very dark inside. But not today. The sun was out, and I intended to take advantage of it.

I bummed a smoke and a light from a guy standing outside. Marlboro Red. Perfect. I lit up and made my way towards the waterfront, only a block away. From Post Alley you would never know Puget Sound and the mighty Olympic mountains were just on the other side of the buildings in between.

I went for a stroll in the sunshine, staring out of the water. Feeling no pain. Whistling past the graveyard. I made my way to Elliott's Oyster House on the waterfront for oysters and beer. I suddenly realized I was lonely.

Not horny, just lonely. The bar was packed. Just how I liked it. I managed to get there just as a young couple was getting up to leave. Good timing on my part. A seat at the end of the bar just before the well. A view of the water and everyone at the bar. I ordered a Pyramid Heff and a dozen Shigoku oysters. A local strain.

The sun was glistening off the glassware and the fixtures in the bar. It was a beautiful day and I didn't have a care in the world. I drank quickly those first few pints to bury the guilt of knowing that I was fucking up.

After staring at the occasional handsome tourist, I got the bright idea of packing an overnight bag and taking the Victoria Clipper up to Vancouver Island, Canada. It left from pier 70. I was at pier 55. Not far at all.

But I didn't have my passport, so I closed my tab and headed back to the shelter to pack an overnight bag and get the things I would need. It took me all of five minutes to pack. This was a bad idea, but I didn't care. I couldn't see it at the time. All I saw was an escape. I was out the door in no time with my passport and my gym bag over my shoulder.

It was a good walk down to Pier 70 and I didn't bother to look up the ferry schedule. I hired a petty cab down in front of Ivar's Restaurant, and he peddled me down there in 5 minutes flat. The ferry was gone. I had missed the last one of the day. *No problem,* I thought. I would catch the Amtrak up to Vancouver instead. A bigger city and more opportunity I thought. For what, I didn't know.

I asked the petty cab if he could wield me over. "Sure," he said. "$20.00." No problem. It was worth it to me. He had a boom box and blared Rick James the whole way. I was loving it. I thanked him, and dashed into King Street Station to read the monitor. This time I was going! I was so excited, and then I read the monitor. The last train had already departed for the day. I was bummed out. My last option was to jump a cab over to Lake Union and buy a ticket on Kenmore Air. They flew up to Canada all the time. I wasn't going to spend $250 just for a half an hour flight no matter how badly I wanted to go North. I wasn't that drunk, not yet. Deflated but not defeated, I would have to wait to go to Canada.

Better to do it when I have more time to enjoy it, I told myself. Truth is, if the train was there, I was getting on it. I went to the King Street Bar and Grill a few doors down to get a beer. It was a bit of a dive, but they had good pizza. I bound down the stairs, I made my way to the bar, and before I got there, I heard, "Cleaves!"

A guy I used to work with was behind the bar. Ted, big Teddy. An affable drinker like myself. Black Irish, a bit of a belly. He wore glasses and had a nice package. Teddy was a looker that's for sure. I had always had a crush on him. He was my type and he was my bartender for the evening.

That's it, I said to myself, I found my place for the night. I could sit here, drink with Ted, and stare at him from time to time. Perfect. Ted was very sexy.

Ted drank behind the bar, with me doing shots from time to time. Teddy also liked cocaine. I just wished he was Gay. At least that night I wished he was. I wasn't greedy. "Just give me 15 minutes," I would say. Teddy knew I was Gay, and he knew I had a bit of a crush on him.

So, this was the beginning of a run that lasted a few months. I refused calls from everyone except for Bob and my sister Patty.

Richard called several times. I answered only once to say that I didn't know when I would return except that I promised I would. I stayed in shitty hotels, in bath houses, and kept my gym bag full of vodka and cigarettes once again. I was going to sound mental health to see my counselor L.T. and always with a water bottle filled with vodka and a mixer. Usually vitamin water to give it color.

I figured that seeing Brian's name on that check, written in the way that it was, was the trigger that probably set me off. Other than just being a dyed-in-the-wool alcoholic, I felt like, in some way, I was taking back control of my life by ordering that pint of Guinness. The goal now was to get stopped so I could finish school and get back on track.

The problem was, as long as I was drinking my pain, that wouldn't happen.

I went in to see Richard to figure out a plan of attack to get me back on course. I told him I was determined to finish what I started. He made it easy for me. You have to go back to inpatient treatment if you want to come back to FareStart. I fought him on it, initially. I just wanted to jump right back in. No dice.

I'm glad he held firm on that. I needed more time to clear my head before he let me back. It was what was best for me. Deep down, I had to agree. The thing was treatment centers were full at that time. I had about a two week wait, minimum. I had vodka in my bag and a little in my pocket, and I was homeless.

I left the meeting with Richard Miller and made my way to the Compass Center to get the rest of my belongings. I took a strong pull of vodka from my plastic bottle. No mixer this time, just straight vodka. I wasn't going back to that place sober.

I retrieved my belongings. I had accumulated a lot of clothing while I was there. So, there I was in the lobby of this place, sorting through my clothes, trying to figure out how much I wanted to carry on my back, and where I was gonna go.

The familiar pang of anxiety and hurt crept back in. *"Oh no you don't,"* I thought to myself. I pulled out the vodka and took another pull. I was so angry with myself. I whittled down everything to one heavy bag over my shoulder and left.

I was getting low on vodka and smokes and I would have to re-up. I made my way up to Capitol Hill, got my supplies, and sat on the bench across the street from the apartment Brian lived in when we first met. It felt safe there.

I lit up a smoke and began to cry. Fuck! It seemed like I was always crying. I spent another week in bath houses and a lousy hotel on Aurora Avenue in Fremont. It was a smoking room. It smelled like stale tobacco. I didn't care. The back window slid open and I could see the sunset over Mount Rainier and points South. It was pretty. It gave me some solace.

I loaded up on shitty frozen food, a couple of bottles of vodka, and stayed for several days. I would end up back here again for longer stay by the grace of Bob. Swooping in to pull my ass out of the fire once again. I don't know why he stayed friends with me, but I am grateful that he did.

For now, all I wanted was to be alone. I had plenty of supplies, so I locked the door, sat down, and poured a drink. It would be a while before I got into a treatment center, wherever that would be. But it had to be done if I was going to return to FareStart and return to health.

I got a call from my buddy who lived on Bremerton Island. He knew I struggled with the drink. He didn't know I was holed up at a hotel. Aurora Avenue doesn't have the best reputation. Dive motels and bars mostly. Especially North of the city. I told him I was waiting for a space to open at another inpatient program and he invited me to stay with him until that happened, I accepted. I was lonely at that point I needed to be out of that hotel. I was isolating.

I let him know that I was still drinking and would not likely stop until it was required to go to detox for three days before inpatient. Whenever that was. He said, "No problem, just get your ass over here." I was happy for a second. I made a drink, slammed it, packed my stuff, and checked out. I took a bus downtown to the ferry terminal and caught a ride over to Bremerton Island. It was about an hour ride.

It was always, always nice to be on the water. Between the fresh air in the vodka doing its trick, I was feeling better. Just being out of that room and around life again was nice. I didn't wanna talk to anybody, but it was nice. The ride over was as lovely as always.

Bremerton is a blue-collar town. There is a Naval shipyard there. It's still active. It's a town of about 40,000 residents on Kitsap Peninsula.

There's not much to do there either. Phil was an ex-Navy guy and a good friend of mine. He lived on what used to be Navy housing on Wheaton Way, a few miles from the ferry terminal. All the houses were cookie cutter and looked the same. Phil's place was a two bedroom in one of these. It was nice. Small, but very comfortable.

He was an avid book collector. They were everywhere. Hundreds of books on every subject under the sun. It was fascinating. I've been to Phil's place before. He was a bit of a homebody. When we first met, he was living at the Dolphin apartments just North of the University district—a funky little neighborhood with shops everywhere about a mile or so from the U-Dub campus. Just far away enough from the students and the lunatics.

Having arrived at Phil's, he greeted me with a big hug and took my bag. "What the hell have you got in here?" He said. *My life*, I thought to myself. Phil put me at ease right away. He knew I was drinking and said, "Make yourself at home, make a drink if you need to." I did. We sat down to catch up and I filled him in on my plan to return to treatment when it opened. Between myself, Richard and L.T. constantly checking for available beds, something was bound to turn up soon. I was grateful to them. I still am.

Phil liked to talk, which was fine with me. I didn't think he got much company now that he lived so far from the city. I could tell that he was happy to have somebody to talk to. I was happy to not be alone. The man could most definitely wear out any subject he was on.

It was impressive. I just laughed to myself. "What do you want for dinner," I asked? I was a culinary student after all. "I could whip something up or get a pizza from down the bottom of the hill?" "Let's go to the supermarket," he said. "I need to load up on groceries and I could use your help carrying it home." "We can get stuff for dinner and cook together." "Sounds good to me," I said. I made a to go drink and put it in my water bottle. I didn't go far without it. It had become a security blanket of sorts.

For some reason I always liked food shopping and cooking when I was drinking. Most of the times I wouldn't eat any of the food I was cooking but I enjoyed the process of prepping and cooking a meal. We got everything back to Phil's house and put it all away. Two giant rib eye steaks, asparagus, scalloped potatoes, and béarnaise sauce. A man style dinner I thought to myself. Simple easy and good.

Phil put on KNKX radio station—one of my favorites in Seattle. They had a Blues segment on Saturday night with limited commercials. It was pretty good.

I garlic-and-rosemary'd the shit out of the rib eyes and pan-seared them to medium-rare. Phil handled the asparagus and potatoes. With dinner ready, he and I sat down in front of his laptop to watch a movie together. He didn't own a T.V. I must have been hungry. I devoured the entire plate. I could feel it metabolizing. Which meant I hadn't eaten in a few days. I wasn't aware it had been so long.

I usually only eat just enough to keep drinking. I always tried not to eat too much because it would stop me from drinking lest I vomit.

Only just enough food to keep me alive. That night I did not drink much more. I was full and groggy. The steak and the Blues radio did a number on me and I fell asleep early. Phil was a late riser and I knew going to bed this early that I would be up before the dawn and in need of a drink.

Sadly, that was my favorite part of this whole shitshow—coming to too early and that first drink. Feeling it steady my nerves and it combined with music would charge my batteries once again. And that's what I did. 5:00 a.m. and I was wide awake. Phil's apartment was completely carpeted except for the bathroom and the kitchen.

He slept with a C-Pap machine on and one of those eye masks to block out the light. He looked like he was on life-support. It was worrisome. The sound of his breathing through the C-Pap reminded me of Brian. I put my headphones in and went to the bathroom to clean up. Not before I made a strong cocktail in a pint glass with a big chunk of lime. Gotta be wary of scurvy. I was in a Navy town after all.

I shaved, showered, and put on clean clothes. It felt good putting on clean clothing. Phil was still out cold and probably would be for several more hours. I had plenty of vodka left. I went outside to smoke.

It was a sunny morning, early, there weren't many people around yet, I enjoy the cigarette and enjoyed the quiet.

I stayed at Phil's until it was time to go into detox. L.T., my C.D.C counselor, called on a Thursday and said that Thunderbird Native American treatment center in Seattle had a bed for me on Monday, but that I had to be sober.

I needed to detox under medical care because of the amount of booze I was drinking daily. There was a detox in Port Orchard, across the water from Bremerton. Just a short ferry ride. I had to get my vitals checked and blood alcohol level to see if I was cleared for detox. I went to Harrison Medical Center and checked in. Detox was holding a bed for me, and would do so provided I stayed in the hospital until my results were in. And provided they prescribed Librium to bring me down from the alcohol safely.

I said my goodbyes to Phil and took a cab to Harrison medical. Roughly two miles away. *Here we go again*, I thought. The hell with coming off almost a gallon a day could only be helped with Librium. I couldn't just stop. I wouldn't. I wouldn't risk a seizure.

I checked in with no trouble. They said they were aware of a bed waiting for me at a Port Orchard Detox. It was gonna be some time. They were busy in the ER. I went outside to smoke. I sat down on the bench feeling defeated.

What would become of me? Was I destined to repeat this cycle for the rest of my days? I put on my headphones, lit up a cigarette and played "Sunshower" by Chris Cornell. I played it over and over. It always broke my heart, but it also reminded me to keep fighting. Not to give up hope. I tried to focus on my return to FareStart in the hopes of beginning phase three in six weeks possibly. Honestly, it was getting harder and harder to focus on anything. My body after a couple of hours was screaming for alcohol. It was agony.

I had to hold on to my chair to keep myself from leaving the emergency room. I needed either Librium or I needed a drink. Which would come first I thought to myself? I had no one with me to make me stay and there were more than a few times I got up to leave. I needed a drink. Goddamnit!

Every time, I just went outside and lit up a smoke. I couldn't bring myself to leave. Although I feared that after another hour or so of waiting, the decision would be made for me. *Please call me in*, I kept thinking. *Please.*

Welcome to the joys of addiction and the hell of coming down. Alone. I was on the verge of bolting when they called me in. Thank God. Librium! Just having it in my mouth was a relief. I knew it would lessen the pain and stop the shaking that was taking over.

They took my blood alcohol level, and it was way too high.

Because I have a mechanical heart valve, a lot of detox places won't take me in for treatment. They felt they weren't equipped to handle it if something went wrong. They weren't. But nothing was going to go wrong. I mean they never really were prepared for me anyway and the only thing that was really required was two pills at the end of the night.

Still I had to search for a detox. Sometimes to no avail. There were many times when I couldn't get to a detox regardless of my blood alcohol level because of my heart valve. I would have to walk into an ER and sometimes wait 12 hours to be seen. All the while, falling the fuck apart and risking a seizure. Many were the times I would just leave to ease the pain with more booze with the hopes of trying again the next day.

Harrison Medical got me into a bed, finally, and with the Librium taking effect, I could relax a little bit. It was only a matter of time before I was sober enough to get into the detox. Imagine that. I was too drunk for detox. That wasn't the case in terms of my balance and being able to speak clearly. My tolerance is so high that I could have an outrageous blood alcohol content and seem as normal as the next person. All or nothing right? I don't fuck around.

Almost a full eight hours later, I could go to detox. They sent me off in a taxi to bring me from Harrison Medical to KRC Kitsap Recovery Center. There I would stay until early Monday morning.

Detoxes are depressing places. If there is any good that comes out of them, it's that almost everyone there is asleep all the time. You could have 25 residents and barely see a soul. They monitor your vitals every few hours whether you're awake or not.

I basically loaded up on Librium and slept when I could. I was grateful to the staff at K.R.C. They were all ex-addicts giving back. One of the good things about K.R.C was that every hour on the hour they would herd all the patients together to go outside and smoke. It rained hard all that weekend. It didn't matter. I was already in hell.

As I mentioned, I got a message from L.T. that Thunderbird

Treatment Center had a bed for me Monday morning, and that a van would pick me up at the Seattle Ferry Terminal, cityside. This was good news. It would solve the homeless problem, and maybe just maybe, I would hear something that would help keep me sober. I was doubtful.

Cautiously optimistic? No. Just doubtful. Thunderbird allowed residents to stay up to six months or longer and even get a job while in treatment. That part was very appealing to me.

Monday morning came. The detox gave me two ferry tickets to get to Seattle.

Chapter Thirty-Three
A New Beginning

One ticket was from Port Orchard to Bremerton, the other from Bremerton to Seattle. I looked at the morning commuters and wondered about their lives. Most heading off to work. Clean and well dressed. And me, heading off to another treatment center. I felt so low.

It was raining early, I had practically no money, no cigarettes , and I was on my way to God knows what. I was thoroughly depressed at this point.

I recall sitting on the stairs of the Seattle Ferry Terminal with my entire life stuffed into two bags. My pictures of Brian and our notes to each other. I bummed a cigarette and waited for the van to come collect me. I can't remember ever feeling so low. A complete failure in life. What is to become of me? Will I always be helped along?

Pain came, then absolute fury. I stood up, grabbed my bags and waited on the edge of the sidewalk for the van.

Thunderbird had my cell number and the driver was half an hour out. I bummed another smoke from a passerby. He must have recognized the look on my face, or maybe he was just a kind soul, but he gave me a handful of cigarettes. That would hold me over until pick up. I thanked him, and off he went.

My pity party was over. Once again, my precious anger swooped in and saved me.

I pulled up my proverbial bootstraps and steeled myself to the task at hand. Twenty-eight days and back to FareStart. Back to life. It turned out that the minimum stay was 45 days. Whatever. Let's just get it done. The rest of my stay there was as I'd already mentioned. Fucking kids, noise, and lunatics bouncing off the walls all day every day. And Native time.

It was a nightmare. We went over the same shit that we did at the previous treatment center. Only they managed to spread a 21-day course into 45. I spent most of my time there fighting for peace and quiet.

The only thing I took from that experience was a lesson in something called "learned hopelessness" – a condition whereby an individual who has suffered a series of traumatic events over a long period of time may be made to believe that things will never get better. I can understand that, but I don't subscribe to it at all.

I can say that when things are going well for me for an extended period, I tend to get a little squirrely. I don't trust it. I run with it, but I don't trust it. I'm always looking around for something out of left field to ruin it. That comes from childhood.

Constantly being unaware of what was to come next. But hopeless? Never.

As the years have gone on, I've learned to roll with whatever comes. What I should say is, I've always known how. I just tend to care about it less and less now.

Forty-five days complete! It was March by this point. My return to FareStart! I was so excited. My first meeting with Richard Miller after treatment felt so rewarding. "I told you I would be back," I said. And I meant it. Something else happened also. I got my own apartment. No more shelter life.

It was an extremely small micro-unit in the Maple Leaf neighborhood of Seattle, just North of the Roosevelt neighborhood which was North of the University district. 254 square-feet. A closet. But I had my own bathroom, a shower, a microwave, and a sink. The rest I could improvise as needed.

What it had was... a lock on the door! I could finally lock the world out and exhale the breath I had been holding in since Brian died. Phil came over with an enormous air mattress, and Bob had a bunch of extra pots and pans and cutlery. A small foldable table, two lamps, and two bookshelves. I was moved in and set up in a matter of hours.

I went up to the local Safeway supermarket to load up on provisions. No frozen food. I went upstairs, put the groceries away, took my long awaited, long coveted walk to the door, and locked it. I locked the door. I sat down on the edge of the bed and cried. Finally. I was so happy, relieved, tired, mentally whipped, and grateful to be alone.

I opened a vitamin water and did what I had been waiting to do for so long. I unpacked. First thing I did was put up my pictures of Brian and me. I unpacked everything else and put it all away. I had suitcases at Bob's house with my most prized possessions in it. The photos and writings between Brian and me. I made a sandwich after unpacking. Yes, it was a ham sandwich, with some potato chips, and I propped up my cell phone to watch Saturday Night Live re-runs while I ate.

The door was to my back, locked. I had a view out of the slider window onto a major construction site. Not pretty but a view, nonetheless. I could see the sky at night. Other than that, I didn't care. I was alone. Sober and ready to rock and roll.

Phase three was beginning Monday morning and so was my return to the gym. I thought to myself, *once more unto the breach.* Only this time, I wasn't letting it go so easily. I left a message with Richard, "See you bright and early Monday morning."

Bright and early.

I couldn't wait.

Having a place of my own after so long, a quiet base of operation, I took off like a rocket. Full blast into the next phase of my life. No easing into it.

Day one of Phase three. I saw Richard across the room at all morning assembly. I couldn't contain my smile. Phase three was extremely fast-paced and I was already scrambling to keep up, trying to remember my kitchen math, and getting ready to cook on the line.

My knife skills were okay but remembering all my measurements right away was difficult. After a couple of days, I was up to speed. I had helped friends cook and had done some prepping in their restaurants before, so when I stepped on the line, it felt natural.

Phase three students were now cooking for the public. I started out on the cold side of the line making salads sandwiches and desserts. Each station had its own Chef Trainer and they were very tough. The lunch menu was expensive, and students were expected to take it seriously.

I loved the pressure and the fun of it all. I had a good time. Next was Sauté and Grill—my favorites. Extremely fast-paced. The whole idea was to slam the student with nonstop pressure to prepare them for life in a professional kitchen. Again, FareStart was no joke, but I was in my element.

The five weeks of Phase three were gone in the blink of an eye. I missed one question on my final exam. I'll take it.

Graduation day! I proudly stood next to Richard as he presented me with my graduation certificate, a food lover's companion and a brand-new set of Chef's knives, gifted to each student upon graduation. I felt such relief.

I felt proud. One, because I completed the grueling program, and two because I made it from the steps of the ferry terminal that day with my head in my hands to graduating and finally having a place of my own.

There was still so much work to be done. We had a graduation dinner and I was able to invite Bob as my guest of honor and introduce him to the entire faculty and student body. I had my turn to stand up and speak, and I said, "Without this individual in my life helping me time and again, I probably wouldn't be here. Both literally and figuratively. He's been my friend, my confidant, my coach and mentor, and he's pulled me back from the edge many a time. Ladies and gentlemen of FareStart, honored guests and fellow students, please help me honor Mr. Robert S. for all that he's done in my life."

It felt so good to be able to honor him in that way. He and I enjoyed a great dinner together, snapped a bunch of pictures, and had a wonderful night.

Having a base of operation all to myself made life so much easier. I threw away the cigarettes and returned to the gym. I took a job right away at Fisherman's Seafood Restaurant on the waterfront. It had an enormous outdoor patio with stunning views of Puget Sound and the mountains. It was located directly under the Great Wheel, Seafood, tourists and sunshine.

The season was beginning, and this place was a shit-show. I hit the ground running. I had as much work as I wanted, I was on the waterfront every day, and I was making good money once again. My body was getting stronger and at the end of every shift, I would walk past the stairs at the bottom of the ferry terminal, and it would bring me right back to that first morning out of detox, waiting in despair for what was to come next. I felt good about myself. It reminded me of where I was a few short months ago, but it also reminded me of my strength and resolve. I was grateful.

I killed it all summer long. Working and saving and going to the gym. I attended A.A. meetings every Friday night in my neighborhood, and even had a sponsor for the first time in years. Halfway through the summer season, I began to think about where I would work come September. Fisherman's was a ghost town after September, according to the long timers that work there.

I applied at one of the best restaurants in the city—El Gaucho—a legendary steakhouse in the Belltown neighborhood just north of downtown by a few blocks. I interviewed with the general manager mid-Summer, and she hired me on the spot for the Fall and Christmas season. Which meant I wouldn't begin until mid-October. I was over the moon. El Gaucho had a reputation for having some of the best servers and bartenders in the business. It had a beautiful sunken dining room with brass and glass fixtures everywhere. It was an expensive restaurant with a stellar reputation, and I was slated to begin relatively soon.

After my initial interview, I was walking along Alaskan Way, en route to Fisherman's, when I received a text confirming my employment and the proposed work schedule for the Fall and Winter. I couldn't believe it. I was so happy in that moment. I felt bulletproof.

My instincts told me to keep a cautious eye, and I told them to fuck off for five minutes and let me enjoy this. That was a great walk in the sunshine. I can still picture it. I worked my dinner shift and took the short ride home on the bus to make a late supper and go over my employee handbook from El Gaucho. Feeling good.

Morning saw me off to the gym before work. If I worked a double shift, and I was that day, I would have to exercise beforehand, or I wouldn't be able to do it at all. It made for an awfully long day, and I was tired by the end of it. It was always worth it when I could shower at the end, plop down on my bed, sprawl out all clean and ready to crash out. That's why it's important for me to make the bed right away when I wake up in the morning.

I plowed through the rest of the season at Fisherman's, sober, in shape, and with a healthy bank account. I was killing it at the gym, and

I felt strong. I could fall asleep looking forward to the morning instead of being afraid of it. I'd saved the most money I had in ages and was in no fear of being homeless for the foreseeable future.

I began to shift my focus to El Gaucho and the difficult two weeks of training that lie ahead. The study of high-end wines again, Cognac, Aperitif, Single Malt Scotch, and expensive Ports and Sauternes. Things I used to know but I hadn't put that knowledge to use in a long time. I would study an hour each night before bed. Double shifts were no longer needed since the season was winding down. I worked my last shift at the end of August. This gave me an entire month to myself to work out, study food and wine, and gather the things necessary to begin at El Gaucho. So that's what I did.

It was more time off than I wanted. An entire month. But I was determined not to be idle. I purchased a copy of the wine bible by Karen McNeal. An old favorite. Just so I could brush up on long forgotten information I would no doubt need. It was an easy read and it helped a lot. A wise purchase. I'm glad I read it as quickly as I did. El Gaucho called and said that they were moving my start date up by two weeks.

What the hell? No biggie, it just caught me by surprise. If I'm honest, I have to say I was a bit nervous. This was El Gaucho after all, and I hadn't really done any fine-dining work in some time. I studied my ass off feeling like I was prepping for a final exam.

Just before bedtime about a week later, I received an email stating that it was a false alarm and that I was to report for training in early October. Again, what the hell? I decided to take myself up to Vancouver, B.C, for the weekend as a small reward for what I had accomplished since entering rehab. For a second time.

I researched the cost of two nights in Vancouver. I know how to travel on the cheap anyway and booked a roundtrip train ride on Amtrak for $37 U.S. *Not bad for a round trip*, I thought. I would have to go cheap on a room, but not too cheap. I don't think I could bear the sight of another seedy motel. So, off I went.

Vancouver may as well have been another world all together. Only 142 miles away, but I felt like I was so far from Seattle. I felt completely anonymous, I felt free. I found a little French Bistro to hide out in the Gastown neighborhood called Jules on Abbott St. I grabbed a quiet table in the back near the Kitchen Expo line. I didn't care, it was dark. I ordered the Moules Mariniere and a pan-seared Steelhead filet with vine-ripened tomatoes and pickled Shimeji (cucumber). I also ordered a glass of Pinot Noir.

Was I insane? Did the last seven months mean nothing? All the struggle, all the fight, the hopeless moments, the despair. Was I willing to possibly throw it all away because I wanted to drink like a normal person?

The alcoholic in me needs no one's help justifying taking a drink. I was determined to drink like other men who could handle it. I fought so hard to get where I was, and my addiction slipped in as if the last seven months had never happened.

Insidious.

I told myself I had too much to lose this time. This time. If I had a nickel. I wasn't going to let either my apartment, or El Gaucho slip away when I had only just gotten them. Oh, how I can lie to myself and whistle past the graveyard. My history shows that even with the best laid plans, once enough of the drink is in my system, all bets are off. I'm a different animal. Kind and gracious to a fault, but all sense of responsibility or duty go directly out the fucking window.

Oddly, this time it didn't. I did enjoy two glasses of wine with dinner, and then strolled over to the West End to find a gentleman's bar. To find a gentleman. I woke the next morning with a slight hangover, a companion sleeping next to me, a bottle of Grey Goose on the dresser opposite my bed, and a pack of Marlboro Reds.

I was surprised to feel as good as I did. My companion rolled over and greeted me good morning. He was handsome. My type. Thank goodness. I have made some mistakes due to alcohol. We showered up and he offered to take me to brunch at a place called Score on Davie in the West end not far from my hotel. Sure, I said let's hit it. I could use a good Bloody Mary.

I reached for the bottle of vodka and put it back down. *No, I* thought to myself. *Those days are over.*

We took a cab to Score. The place was bumping. They had good music and their famous Bloody Marys on display. They were huge. They had all kinds of weird shit on them. Mini sliders, giant onion rings, spicy chicken wings. WTF? When in Rome. I just wanted vodka and bloody mix. Or bloody Caesar, was it? Oh Canada.

We ordered a couple of Bloody Caesars, and sat back to take in the crowd. It was very busy and very Gay. I felt proud of myself for not taking a swig from the vodka bottle before I left the hotel. Small victories. It wasn't because I had company. That wouldn't have stopped me. I was determined once again to drink like a normal person. Well, I am not normal people. My date had two Bloody Marys to my six, and in no time at that. I ate a full breakfast, which would normally stop me from drinking but not today.

Between the music and my handsome breakfast companion, I was in fine form. That ended up being a long, leisurely brunch. I planted a kiss on my date and didn't come up for air for quite some time. A handsome distraction, nothing more. "You seem to like me. A lot. A whole lot," I said towards the end of our time together. Or more specifically, the reason behind the end of our time together was that he kept saying to me, "You know what I want to ask you, don't you?" "No, go ahead," I said. He kept repeating it over and over until it finally dawned on me...

Was this motherfucker about to propose to me?

No!

He couldn't be serious! He was.

"Are you out of your Canadian mind?" I said to him. He was deadly serious. "I want to marry you! I've never met anyone like you. You are a hurricane."

Check please! That was the last I saw of him. Too bad. He was cute. Cute and crazy. Isn't that always the way? I spent the rest of that day strolling around the West End and then Gastown and the waterfront. Vancouver is beautiful. If I could live anywhere in that city, it would be Gastown. Summertime in Vancouver is just lovely.

I got back to the hotel mid evening around 7:00 p.m. I packed everything up for departure in the morning and reserved a taxi for pickup at 8:00 a.m. I laid down the bed, turned on the T.V., and promptly fell asleep. It was a long day of walking around, and what with marriage proposals and all, I was a bit tired.

The journey home was fast thank goodness. It felt good to be back in my own place again. I still had some time before El Gaucho and the winter season started so I pulled out all my study material and got to work.

It's always a pain, learning a new menu verbatim. It takes time, repetition, but this was my wheelhouse. I was excited and proud to be part of the El Gaucho team. I still felt a little off kilter and guilty about drinking, so I shelved the studying for a bit and went to the gym to sweat it all out. That always helped. For the time being.

The mental transformation is remarkable. After two hours of kicking my own ass, I felt great. Ready to rock and roll. No more booze, no more smokes. Only exercise and studying.

October, first week of training. Tuxedo at the ready. It went off without a hitch and after the two weeks I was ready to go. El Gaucho was gearing up for the Fall and Christmas season and the day after Halloween, it was on. Again, I found myself in my element. All the nervousness was gone, and my instincts kicked in. Gaucho's atmosphere, menu and decor screams money.

People knew what to expect and were willing to pay for it.

Educated diners that rarely if ever complained. They had no reason to. An El Gaucho server doesn't give you one. The money was ridiculous. I made back everything I spent in Vancouver in two shifts. The next two months were a blur. I worked almost every day. Or night I should say.

Dinners only at El Gaucho. Guests were in the holiday spirit. Staff was in the holiday spirit, and I was stacking money hand over fist. I was already planning my next trip up to Vancouver. I stopped drinking and was steady at the gym again. The plan was to finish the season there and return to Fisherman's for the beginning of Summer.

It didn't work out that way. They went through a complete overhaul at Fisherman's, and fired almost an entire kitchen crew and most of the floor staff. Most of last season's new hires, including myself, wouldn't be hired back. I was surprised, and asked if it was a performance issue? I know it couldn't have been. I was one of their top salesmen. "Nope," they said, "Just a companywide decision." They had so many staff members and I think I just got swept up into that decision with so many others. Too bad, I liked it there. Working on the water.

Epilogue

At the gym one morning, warming up on a stationary bike, I decided to check out the service industry app called Poached. It listed all service industry gigs from barista to cooks to waitstaff to bartenders to waiters.

A French Bistro called Maximilien was hiring waiters. I kinda knew one of the owners, Willie, from cocktailing at Il' Bistro Italian Restaurant in the marketplace. It was literally just down the stairs from Maximilien. I decided to go and apply in person right after my workout. I had known of the place for years, but never thought to apply. It seemed so small inside and it was, until you went outside onto the patio. A stunning 180-degree views of Puget Sound, the Great Wheel, and the mountains. I now understood why they were so busy. What an amazing view!

I met with Axel, the other owner, and he recognized me from Il' Bistro. Good news I thought. We set up "stage" for the following week. A tryout. He needed two waiters for the season beginning May 1st. Halfway through the stage, Willie, the younger of the two owners, pulled me off the floor and sat me down. He had paperwork in his hands. We've seen enough. We want to hire you for the Summer season and possibly beyond that. Are you interested? Yes, I was! Great news.

This place was a moneymaker. I filled out the necessary tax forms, etc., and with firm handshake I said, "I will see you May 1st." I was hired on as a full-time waiter. Wonderful. *The plan was still on track*, I thought. Summers on the water, or close enough by and Winters at El Gaucho. Maximilien didn't need me until May, which gave me almost a month without work.

I had enough money stashed away to cover bills until work progressed. The last thing I wanted to do was pick up a drink, so I doubled down at the gym, studied their menu, and changed my schedule to early morning wake-up times. I had a feeling there would be a lot of double shifts at Maximilien, and I wanted to be up early to work out beforehand if necessary.

There's something oddly satisfying about going to bed at 9:00 p.m. with a book in hand. I was enjoying the early mornings again. Plus, I wanted to leave no stone unturned in my preparation for the summer. I knew what was coming. They had nonstop business, but this time the menu was expensive for lunch. Unlike Fishermen's.

Training lasted a total of two days with no menu or wine exam. Just go! I love the French for this. You were expected to know your shit and to work hard and get it done. No problem. I hit the ground in fourth gear and burned rubber.

We were busy, the sun was shining, and the marketplace was packed. I loved it. We served the usual Bistro fare: Foie Gras, Oysters, Cassoulet, Steak Frites, and French Onion soup. Easy to sell and expensive. I started making real money right away.

I was as busy as I could be between work and the gym. No alcohol at this point. The money at this place even rivaled that of El Gaucho. I was surprised. This only motivated me to get after it even more. And for three months, I worked, exercised, slept, and saved money. I began thinking about my return trip up north, only this time I had planned to stay longer and at a much better hotel. Without an end game or a plan, I can become mentally idle or stagnant and it's a dangerous place to be for an alcoholic like me.

The trip up North at the Summer's end was my goal, my prize. The finish line. The plan was to complete the season at the end of August or mid-September, giving me two plus weeks off before El Gaucho started up again.

I was excited to be returning to Vancouver for a week. After all, I had solved the problem of letting alcohol get in the way, hadn't I? I tore the rest of that summer up. I made a shit load of money in a short amount of time, finished up earlier than I needed to at Maximilien, and closed my last shift for the season. I went down the stairs to Il Bistro for an Old Fashioned.

Just like that. As natural as can be. No thought, no hesitation. I can handle it now. One or two and homebound. And again, it always starts off that way. Sometimes it lasts a week or two. Or even a month where I can drink this way. Before I no longer am able or willing to stop.

But this time was different I told myself. This time.

Walking down the steps towards my drink. Towards another season in hell. I woke the next morning and without batting an eye, I made a cocktail. I had no feelings of shame or guilt about it at all. I felt I deserved to drink the way I wanted considering all that I had accomplished that year. Things were different now, I had a place, I had money. I wouldn't fall again. I believed it.

I drank pretty much every day up to and including my trip up north. I never booked it. I just woke up on a Friday morning, packed a bag, and after a few drinks, I hit the shower and was in a Lyft and on my way to King Street Station to catch the train to Vancouver.

I had no hotel reservations anywhere, but I didn't care. I could get a room once I got into the city. I wanted to stay at the Sandman Hotel on Davie in the West End. I just assumed they'd have a room for me.

I missed the train, but one of the Bolt buses as they were called was leaving soon, so I purchased a one-way and off I went.

I had some Vodka in my bag and bought a cranberry cocktail juice in a plastic bottle from one of the vending machines inside the station. I loved it in there. There's not much there really, just a bunch of benches and a few monitors. What it offered was the attraction of leaving. It offered escape. It offered a route to Canada – a whole other world for me that was so close but made me feel so far away. That's exactly what it offered, and that's why I always got excited walking through that place. Especially on my way back to that fucking shelter. It was a very brief oasis in a dark time. It reminded me of what awaited. Freedom.

I now had the means to do exactly what I wanted. Standing there waiting to leave for the hour-and-a-half ride up with my cleverly disguised drink in hand, I turned in the direction of the shelter. I couldn't see it, but it didn't matter. Fuck you I said. Fuck you shelter life, never again.

I got on the bus with my drink, sat down, and selected the band Triumph from my playlist as we took off North. An all-time favorite band. Goodbye Seattle, for now. Maybe for good, the way I was feeling. I made it to the Sandman Hotel by way of taxi once I set foot on Canadian soil. Unbeknownst to me, it was Gay Pride weekend. How did I miss that? I had no idea really.

Davie Street was packed with people. There were balloons and rainbow flags everywhere. It was wonderful. What a pleasant surprise! I popped my head in to Score for a quick drink before checking into my hotel. The staff all had their Pride gear on. The place was jammed. I needed to get to the hotel so I could unpack and figure out a game plan.

It was Pride weekend ,and I didn't have a reservation. Sold out. Bummer. In fact, the whole city was practically sold out. What was I gonna do? Hotels have cancellations all the time, so I pestered the concierge to find me anything. Anything. At that point, I wasn't all that concerned with the price. I just wanted a room.

I made the mistake of saying to him that money was not a problem, and that I'd be at the hotel bar. Let me know when you have an opening. I didn't have long to wait. Lucky for me. Half an hour later, I heard her voice behind me, "Mr. Cleaves, we have a room available. It's a corner suite with a great view. But it's not at our hotel. It's at the Sunset Inn around the corner."

"I'll take it," I cut him off. Let's go! I didn't care at that point. I needed to shower and to stretch out.

I checked into the room and I said to myself, *this is gonna cost a lot of money*. It was gorgeous. A full kitchen, living room, California King-size bed in the master suite, and a shower that could hold at least six men. *Challenge accepted,* I thought to myself. I threw my bags on the bed, raided the mini bar for a drink, and sat down on the couch looking out at the city. I quickly buried the thought of what this was gonna cost by making an extraordinarily strong drink.

A shower was in order and a change of clothes before I went out on the town. I put on some Beth Hart and climbed in to wash up. The shower was amazing. It took me forever to figure it out. Eight different shower heads all flush with the tile and with two coming out of the ceiling was a bit of a surprise. It took me ten minutes to figure the damn thing out. I thought to myself, this is how they're going to find me. Drowned by shower heads.

Once I figured it out, I had a grand old time. I was really fucking clean when I eventually got out. I climbed out and put on a massive white terrycloth bathrobe. It covered every inch of me. I felt so clean, so relaxed. I took my drink over to the balcony and sat down to admire the view. Suddenly I was in no rush to hit the city. I was going to pay dearly for all this square footage, and I intended to enjoy it. Several hours later and after a Disco nap, I woke up and got ready to join the revelers for the first night of pride.

Canadian men are a very friendly, kind sort, but they're not exactly aggressive when it comes to meeting people or striking up conversation. I tended to be a little more forward. I was always taken aback by their politeness. *Canadian men are sweet,* I thought.

Pride weekend was exactly what I imagined it was going to be. Drinking, crowded streets, packed out bars, and noise. And I took in my fair share of it all. Every store, shop, restaurant and bar were busy. It was surreal to see a Kentucky Fried Chicken filled with homos. I wanted to pop my head in and just listen for the innuendo. Too crowded.

The entire week ended up being a blur after a couple of nights. I never did fill the shower full of Canadian men. I'll have to try harder next time. After a while, Pride week seemed to lose its fascination on me. I tore it up alright, no issue there, but I felt like I couldn't find what I was looking for. I felt like the next place I went, I was going to find whatever the hell it was. Some sort of never-ending search. It was always that way though, wasn't it?

I got back to my room on the last morning and realized that's all I wanted to go home. I made my last drink there and checked out of the hotel. At that point, I wasn't concerned with the bill. I just wanted to go home. I don't know what turned my mood so sour. Loneliness perhaps. Knowing that I wasn't doing the right thing. It is entirely possible for me to have a moment of clarity while I'm still drinking. It is the strangest thing. It hit me from out of nowhere really. I was surrounded by a city full of Gay people and I just wanted to go. So, I did.

All I could say about the hotel bill was, ouch. Absolutely worth it, though.

With no ticket or reservation, I took a cab over to the train station. No trains but once again I scored a ticket on a Bolt bus. Lucky really. The next one after wouldn't be until the following day. I settled into my seat for the quick ride back to Seattle.

For split second I felt bad for my fellow passengers. I didn't brush my teeth and my breath I could only imagine reeked of booze. The feeling quickly passed. I had no one sitting next to me, though, so it wasn't so bad. I searched through my bag for a charger to plug my phone in and came across a pint of Bulleit Bourbon.

How do you get in there you little bugger? I was happy to see it. I took a quick, sneaky pull and buried it back into my bag. I downloaded a movie on my phone, something about a trio of British adventurers trying to survive the jungles of Belize. I watched intermittently. It wasn't going so well for them. I would close my eyes for a bit, opened them to see the Brits in ever increasing danger.

Every time I check back in, they were getting more and more fucked up. These guys are dead, I thought to myself. Customs was quick and painless, thank God, and I managed to sleep for a little while. I opened my eyes and we were pulling into Chinatown Station or the International District as it is called here in Seattle. I don't know why? There's nothing but Chinese motherfuckers there. And really good food. I thought about grabbing some food to take home, but I just flagged a taxi instead.

I just wanted to be home. Absolutely no traffic on the fifteen-minute ride home. Thank God. I had the cabbie drop me off at the gas station across the street to buy smokes and a few bottles of wine just in case. They always stared at me like I was crazy when I ever I went in there. If I was drinking, it was two or three times a day to buy more booze. Fuck them.

I spent the next month in isolation. Drinking, smoking, and listening to music. Trying to figure things out. I let all my obligations go. I wouldn't be returning to El Gaucho anytime soon and I didn't care. I'm not sure how to describe how I was feeling.

It wasn't self- pity. It wasn't righteous indignation. It wasn't anything. I was completely indifferent. Indifferent to it all. I simply no longer cared. All I wanted was to sit in my tiny chair with my tiny table in my tiny lamp and drink. Nothing else. No one else. I would sit there for hours at a time.

At one point, I did a 12-hour stretch sitting in that chair. I must be tripping I said to myself. There's no way. But I did. I would read from time to time, mess around online, and scribble nonsense into a journal. But mostly, I just sat there, thinking. I didn't give up. I would never do that. I simply felt nothing.

The days flew by. I lost all track of time. I would only leave to get more booze or smokes, and as quickly as I could, return to my chair. Apparently, an entire five weeks flew by. The only way I really knew was via a notice from my building that the rent was late. I looked around my tiny apartment, if you could call it that, and it was a mess. Empty wine and vodka bottles. Laundry piled up, and in the corner, where I sat and contemplated life, a pile of cigarette ashes. That was the last straw for me. The cigarette ashes.

Get up Cleaves! I said to myself. *Clean this fucking apartment.*

It was very uncharacteristic of me to keep such a messy existence. It was early morning. I got up, made a strong drink, put on some rock and roll, and got busy. I cleaned for a solid three hours. That's a lot for such a small place. By the end, the laundry was all done, floors scrubbed, and every surface was wiped down and sanitized. It smelled clean. Time to clean myself. Another double vodka and into the shower I went.

This time it was Adele on my playlist. I started crying. I swallowed the pain and walked directly out of the shower with the curtain open and the water still running. I had to change that shit. It hurt too much. Van Halen, "Mean Street." I snapped out of it. It was nice to walk back into a clean room. I was happy for that.

I went over to the slider and opened it up all the way. Leaning on the railing, I lit up a cigarette.

What now? What next? Work, drink, destroy, rebuild, repeat? I had to get out of that room suddenly. I brought a container of wine and my smokes with me to little park just in front of my place. I needed some fresh air. It was nice to be outside. Something different to look at. I felt better, I felt hungry. I had the ingredients to make a meat sauce and some pasta for dinner, so that's what I did.

It was nice to feel like I was doing something even if it was just making dinner. I didn't eat much of it, but I did eat. As always, just enough to keep drinking. I didn't like the space I was in mentally. No forward, no backward. I felt stale, stagnant, in limbo.

The drinking had become a natural part of my existence at this point. Some people get up, have breakfast, and start their day. For me, it was a double vodka and tonic and a shower.

I could feel myself tiring of this existence. My conscience was climbing out of the mire. Something had to give. This is around when St. Matthew's House was introduced to me. Drinking was now an all day, everyday thing. Alcohol had once again become a necessity. I required it to function. I let it become this way and it progressed to the point of almost a gallon of vodka again.

I accepted the offer for help from the Olson family and from St. Matthew's House. I would be off to Naples, FL. to try, once again, to get and stay sober. I was grateful for the Olsen family. They seemed to genuinely care about me. I met them at a very dark time in life and still they were so open and caring. Right away. It took me aback, initially.

Here I am, destroying myself and not giving a shit, and these people are opening their lives to me and offering so much. It's something I will not soon forget. Good people do exist.

So, off I went. All the while saying to myself, this is the last time. If this doesn't work, then that's it. I'm never going into treatment again.

And the rest, Dear Reader, you already know.

St. Matthews introduce me to an anger I never thought possible. Absolute fucking rocket fuel. I hated "Christians" when I left on February 7, 2020.

At 50 years old, I was in the best shape of my life because, at every chance I got, I burned off my anger at these people by using the gym. Nonstop. More, more, more. I put on 20 pounds of muscle, and I beat the heavy bag like it stole from me. I felt farther away and angrier at God than I ever had before. In fact, I don't think I was ever really angry with him until I experienced what I did at St. Matt's. I looked at everyone as the enemy.

Moving forward, I thought to myself. I would no longer tolerate anything from anyone. I felt like a walking time bomb. No longer would I suffer paper tigers. No more assholes with metaphors, no more hypocrites, or pharisees. No more false prophets, dime-store philosophers, or armchair warriors. I was fucking done!

I returned to Seattle, where I currently reside, villainized by Mr. Olson. I was called a user and a liar for leaving the program. To which I say, if you've learned anything about me from reading this, then you know that I will not be bullied. I will not be brainwashed, and you can't intimidate me.

I am too strong. I've seen too much. I am not afraid.

The only thing that scares me is me. The monster that lives inside – The Closet Maniac.

My anger and my rage are what scare me the most. I consider them gifts, albeit dangerous ones that I have to control on a daily basis. I continue to use these gifts to keep my body strong lest someone try to hurt me, and I use them to keep moving forward. Ever hopeful but ever vigilant.

So, dear friends,

I'm not sure what lies ahead, most likely another series of ups and downs. Sobriety and destruction. I've been both the windshield and the bug. Flush and broke. I've been lucky enough to have real love in this world, and I have come to find it is the only thing that matters.

So, if you will, here is some advice from a walking bundle of contradictions:

Love hard and forgive often. Time is luck and whatever time you may think have, YOU DO NOT!

Pick up the phone and call someone you're fighting with. Swallow your pride, beg for forgiveness if you need to.

Take the plunge, eat the cake. Ask him on a date, ask her on a date. Say I love you. Say I'm sorry. Hold on to the ones you love as tightly as you can because, in the blink of an eye, it is all gone and nothing in this world is more expensive than regret.

So, moving forward in this life of mine, I find myself in two places at the same time.

Two Edwards.

The one who wakes up sober and has coffee in the morning, feeling his strength and hope rise. Boundless and full of vigor and with eyes wide open. The same "Kind Soul" that I ever was.

And the other Edward – the one that burns with white-hot rage. The "Closet Maniac" who will never stop, never slow down, the one who will always be searching:

…for Brian,

…for peace,

…for a way to assuage the anger in me that wants to absolutely fucking kill you.

The Kind Soul that will cry at the drop of a hat. The Closet Maniac who wants to do things that scare the shit out of him.

I now know what it means to live life completely "in the moment." I keep one eye on the future, but I make no plans. Throughout this process, I'm beginning to let go of the past. I will never let go of my precious anger, however. I only hope that I can hold onto it instead of letting it loose on those I feel deserve it.

I'm not sure where I will end up, dear friends. Rest assured that I will always pull through. No matter what.

Life is far too delicious, and its players are way too lovely and tempting for me to leave just yet.

There is still life left in these old bones, and I intend to put them to the test time and again. So, if you see me out and about, say hello. Sit down, have a drink. I won't bite.

Until then, I'll be off searching.

For what, I still don't know.

THE END

About the Author

Edward Cleaves lives in Seattle ,WA. He spends his days writing, making his friends laugh and riding the ferries around Puget Sound and the beautiful Pacific Northwest.

For more information, please see my website.

edwardcleaves.com